LAND ROVER DEFENDER

MODIFYING MANUAL

LAND ROVER DEFENDER

MODIFYING MANUAL

A PRACTICAL GUIDE TO UPGRADES

LINDSAY PORTER

First published in January 2012

A catalogue record for this book is available from the
British Library.

ISBN 978 1 78521 858 3

Library of Congress control no. 2011935260

Haynes Group Limited
Haynes North America Inc.

Website: www.haynes.com

Authorised representative in the EU:
HaynesPro BV, Stationsstraat 79 F,
3811MH Amersfoort, The Netherlands
gpsr@haynes.co.uk

Printed in the UK

Contents

Introduction

This is a manual for people who, like me, are completely nuts. Nuts about their Land Rover Defender. Nuts enough to enjoy owning it – not the most practical of everyday vehicles, is it? And even nuts enough to want to change it round a bit, personalise it, make it do just what you want it to do and be how you prefer it to be.

And that's one of the most attractive things about the traditional Defender. Not only is it supremely tough, rugged and long-lasting; it's also crying out to be modified. Because it's a great big kit of hand-assembled parts, it's also easy to unbolt some of those parts and bolt some different ones on in their place. Indeed, there's a massive range of modification parts available, some produced by large companies, some by small, and all of them designed to satisfy a need for on- or off-road performance, appearance or even comfort – which the uninitiated might think would be the last thing a Defender owner would think about. But they'd be wrong.

There's really no limit to how far an owner can go in modifying his or her Defender, except the depth of their pocket. And there's no limit to the number of changes that you can make. Indeed, it wouldn't be possible to include every possible permutation of Defender mods in a single manual, so I haven't tried. Instead,

I've attempted to compile a range of the most typical, useful and attractive options available and to show how we went about fitting them. And if anyone was to say 'That's not how I would go about it,' or 'Those aren't the parts I'd choose to fit,' I'd have to agree that there's no one way of modifying a Defender, and that's part of the appeal. Everyone's Defender is different to everyone else's. So I hope you'll use the information here as your guide, inspiration and starting point and, while keeping things safe and responsible, have fun in modifying your Defender and making it unique!

WHO – OR WHAT – IS DIXIE?

First, because to the eyes of those who know their UK Defenders it doesn't look 'right', an explanation regarding the vehicle featured in many pages of this manual. My white Defender, known in *LRM* as DiXie, was built in 2006 as one of the last, export-only 300 Tdi four-cylinder Defenders. At that time the only Defenders 'officially' available in the UK were those powered by the Td5 engine.

Although DiXie got as far as the quayside at Rotterdam, the original sale fell through and it was re-imported, unused, in 2008, when I bought it. At that time it was permissible to make a left-hand-drive, imported Land Rover street-legal by putting it through the Special Vehicles Approval

system, also used to approve kit cars. So, although the 300 Tdi was last officially sold for the UK market in 1999, mine started out as a genuine, factory-built, 2008-registered 300 Tdi, which we later (and quite legally) converted to right-hand drive. Then we went on to add a bit more to it, and then a bit more. And so this manual was born...

ACKNOWLEDGEMENTS

It would be easiest to say that all the people I need to thank appear in the photographs in the pages of the manual. But it wouldn't quite be true. First, I'd like to thank my wife Shan for her shared enthusiasm for our Defender and her unfailing encouragement with the huge amount of work that went into the vehicle and this book. Things don't always go smoothly – in fact they often don't – but when you've got someone alongside who smoothes out the bumps, it doesn't half help! Shan also takes some cracking photographs when required.

And I'd like to thank Zoë Palmer, who's been my assistant for 20 years at the time of writing, and who knows more than most people about the mechanics of putting a book together – and a fair bit about putting Land Rovers together too. She's put a lot of invaluable work into this book and, as always, has made a real difference.

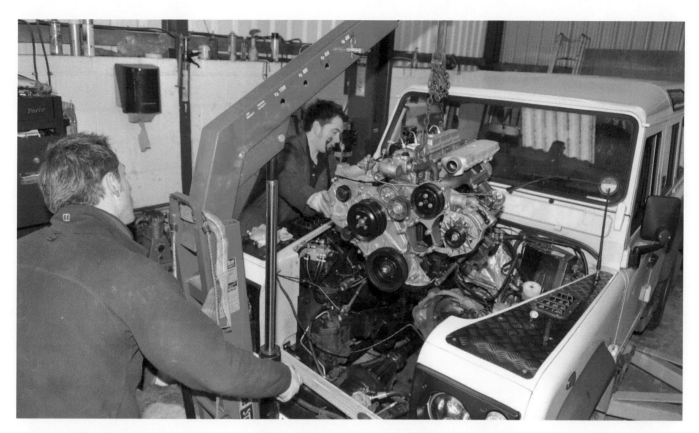

Then my grateful thanks are due to the great crowd at *Land Rover Monthly* magazine (written for enthusiasts, by enthusiasts, they say – and it is, too!) who are smashing to work with and who have paid me for a good few years to produce how-to stuff for the magazine. It was there that most of this material appeared in its original, magazine-orientated form. On which subject, my editor at Haynes, Steve Rendle, has done a great job of working with me and Zoë to carve my stuff into a suitable form for this manual. Steve really knows his stuff!

At *LRM*, my good mate Frank Elson, a wrinkled old so-and-so like myself (though he tells anyone who'll listen that he's a touch younger than me), has been a great source of encouragement and kindly wrote the foreword for this book. Frank is a legend in his own Land Rover, a good mate and a good bloke all round.

On the workshop side, Ian Baughan and Tim Consolante have assisted greatly with their unequalled workshop and 'electrics' expertise respectively, but most of all thanks are due to Dave Bradley-Scrivener, who works for me at weekends and whose efforts have gone above and beyond the call of duty to make sure the workshop work for this book was completed in time. He's a great bloke to work with, he always gives of his very best and Shan and I greatly enjoy having him work here.

Also, it's not too much to say that you, the Defender enthusiast, are also to be thanked for your unwitting assistance. I've

heard from many Defender nuts and met a good number at shows and every single one I've come across has been a good-hearted enthusiast and, in short, an utter nutter like myself. Thanks to you all!

Postscript. When asked what he thought was wrong with the all-new Defender, Charlie Thorn, who's an *LRM* stalwart, contemporary of Frank Elson and myself and an all-round Good Bloke, put it simply enough: 'The tops of the wings aren't flat so there's nowhere to put your cup of tea while you're tinkering with your Land Rover.' So true, and it says it all, really...

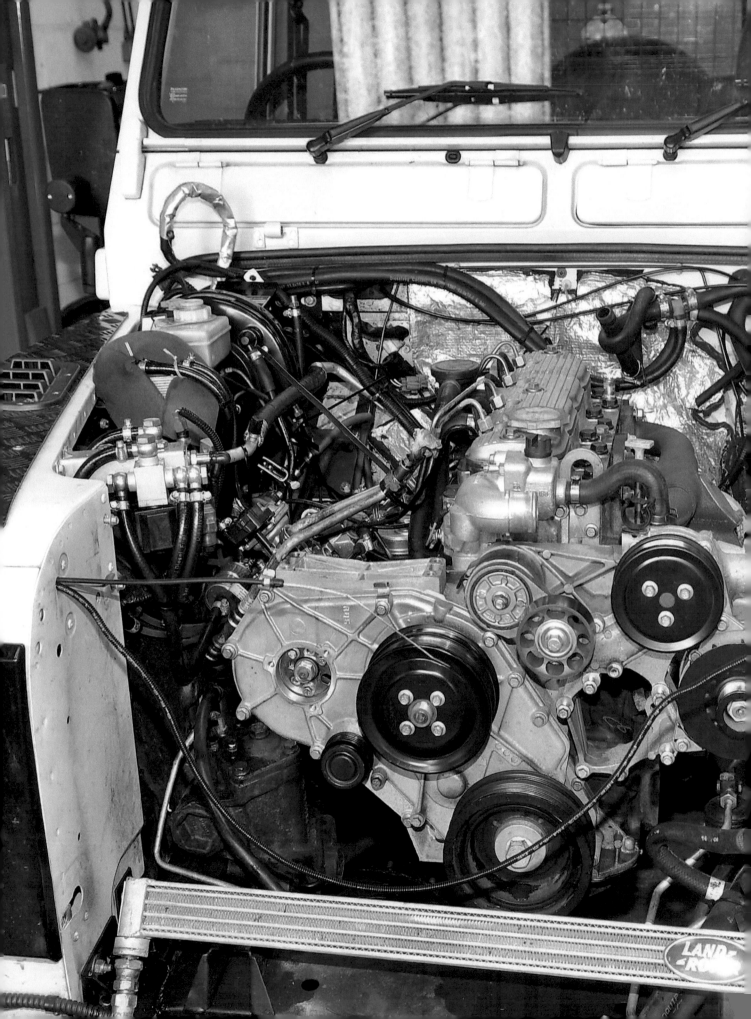

CHAPTER 1

Engine

Introduction to turbo diesel tuning

by Allard Turbo Sport

Diesel engines will always be limited in their rev range compared to petrol engines, and although they can be tuned in a similar way – *eg* with cylinder head modifications, change of camshaft etc – these methods aren't particularly cost effective due to the amount of labour entailed, and the renowned longevity of diesel engines can be considerably reduced by this type of modification. This is why Allard concentrate on intercooling (charge cooling) and optimisation of the air/fuel ratio. Intercooling provides the most cost-effective way of substantially increasing performance from tick-over to maximum rpm, at the same time as having the potential to improve fuel consumption, reduce the thermal load on the engine and reduce smoke emissions. Allard have developed a range of complete intercooler conversions or an uprated intercooler if one is already fitted as standard.

Because of the way turbo diesels are set up at the factory to suit the average driver and urban driving conditions, many vehicles can have their performance improved by up to 25% with only a small increase in fuel consumption and a mild increase in maximum boost pressure.

On Puma-engined Tdci and on Td5 engines, both with an electronically controlled fuel pump, up to 25% improvement is possible when an uprated ECU is used in conjunction with an uprated intercooler.

On a turbo diesel engine the fuelling curve relative to airflow into the cylinders is the critical factor. Too much fuel without sufficient airflow will produce an over-rich fuel air/ratio, leading to smoke. It's important to have good boost available at low rpm to create sufficient airflow, but actually boost pressure and maximum boost are very much less important, provided sufficient cooled airflow is achieved.

Increasing boost at lower rpm can be very beneficial, but in many cases just increasing

maximum boost, even if fuelling can be matched to it, won't necessarily increase power very much. There can be many reasons for this. One of the most significant is that modern turbochargers are of the low-match type, with relatively small compressor wheels working at very high speed. An increase in boost will increase the speed of the turbocharger, which can increase the air delivery, but air temperature rises more rapidly and the compressor runs out of its speed versus boost efficiency envelope. The rise in air temperature quickly offsets most of the increase in mass airflow, resulting in minimal increase in power and increased thermal and mechanical loads on the engine. The introduction of variable geometry turbochargers (VGT) will improve volumetric efficiency over a wide rpm range, but the importance of an effective intercooling system will still be essential to increase flow, reduce thermal loads on the engine to minimise exhaust smoke, and improve specific fuel consumption.

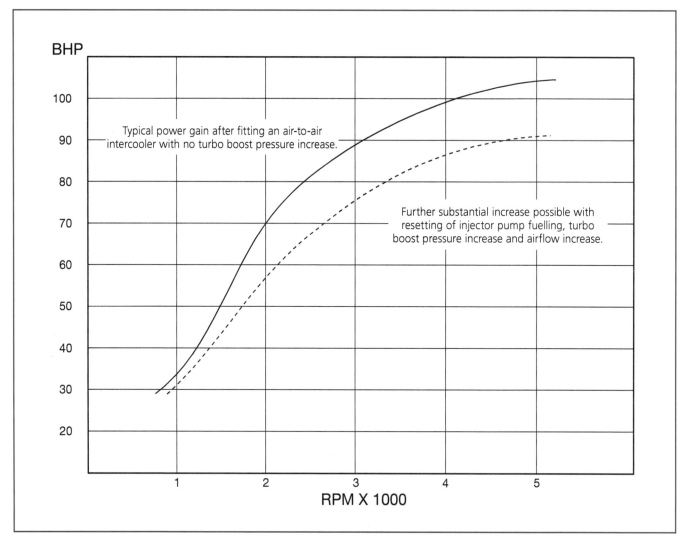

Typical power gain after fitting an air-to-air intercooler with no turbo boost pressure increase.

Further substantial increase possible with resetting of injector pump fuelling, turbo boost pressure increase and airflow increase.

Aluminium replacement intercooler

An intercooler (heat exchanger) can provide uprated performance at the same time as reducing fuel consumption, exhaust emissions and thermal load on an engine.

Allard intercoolers are manufactured in aluminium to a high quality, robust design. The tubes in the core are spaced and shaped to provide minimum flow resistance at high airflow rates, yet at the same time achieve optimum cooling of the turbo compressed air. The finning, both between and inside the core tubes, presents a very large cooling surface to the compressed air, resulting in a substantial temperature drop across the core.

These step-by-step details show how to transform your turbo diesel Land Rover's performance in only an hour's work, by fitting an Allisport aluminium intercooler.

Elsewhere in this manual you'll see a 300 Tdi Defender being converted to automatic transmission. A downside is that the relatively weedy power output of the 300 Tdi engine is diminished further by the power losses in the auto transmission – perhaps by around 10%.

According to Allisport's boss Andrew Graham, there are three main reasons why this conversion helps to make up the difference:

- Like the standard intercooler, it's made of aluminium, but while the original unit uses very heavy cast alloy end tanks, which have the effect of retaining heat, the Allisport units are made from lighter aluminium sheet and radiate heat much more effectively.
- Allisport also make the end tanks smaller, allowing the core to be larger, giving over 50% more cooling capacity.
- Not all of the tubes in the standard unit are complete – some of them are blanked off. It would be interesting to know what Land Rover have in mind by deliberately strangling performance in this way.

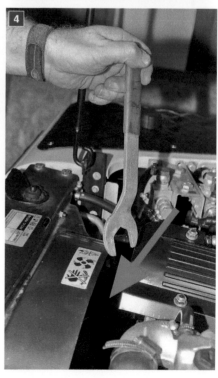

1 To get at the intercooler you need to remove the fan shroud, while to remove the fan shroud you have to drain some of the coolant and remove the top hose. A Pela Extractor (see page 13) was used to draw fluid out without having to messily drain coolant at the bottom end.

2 This is a relatively new engine so we were confident the hoses would come free. If your hoses are stuck in position you might want to leave this end of the hose in place, hope to get away with freeing the radiator and fold the hose back on itself.

If all else fails you'll have to cut the hose off and fit a new one.

3 While you're in the vicinity, detach and remove the top intercooler air hose, which is always easier to remove because it won't have been heat-welded into place.

4 Using the correct spanner to free the fan makes life so much easier. I bought mine second-hand on eBay for a few quid.

WHAT DOES AN INTERCOOLER DO?

- Like almost everything else, when air heats up it expands and when it cools it contracts.
- Cooler air, because it's 'concentrated', contains more oxygen (by volume) than hot air.
- A turbocharger has the unfortunate side effect of heating intake air as it goes through the turbo. So the intercooler sits between the turbo and the engine air inlet, cooling the hot air down again.
- An intercooler is a radiator that has the injection system's intake air passing through it. The intake air is cooled in the same way as the coolant radiator – by air from outside the vehicle passing through it.
- The better the intercooler, the cooler the intake air and the more efficient your turbo diesel engine will be.

5 The fan nut (arrowed) is reached behind the cowl, as shown in the previous photograph. It's important to note that it has a left-hand thread. You fit the spanner then shock the nut free by hitting the spanner with a hammer, turning it the 'wrong' way of course. After spinning the nut free, the fan is carefully left inside the shroud. Then remove the screws holding the top of the shroud in place.

6 Note that the hoses positioned in these clips have to be detached by reaching down into the depths.

7 As you lift the shroud out it's important to reach down and hold the fan, taking great care not to damage the radiator.

8 Here the shroud and fan have been lifted out as a complete unit (the fan retaining nut is arrowed). Place them to one side.

9 It's not essential, but access to the bottom of the intercooler is a lot easier if you remove the radiator grille.

10 First the top radiator mounting plates have to be removed. Take out the two screws holding each one in place then just lift them away.

11 Two machine screws at each end of the radiator top plate are then removed and the top plate itself is simply lifted off.

12 The bottom air intake hose from the intercooler is next detached and removed.

13 With nothing now holding the intercooler in place except the friction of its seals, it needs to be worked carefully upwards until you can lift it out.

14 The old intercooler (left) alongside the new aluminium one, which has fewer but larger and longer air tubes than the original. Note the foam strip seal glued to the left-hand edge of the old intercooler. A similar seal needs to be added to the new intercooler, for which we used self-adhesive foam strip available from R.H. Nuttall Ltd of Birmingham.

15 The new Allisport intercooler is lowered into place, making sure that the pegs are located correctly at the bottom. This is where having the radiator grille removed can really help.

16 The bottom intercooler hose is then put back, only this time the centre mounting bolt is fitted to the inner wing (we discovered it had been left off previously). As you can see, you need to access both sides of the wing at once to hold the bolt while turning the nut.

17 This is the Pela Oil Extractor that was used to withdraw a suitable quantity of coolant before removing the hoses. A plastic tube was fitted to the hole in the top of the extractor (now being used as the pourer), and when the handle was pumped coolant was sucked up and out. Brilliant!

18 Because of the air conditioning condenser 'radiator', this is all that could be seen of the Allisport intercooler, so airflow through it must unavoidably be restricted. This problem will be overcome when I fit a full-width Allisport intercooler.

CONCLUSION
The results are far better than I dared hope! As I drove slowly off down our narrow lane, with the engine cold and little air passing through the rad aperture, I noticed that performance seemed just that bit more lively than before and about what it had been before the auto 'box had been fitted. Then, as the engine warmed up and the

speed increased a little, the extra 'oomph' became impressive. There's certainly a few more revs at the top end, but the most noticeable improvement comes through mid-range torque, where you need it most. The Defender feels so much more lively and pleasant to drive than it was before, so my recommendations are: (a) if you want the simplest and most unobtrusive way of improving your turbo diesel Land Rover's performance, this is it; and (b) I can't wait to find out what a full-width, and thus even more efficient intercooler will be like.

FULL-WIDTH INTERCOOLER
A full-sized Allard intercooler is another modification I'm more than happy to recommend. Even compared with the aluminium standard-sized intercooler, there's much more torque low down, delivery is smoother across the range and there's even a higher comfortable cruising speed on the motorway. I haven't had an opportunity to carry out an economy check yet but I'm convinced, from the ease with which the engine pulls, that there's the potential for much better economy as well as brisker and more relaxed driving.

19 Allard can supply intercoolers for all Defender models. This is the standard 300 Tdi version. As you'll see in a moment, ours is also a 300 Tdi intercooler but specially fabricated to allow for the shape of the components fitted to the standard Land Rover air-conditioning system.

20 Here, as Lloyd Allard offers up the intercooler to establish where he wants to mount the fixing brackets, you can see the cutaway that allows for vehicles fitted with standard Land Rover air-conditioning.

21 Because this was very much a one-off installation, and because a pipe-flaring tool is simply too large a piece of equipment to lug around, we had to improvise in making a flare on the end of one of the rigid pipes. Using grips, I worked all the way round the end of the aluminium pipe, flanging it. Now, there's no chance of the pipe blowing off.

22 When fitted the intercooler is a real work of art.

Earlier pre-TGV versions of the 2.8 didn't have the benefit of the variable vane turbo.

IS IT A LAND ROVER ENGINE?

International Motors built the HS 2.8 TGV in South America – some in Brazil, others in Argentina – on behalf of the Ford Motor Company. When Ford owned Land Rover they of course owned the rights to the Land Rover 300 Tdi engine too. International Motors (not, it seems, actually a part of Ford) built 300 Tdi engines for Land Rover and for the MoD but also took the design further, enhancing it to make other similar engines, including this larger-sized, 2.8-litre turbo diesel, direct-injection engine, the HS 2.8 TGV. It is thus a development of the Land Rover 300 Tdi engine. Its transmission mountings are compatible and the engine mounting positions the same, even if many of the details are different.

The 2.8 TGV engine is no longer in full-scale production, International Motors having replaced it with a fully-electronic 3-litre version with cross-flow head. It would be extremely difficult, we understand, to fit the 3-litre engine to a Land Rover even if you wanted to, possibly because of its height and certainly because of its heavy reliance on electronic control. However, the 2.8 engine is still available at the time of writing and used examples are likely to be available for some time to come.

The 2.8 engine outperforms the old 300 Tdi both in terms of power and durability. There are a number of improvements on the old engine that enable the HS 2.8 TGV to perform as well as it does. The increased displacement obviously, the use of improved internals like special pistons developed by Mahle in Germany and a crankshaft that's forged rather than cast, to name but a few. Then there's the fitment of a new, much larger, Garrett variable nozzle turbocharger, which reduces turbo lag and delivers better performance across the rev range.

300 Tdi
Maximum power 111bhp @ 4,000rpm
Maximum torque 195lbf/ft (285Nm) @ 1,800rpm

HS 2.8 TGV
Maximum power 135bhp @ 3,800rpm
Maximum torque 277lbf/ft (375Nm) @ 1,400rpm

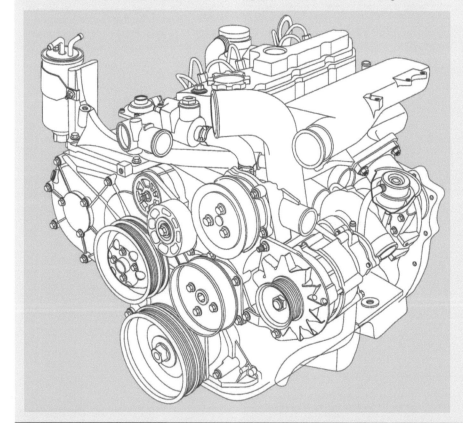

The shiny new engine, plus exhaust components, an instruction book and a box of bits, comes in an impressively large crate that won't fit in the back of a Land Rover Station Wagon and was a tight squeeze even in my VW Transporter. However, off it went to one of the best young Land Rover technicians I've come across, Ian Baughan at IRB Developments.

DAY ONE

1 Remember to start by disconnecting the battery.

2 Stripping out the engine bay is basic common sense, but if you're unfamiliar with Land Rovers it's a good idea to take lots of photographs to remind yourself exactly where every bolt and bracket belong.

3 Different people have different preferences on how to remove the Defender's engine, but the conventional out-of-the-front approach is the most straightforward. So off came the grille...

4 ...and the grille surround. To remove the bottom fixing bolts you have to lever out the plastic inserts for the grille screws.

5 You may need to remove the threaded stud that's fitted to some Defenders. To avoid damaging the threads use a proper stud removal tool if you have one; alternatively you could lock two nuts together on the outer thread using a pair of spanners then turn the inner nut to wind out the stud.

6 This enables you to lift off the top or bonnet-slam panel. The radiator top brackets are left attached to this because there's no need to remove them.

7 You can then lift out the radiator assembly complete with intercooler and store them safely out of the way at the back of Ian's workshop.

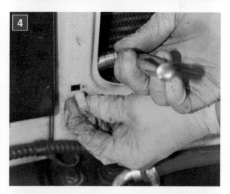

8 If your Defender has air conditioning, it must have its gas extracted by a specialist. They'll be able to store it for you, ready to refill the system later. (In my case the system had been drained down some time ago when auto transmission was fitted.) The three a/c belt tensioner fixing bolts can then be slackened, the tensioner turned to release the tension on the belt, and the belt lifted out of the way.

9 The air conditioning compressor can then be unbolted and removed...

10 ...followed by the cradle beneath it, which has to be unbolted ready for refitting to the 2.8 TGV engine in conjunction with the conversion kit.

11 The air filter assembly also has to be transferred over. It's unbolted from the cylinder head, the two head bolts having to be removed completely, and disconnected from the support bracket beneath.

12 Take careful note of which crankcase bolt is used to fix the support bracket so that the same one is used on the new engine.

13 At first glance the inlet manifold on the 2.8 TGV engine looks the same as that on the 300 Tdi, but it's not. Ian had the bright idea of unbolting the 300 Tdi's inlet manifold...

14 ...and removing it from the engine while it's still in situ in the vehicle.

15 The inlet manifold has to come off anyway, but by removing it now access to items such as the exhaust pipe at the exhaust manifold is improved.

16 With all belts now removed, three fixing screws are taken out and off comes the power steering pump pulley for use on the new engine.

17 Finally, at least for this part of the work, this rail for transmitting coolant to the back of the engine (for the heater) was removed, ready for reuse later.

What with trying to interpret the instructions, which weren't that well translated from the Dutch, and working out what would need to be reused and what wouldn't, this got us to the end of the first day's work.

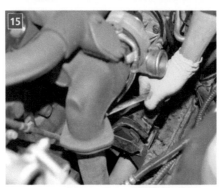

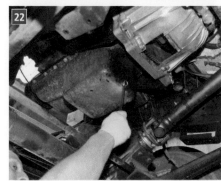

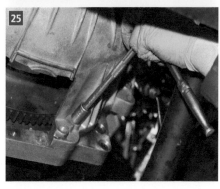

DAY TWO

18 With my Defender now up in the air, the exhaust system is disconnected at the front pipe.

19 Then, because this is an automatic transmission, the access plate for the torque converter on the bottom of the gearbox was removed. (It only looks like this on Ashcroft Transmissions' Defender conversions – it's different on Discoverys with auto transmission.)

20 This is where you need two pairs of hands – one person to lock the front of the engine so that the crank can't turn...

21 ...while the other removes the bolts fixing the torque converter flex plate to the flywheel.

22 Slacken the engine sump drain plug and drain the oil out. Ian was a bit embarrassed to be using a bucket, but his oil collector was full!

23 The engine mounting on the right-hand side of the engine can be glimpsed adjacent to the oil filter position...

24 ...while this is the location on the other side.

25 Some of the bell housing bolts, in particular those on the bottom, are very easy to reach...

26 ...whereas others require a little more effort, though compared to engine bay access on most vehicles none of them present a challenge. Remember to support the engine and transmission where they join, because with all the bell housing bolts removed you'll see a bit of a sag start to occur, and on manual transmission Defenders (ie the majority of them) you risk putting harmful strain on the transmission first motion shaft, the one that fits into a bush on the back of the engine crank.

27 The first phase of the work is now complete. The 300 Tdi engine in my 2006-built export model Defender is now ready to be lifted out.

28 Hook up to the lifting eyes on the engine, and as you lift it out check that nothing gets snagged or damaged – the power steering reservoir, for instance, is a mere sliver away – and that nothing is still connected.

29 With the 300 Tdi engine securely propped with a wooden block beneath the front of the sump, the engine crane was turned round and connected to the International HS 2.8HGV engine.

30 In this instance, being an auto transmission, the flex plate and support ring have to be removed from the 300 Tdi engine's flywheel. In all cases this is followed by the flywheel and backplate, complete with rear engine mountings.

31 These are most of the parts that have to be removed from the 300 Tdi engine when carrying out this conversion.
- In the background is the engine backplate complete with engine mountings. (Mine is a special backplate adapted for the auto gearbox conversion; on most engines it will just be the standard type.)
- To the right is the inlet manifold.
- Front left is the engine lifting eye...
- ...and to its right the flywheel and auto flex plate.

In the centre is the air conditioning pulley, while the a/c tensioner also has to be transferred where a/c is fitted.

32 The International 2.8 engine, though developed from the Land Rover engine, has been used in a number of Ford vehicles in the Americas and comes with engine mounts that are removed and discarded.

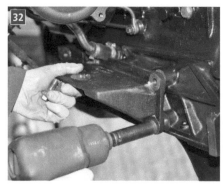

33 On this, the turbo side of the engine, the 300's engine mounting assembly simply bolts on to the same mounting threads.

34 On the other side, things are just slightly more complicated. The 2.8 has its own in-built oil cooler instead of using the one built into the radiator as on the Tdi engine. This assembly has to be slackened and moved over...

35 ...to gain access to the redundant engine mount on that side of the engine.

36 In the same area, a modification supplied by the engine suppliers at the time, Prins Maasdijk, had to be added. This was because the oil filter in its original position fouls on the Land Rover's engine mount. After removing the oil filter, this adaptor plate is screwed to the oil filter mounting position.

37 Then, this mounting plate is bolted to two threaded holes already present in the engine block. Kits should come with all the necessary fixing bolts.

38 The remote oil filter head is then screwed to the adaptor plate.

39 Next you need to work out how the oil pipes are to be run. Ian decided that the Land Rover engine mounting should go on, so that we could see for ourselves where the pipe runs could go.

40 We screwed in the first of the elbows, working out how far it would have to be screwed in to provide a tight seal while still facing in the right direction...

41 ...then added thread seal to the thread before screwing the elbow back in again. Just before each pipe was fitted to its elbow, we put another wipe of thread seal on each thread. It's important to note that this is thread seal rather than thread lock, which has different qualities.

42 Here you can see how the correct orientation of the elbows allows the pipes to run more or less horizontally, clearing the chassis rails and engine mounting. They'll be clipped neatly in position once the engine has been fitted.

43 The standard oil filter fits neatly in this new location.

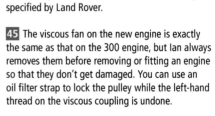

44 The backplate from the Tdi engine was bolted to the 2.8 engine block to the same torque settings as specified by Land Rover.

45 The viscous fan on the new engine is exactly the same as that on the 300 engine, but Ian always removes them before removing or fitting an engine so that they don't get damaged. You can use an oil filter strap to lock the pulley while the left-hand thread on the viscous coupling is undone.

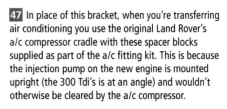

46 This bracket supports the oil filter on the International engine but can be removed and discarded before the engine is fitted into your Land Rover.

47 In place of this bracket, when you're transferring air conditioning you use the original Land Rover's a/c compressor cradle with these spacer blocks supplied as part of the a/c fitting kit. This is because the injection pump on the new engine is mounted upright (the 300 Tdi's is at an angle) and wouldn't otherwise be cleared by the a/c compressor.

48 The inlet manifold used on the 300 Tdi (top) and the International 2.8 engine (bottom). Note the differences in the inlet stub.

49 The 300's inlet manifold has to be bolted to the 2.8 engine's cylinder head.

50 Mounting bolt positions are exactly the same on both engines...

51 ...and the heat shield fits against the 2.8 engine's exhaust manifold and can easily be transferred over.

52 It's necessary to remove the straight coolant hose from the back of the 2.8 engine's cylinder head and to fit a 300 Tdi hose, which is upswept to clear the heater hose pipework.

53 The clip and mounting bracket for the same heater hose are also a straight transfer from old engine to new.

54 On a/c versions, three screws have to be removed and the cover plate taken off the engine (arrowed) so that the air conditioning belt tensioner can be fitted.

55 The a/c idler pulley is screwed into an identical threaded boss on the new engine.

56 On the right is the old air conditioning belt which is driven by the crank pulley on the 300 Tdi engine, while on the left is the new belt, shorter

because it's driven by the fan pulley (which is itself driven by the crank pulley via a separate belt).

57 The engines are similar, but different. This is the rear crank seal on the 2.8-litre engine. The two extra screws indicated, not fitted to Tdi engines, are there to prevent the oil seal leak that's so common on Land Rover engines.

58 The spigot bearing housing is a larger size on the 2.8 engine. The conversion kit includes this adaptor bush plus a new phosphor-bronze bearing into which the first motion shaft on the gearbox will be slid as the engine is installed.

59 With automatic transmissions, of course, this isn't the case. This is the adaptor plate assembly fitted to the (modified) flywheel used on auto transmission conversions.

60 Lock the front end of the crank while the flex plate is fitted to the flywheel.

61 Now for the easy bit. The 2.8 lump is so similar in outward construction that it's really simple to install it in the Defender's engine bay (this applies to Discoverys as well), but it's a bit of a squeeze in places and you have to pay attention to avoid damaging anything that's already in there.

62 After slipping it past the power steering reservoir, concentrate on aligning the engine with the transmission. Although still quite a fiddle, this is so much easier in the case of an automatic transmission than a manual transmission with the first motion shaft that has to be aligned with and inserted into the back of the engine.

63 You can just see the trolley jack on the floor, used to raise and lower the transmission bell housing so that it becomes parallel with the engine before inserting the bolts holding the two units together.

64 With an automatic transmission, the flex plate in the torque converter has to be bolted to the engine flywheel. In order that the bolts can be tightened you need to lock the front end of the engine.

65 One of the fiddly fitting jobs involves mounting the air cleaner bracket to the engine, since the engine dipstick is in the way. The instructions supplied with the kit point out that the dipstick tube needs to be bent to clear the filter, and though it seems a daunting prospect it's actually easier than you'd expect!

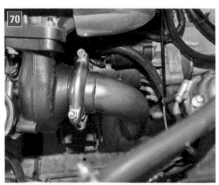

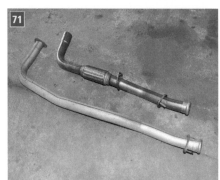

66 This standard 300 Tdi's air conditioning pump cradle would foul on the top of the 2.8 TGV engine's fuel pump but the Prins Maasdijk kit included steel spacer blocks (arrows) to provide the necessary clearance.

67 Now to a problem you're not going to encounter unless you have an Ashcroft automatic transmission fitted. The lack of clearance above the fuel pump when air conditioning is fitted means that the fuel pump-mounted throttle position sensor fitted by Ashcroft can't be used. Ian therefore took the original 300 Tdi's throttle pedal and cut off the cable fixing...

68 ...before welding it to a Td5 throttle pedal which, being 'fly-by-wire', has no cable mounting but does have its own integral throttle position sensor.

69 On my Defender the mountings for the Td5 pedal were already there, but even if they hadn't been mounting it wouldn't have been difficult.

70 Loosely clamp the exhaust downpipe supplied with the kit to the exhaust outlet.

71 You can see the rest of the exhaust supplied by the Dutch engine supplier (top) and how much shorter it is than the standard unit beneath it. This is because of their different exhaust outlet positions from the engine.

72 Next loosely clamp the new exhaust to the existing system...

73 ...only carrying out final tightening once all the clearances have been properly established.

74 Because there's no turbo inlet pipe with the kit (or at least, none that fitted the Defender) Ian made up his own. The one being held was made in mild steel as a template, while beneath it you can see the final version in stainless.

75 We made a simple, folded, bolt-on bracket...

76 ...and clamped down the new stainless steel pipe.

77 The original air inlet hose is simply fitted to the new pipe.

IMPORTANT NOTE: if you're carrying out this work yourself and don't have access to advanced pipe-

bending equipment, make sure your engine supplier provides you with the correct parts – or you'll be stuck!

78 OK, so the stainless steel pipe introduces fresh air into the turbo but now you need a pipe to go from the turbo to the intercooler. Ian fabricated a new pipe and used the silicone 90° bend supplied with the kit to connect it to the turbo.

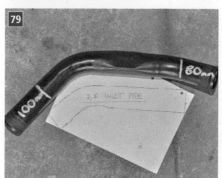

79 Without supplying details, the Dutch engine supplier suggested that the existing pipe could be cut down. After comparing it with the pipe Ian made, then yes, I think they were right. I don't think it would fit quite as elegantly as the pipe we made, but by cutting 100mm from one end and 80mm from the other you'd certainly have a serviceable intercooler pipe.

80 The next problem involved fitting the intercooler pipe elbow to the turbo. The stub on the turbo is a different size to that on the original 2.5 L engine. Prins Maasdijk, the suppliers at the time, suggested squeezing the elbow down with a pipe clamp but we were of the opinion that this would almost certainly create air leaks, and didn't seem to be good practice anyway. Instead, Ian made an aluminium sleeve with an outer flange...

81 ...that ended up being cut in two and fixed to the turbo stub with epoxy resin.

82 Because of its increased flexibility, silicone hose does make it easier to get the hose over the flange.

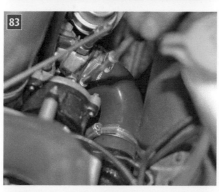

83 However, you have to remember not to over-tighten the hose clamps, because they can dig into and eventually cut through soft silicone hose.

84 Another hose not supplied with the kit (or at least not for the right-hand drive version of the Defender) is the vacuum hose that goes to the servo. Ian used one-shot hose clips to fix the hose in place...

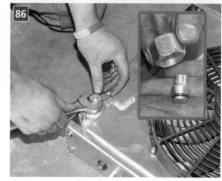

85 ...then refitted the connector to the servo body.

86 The 2.8 TGV engine has an oil cooler plumbed directly into the cooling system. This means that the oil cooler stubs on your radiator become redundant. The Prins Maasdijk engine kit included a pair of nice blanking plugs (see inset) for the radiator. Note that this is a replacement aluminium radiator, but the same principle applies.

87 As we refitted the radiator, we connected up the various hoses as we went along.

88 We also made up mountings for the air conditioning condenser on the air conditioning nose frame...

89 ...and fixed the auto transmission oil cooler to the same frame. You have to make sure that the cooler fits in the airflow and isn't hidden behind part of the grille.

90 Then we broke out the Morris' antifreeze, mixed it 50:50 with water and removed the filler plug from the top of the radiator.

91 It's crucially important that Land Rover diesel engines are topped up with coolant 'by the book'. This is because any air pockets in a diesel engine's water jackets can lead to rapid failure. Once coolant starts to appear in the header tank, replace the radiator filler plug, remove that from the thermostat and top up again there. A lot of hose squeezing should also take place, to encourage as much air out of the system as possible.

92 Morris' 10W/47 semi-synthetic engine oil is much more economical when purchased in 25-litre drums, but you can also purchase much smaller top-up containers.

93 Because of having to change the power steering pump, the opportunity was taken to refill with Morris' Dexron II automatic transmission fluid, which is also used here as power steering fluid.

94 After running the engine up to temperature, and checking for leaks or any other problems my Defender was ready for its first test drive, a trundle around the farm buildings surrounding Ian's workshop unit.

VERDICT
At the time of writing this I've only done a few hundred miles and, after spending all those thousands on the engine, I'm treating it gently for now. But already the difference is very noticeable. There's no more groaning lack of power when pulling away from rest or uphill, and overtaking is something you don't have to plan months in advance.

The engine sounds different too. It's recognisably a Tdi-derived lump but it's got a deeper note, and it's smoother and noticeably quieter when the vehicle is on the move.

I love the fact that it's got top-quality Mahle pistons and a forged crank, that the rear oil seal can be expected to work properly, that the head is more efficient and the water jacket has been developed. And not least, of course, that I can look forward to some seriously improved performance over the standard engine, once the new one has loosened up.

It was also hugely encouraging that someone as accomplished and such a perfectionist as Ian Baughan fitted the thing. His Land Rover engineering skills, developed at the factory itself, are as good as you can get.

Whether you can justify the several thousand pounds that these engines cost is something only you can decide. My Defender, though built in '06, was fitted with a 300 Tdi from new because it was built to 'rest of world' spec. And it had only done 8,000 miles when the new engine was fitted, so in this case it was money well spent.

You have to remember, whenever you're carrying out non-standard modifications, that there will always be unforeseen complications. Even, as in this case, when you're buying a kit of parts, there may still be areas that present difficulties that you simply have to solve yourself.

FOOTNOTE
The Dutch suppliers, Prins Maasdijk ceased their connection with replacement International Land Rover engines shortly after mine was fitted. A UK supplier, Motor & Diesel, whose fitting kits are known to be of very high quality, are now the people to contact for the supply of engines and components.

Ian Baughan of IRB developments holds up a standard Puma engine's intercooler in front of a full-sized intercooler fitted to the vehicle.

First, a note about why so-called 'porting and polishing' of cylinder heads isn't included here. Petrol engines are much more 'revvy' than diesel engines and respond well to having the cylinder heads polished to improve gas flow. However, it's a relatively arcane and complex business about which whole books have been written. And in any case, the diesel engines covered in this manual are much easier and more cost-effective to tune by other means, as shown here.

1 We show elsewhere in this manual how to fit a full-sized intercooler from Allard Turbo Sport. This is one of the IRB Developments versions. Just changing the standard intercooler for an aluminium performance version will make a big difference, while switching to a full-sized intercooler is another forward leap – though not by as much, proportionally, as replacing the standard intercooler with a standard-sized but more efficient one.

AIR FILTERS

2 Don't overlook the fact that a more efficient air filter will allow air to flow more easily into the engine. This is a Puma engine's version.

3 A K&N high-flow air filter is fitted to the standard 300 Tdi filter housing on my Defender.

EXHAUST GAS RECIRCULATION VALVE

4 Getting rid of the EGR valve is a simple and relatively inexpensive way of improving your Defender engine's performance. This is one of the kits available from Allard Turbo Sport.

This is Allard's unparalleled advice on why you should consider replacing your EGR valve:

'All EGR systems reduce air flow, combustion efficiency and consequently engine power. The exhaust gas re-circulation system is an attempt to reduce the level of nitrous oxide being emitted through the exhaust system. To achieve this, a proportion of the exhaust gas is diverted by the EGR valve unit (only at part load and light load conditions – at full throttle the vehicle ECU will tell the EGR to close – it is also engine coolant temperature dictated – too hot or cold and the EGR will stay closed), from the exhaust manifold to the inlet manifold, to mix with the inducted charge. The EGR system also helps reduce diesel knock by slowing down the combustion process – but on a Land Rover diesel engine you probably won't notice the difference.

'The system works well as far as reducing the oxides of the nitrogen on a new engine, but in general on older engines of over say two years (35,000 miles), the effectiveness is compromised by the sludge build up inside the inlet manifold. This further reduces engine performance and airflow, which in turn reduces combustion efficiency and increases other unwanted emissions, principally CO_2 and particulate emission. The sludge is a combination of oil and exhaust emission (soot) meeting at the EGR valve inlet; the oil can be found leaking from the front bearing of the turbocharger (compressor side) but mainly from the breather system which is directly connected into the induction tube between the air filter and turbocharger on a Tdi engine.

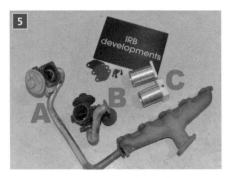

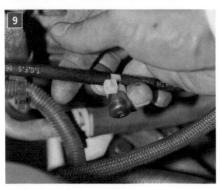

Many people think that simply replacing an EGR valve will solve the problem; well that's simply not the case. This is because the turbo bearings continue to wear and, with the breather system left connected, the engine will continue to discharge oil into the turbocharger inlet, which then leads into the inlet manifold/EGR valve.

'The EGR valve itself is generally a reliable part and can last the life of the engine. The only way of solving the problem of sludge build-up is to ultimately renew the turbo (if it has started to leak oil) and fit a separate engine breather system.

'From the point of view of obtaining optimum power output, it is obviously detrimental to introduce hot exhaust into the inlet manifold, even if this is only under light load conditions. Any associated pipe work restrictions also contribute to this. Also, on older engines, there are increasing failures with leakages from the EGR valve and to replace one can cost more than a "removal" kit.

'However, leaving a failed EGR valve on an engine will also lead to massively increased engine bore wear!

'A better alternative to the EGR System is to fit an EGR valve replacement kit for improved performance, thermal efficiency, fuel consumption and smoke emission. This will:

- Get rid of all the problems associated with faulty or leaking EGR (exhaust gas recirculation) system.
- Eliminate tar and sediment build-up inside inlet manifold, which in turn reduces air flow.
- Improve thermal efficiency, by reducing heat build-up in the inlet manifold.

'All these benefits combine to give improvements in overall fuel consumption and performance with a reduction in exhaust smoke.'

5 Here are a standard Td5 EGR valve (A), one from a 300 Tdi (B) and a replacement for the valve, one with connector stub and one without. IRB developments offer two inlet options for Td5 (C). One is a standard inlet stub and the other, with a thicker base, offers the option of fitting a turbo pressure (boost) gauge.

6 On the left is a rather inferior connection for the turbo hose, while on the right the IRB Developments version is machined so that the hose, once it's clip has been tightened, can't slip off under pressure.

7 This is where a Td5 EGR has been removed, leaving the plain connector shown in the previous shot in its place.

8 The blanking plate fitted in position on the heat exchanger (EU3 Td5 engine).

9 An IRB Developments closing-off cap where a vacuum pipe used to go to the top of the EGR valve.

Td5 EGR SYSTEMS
Two types of EGR system have been fitted to Td5s, and these are the fitting procedures:

ALL VERSIONS
- Remove the three bolts holding the engine acoustic cover in place.
- Take out the four screws and remove the cooling fan cowl.
- Disconnect the vacuum hose from the EGR valve and blank off. Ideally there will be a blanking plug supplied with the kit.

LATER TYPE, KNOWN AS EU3 (2001–6)
There are two vacuum hoses to/from the EGR valve.
- Cable-tie the redundant vacuum hose(s) neatly in place after you've finished the job – hoses will be removed if done with a proper kit.
- Remove the four 6mm bolts attaching the EGR valve to the inlet manifold (8mm head).
- Detach the jubilee clip holding the engine air intake hose and remove it from the EGR valve.

EARLY TYPE, KNOWN AS EU2 ('98–'01)
- Detach the two 8mm bolts from the EGR recirculation pipe, where it fastens to the front of the cylinder head, and remove the two 5mm Allen bolts securing it to the exhaust manifold.

IMPORTANT NOTE: Especially with older engines, there's a real risk of at least one of the two 5mm Allen bolts shearing off when you try to undo them. To reduce the risk:
- Only work when the engine (and thus the exhaust manifold) is cold.
- Apply copious amounts of releasing oil, preferably a full day before attempting to remove them.
- If the bolts don't move and look as though they might shear off, apply localised heat using a heat gun to help break the sealed thread.

EU3 ENGINES (2001–6)
The EGR recirculation pipe will probably be fitted with a heat exchanger. If so:
- Remove the pipes but leave the heat exchanger in place. Your supplier should provide additional blanks to seal it off.
- There will be another vacuum pipe running to an additional actuator on the side of the EGR valve body. As with the other vacuum pipe(s) described above, this must be blanked off.

LATER EU2 AND EU3 ENGINES ONLY
- The two electronic modulators must both be disconnected electrically from their black and green plugs. The ECU will no longer recognise them.
- Alternatively you can completely remove the EGR electronic modulator assembly, but if you do so you must fit a new pipe without a T-piece in it. These are available from Land

Rover dealers, parts numbers ANR6916 (RHD vehicles) or SQB103360 (LHD vehicles). The other option is to use the EGR removal kit from IRB Developments, who've had a purpose-made blanking cap moulded (Step 9 photograph opposite). The IRB kit also comes with a blanking cap for the air box (the Td5 also has a pipe from the air filter to the solenoid valve).

EXHAUST

There are two main reasons for fitting a modified exhaust. One is to fit a 'performance' exhaust. The other is to fit stainless instead of mild steel to increase the exhaust system's longevity. However, be careful. Though a stainless steel exhaust will last far longer than one made from mild steel, some cheaper stainless steel systems are made from less expensive materials and will still rust, albeit at a slower rate than their mild steel counterparts.

Exhaust pipe size is also relevant because it's no good increasing the flow of fuel and air into the engine if the burned gases can't easily get out again.

10 These two exhaust centre-sections look virtually identical on the outside…

11 …but the difference in diameter becomes apparent when you look at a cross-section.

12 Another option is to replace the large centre exhaust silencer box with a much smaller equivalent.

13 IRB recommend mandrel bent exhaust systems. These are little more expensive than those formed with a regular pipe bender, but don't decrease the diameter of the pipe on the bends and allow a smoother gas flow.

FITTING A SNORKEL

14 These are the components supplied with the Bearmach snorkel we fitted to my Defender. Designed for fitment to the right-hand side they comprise upper mounting bracket; air ram assembly; gasket for mounting bracket; bolt (M6); stud (M8); three nuts (M8); three washers (M8); four self-tapping screws; foam gasket; snorkel body; template; sealing gasket; and hose-clamp for air ram assembly.

15 This Britpart snorkel is not only different because it fits to the left-hand side of the vehicle (and is intended for pre-300 Tdi models only) but also because it has a slightly different approach to fitting. Britpart and Bearmach can both supply left-hand and right-hand snorkels, suitable for both versions of Defender.

16 There are no visible bolt heads on the Bearmach unit because fixings have to be accessed from inside the wing, which means tapping through the plastic rivet heads then removing the wheel arch liner.

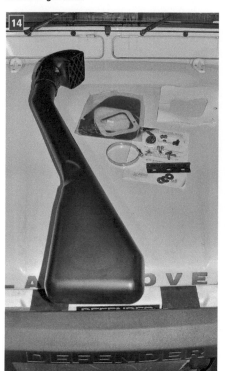

17 In all cases the air intake cover has to be levered free, taking care not to damage the paintwork.

18 The template supplied with the Bearmach unit must be checked against the threaded holes in the snorkel. We used masking tape to cover each pre-stamped hole in the template and then marked new hole centres with a scriber.

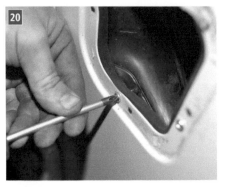

19 After removing screws and freeing the inlet pipe from inside the wing, the Bearmach kit has a foam seal that fits between the wing and the inlet pipe.

20 The round-head screws holding the inlet pipe in position have to be removed again and replaced with countersunk head screws because the snorkel fits flush into the recess in the bodywork.

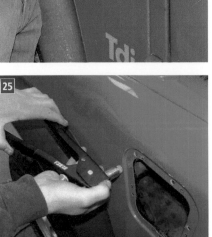

21 Use the template to drill pilot holes for the four bolt positions.

22 Before fitting the 200 Tdi's snorkel, apply masking tape round the aperture then offer up the snorkel. Mark through the holes with a pencil...

23 ...before lightly centre punching...

24 ...then drilling the correct size holes...

25 ...for the rivnuts supplied with the kit. You could, of course, use regular nuts and bolts using the method shown here for the Bearmach snorkel.

26 Offering up the Bearmach snorkel, having temporarily screwed in the threaded studs supplied, showed that it didn't fit!

27 Holes have to be filed out until the snorkel body matched the shape of the wing top.

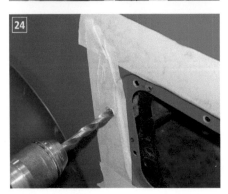

28 I had some quick-drying Tetrosyl aerosol primer on the shelf. Some was squirted into the aerosol cap and painted on to protect raw edges of aluminium from corrosion.

29 The Britpart kit requires sealant between the air inlet pipe and the body…

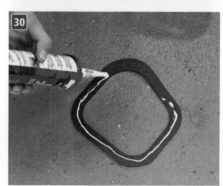

30 …and more sealant is added to the external gasket…

31 …on both sides of it…

32 …before offering up to the snorkel and screwing the fixing bolts into the rivnuts.

33 This is how the Bearmach snorkel fits together.

34 The four studs each have a couple of nuts run along them before being treated with some Würth permanent thread lock…

35 …immediately before the two nuts were used to tighten each stud in turn into the body of the snorkel, before removing the two nuts again.

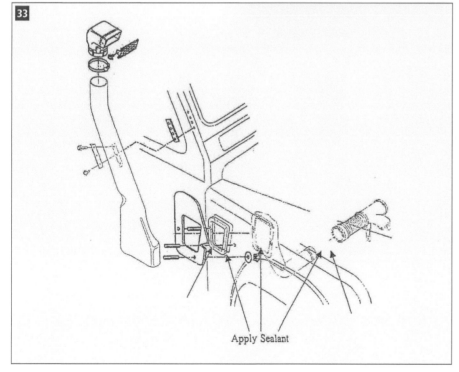

Apply Sealant

36 The concealed studs pass through the holes in the body, and it's a bit of a fiddle to reach inside the wing to fit the washers and lock nuts supplied.

37 Both snorkels come with an angle bracket to be screwed to the body of the snorkel.

38 This time we used Würth medium-duty thread lock in case the bolts ever need to be removed.

39 Without significantly moving the position of the snorkel on the wing the snorkel upright didn't line up with the angle bracket when fitted to the windscreen frame, so we used spacers to make up the difference.

40 The hole positions are centre punched …

41 …before drilling tapping-size holes and screwing in the stainless steel self-tapping screws provided. I've got a box of nut caps I bought on eBay and I raided it to finish off the bolt heads.

42 The effectiveness of the snorkel depends on the quality of its seal both inside and outside. We decided to make the outside seal doubly effective by piping some Würth Bond & Seal around the joint.

43 The inlet on the snorkel is held to the top of the pipe with a screw clamp. While having it facing forward could well add some ram-effect, it will also allow the ingress of rainwater and could block up in blizzard conditions. Turning it 180° to face the other way is an option.

44 The final result is a snorkel whose appearance you'll either love or hate. A test drive suggested to me that the snorkel actually did make a small but noticeable difference to power at speeds over about 30mph when, presumably, the ram effect increases.

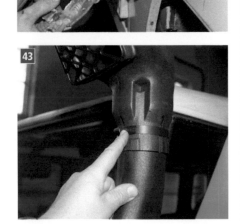

Turbocharging options

A turbocharger is a pump. It consists of a turbine, driven by the exhaust gas from the engine and a shaft from the turbine driving a compressor wheel. The compressor forces a greater mass of air into an engine than would otherwise be the case.

The turbocharger needs to be correctly matched to an engine. If a turbo is too large, you'll experience turbo lag because of the delay before the turbocharger's turbine wheel spins fast enough to produce usable 'boosted' pressure. If turbo lag is overcompensated for by using too small a turbocharger, it won't supply sufficient air at higher revolutions and there'll be a real risk of over-speeding and thus damaging the turbocharger.

So in simple terms most fixed-blade turbochargers are a compromise, with a bit too much turbo lag than would be ideal and not quite as much boosted pressure as would be ideal either. Incidentally, the blades on the turbo are sometimes referred to as 'vanes', while their setting is referred to as 'geometry'. The geometry of the blades on the turbo is sometimes referred to as its 'aspect ratio', or A/R.

A variable vane (or 'variable blade', or 'variable geometry') turbo does what it says and can adjust itself internally to mimic the effect of making the turbo either smaller or larger, according to requirements. This is done because the optimum aspect ratio at low engine speeds is very different from that at high engine speeds. If the aspect ratio is too large, the turbo will fail to create boost at low speeds; if the aspect ratio is too small, the turbo will choke the engine at high speeds, leading to high exhaust manifold pressures, high pumping losses, and ultimately lower power output.

By altering the geometry of the turbine blades as the engine accelerates, the turbo's aspect ratio can be maintained at, or near, its optimum. Because of this, variable vane turbos have a minimal amount of lag, a low boost threshold, and are very efficient at higher engine speeds.

What's more, variable vane turbos don't require a wastegate. These turbos are particularly well suited to diesel engines, as the lower exhaust temperatures mean they're less prone to failure.

On the road a variable vane turbo can transform the low speed performance of your Defender. Instead of the usual delay between pressing the throttle and experiencing acceleration, you notice an instant pickup, which makes the vehicle so much more satisfying to drive.

1 At the time of writing, IRB Developments is the only company offering the full range of Land Rover Defender turbocharger upgrades, comprising: (A) Variable vane for 200 Tdi – goes into a separate exhaust manifold; (B) Variable vane for 300 Tdi – the turbo body is the exhaust manifold; (C) Stage 3 Td5 turbocharger, a 'race' specification turbo for people who want 200-plus bhp (with matched mapping and intercooler change) – the turbo body is larger and there's very slightly more turbo lag; (D) Stage 2 Td5 turbocharger, which provides a smooth pickup, more responsive throttle and a noticeable power gain (theoretically there's a Stage 1 version that provides greater smoothness but no real power gain); and (E) Upgraded Tdci (Puma) turbocharger, electronically actuated, which has a larger exhaust wheel and compressor wheel than standard so, at the same boost pressure, provides greater airflow.

2 The 200 Tdi's turbocharger can also be fitted to earlier Turbo diesel engines, but according to Ian Baughan it's a really bad idea because the engine would be highly likely to blow up! These are the standard units, from 200 Tdi to Tdci, reading from left to right. IRB's upgraded turbochargers are a direct replacement for the standard turbocharger (the only change required on some turbos is a new oil feed pipe, supplied as part of the kit).

3 Close-up of a standard Tdci turbocharger (left) and the IRB upgraded version (right).

4 Compressor wheel and porting on the standard version.

5 The modified version is quite clearly larger.

6 This Td5 engine has an IRB turbocharger fitted to it, while above it is the original turbo that was removed from the engine. As you can see, one is a direct replacement for the other, though fitting a variable vane turbo will only give of its best if other 'breathing' and fuelling modifications and adjustments are also made.

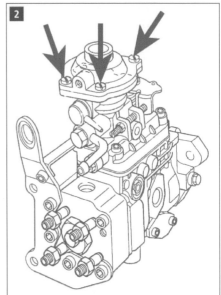

1 I was delighted when Alan Allard himself popped over to my workshop to finalise the fuel injection pump tuning. If we'd needed it Alan could have checked the boost pressure on the turbocharger and then adjusted it as required. However, we agreed that in the interests of longevity, and since the engine itself was almost brand-new, we'd leave the boost pressure as standard.

2 Alan was quite certain, however, that the engine would be under-fuelled. The light ram effect from the snorkel, the cleaner passageways of the K&N air filter and the straight-through exhaust pipe and, most of all, the extra oxygen supplied by the larger intercooler all meant that the engine was receiving extra O_2 but no extra fuel. So he started by removing the screws from the top of the fuel pump, which is very similar to the standard 300's pump.

3 Removing the cap revealed a plate and diaphragm…

4 …and beneath it a plunger, with a taper machined on to its lower end, a plastic spacer and a spring. When the engine is at idle, the spring holds the plunger fully upwards and the taper (arrowed) bears against a fuel valve pin in the pump. Because the plunger is in the 'up' position, the taper is at its widest end, and this keeps the valve almost fully closed. As the engine accelerates the plunger is pulled downwards against the force of the spring, exposing the narrower part of the plunger to the fuel mechanism and allowing more fuel to flow.

5 As you can see, the taper is eccentric to the shaft, so that if the shaft is turned a larger or smaller amount of fuel is allowed to flow through the pump. Of course, to Alan this is child's play, but if you don't know what you're doing work with someone who does. Interestingly, you can see that there seems to be some dirt build-up on the taper, and the fuel valve pin was certainly very sticky.

If the proof of the pudding lies in the driving then I'm delighted to say that the pudding is well proven. There's much more torque low down, delivery is smoother across the range and there's even a higher comfortable cruising speed on the motorway. I haven't had an opportunity to carry out an economy check yet, but I'm convinced, from the ease with which the engine pulls, that there's the potential for much better economy as well as brisker and more relaxed driving.

ECU upgrades

The ECU, or electronic control unit, controls many aspects of the Td5 and later four-cylinder Puma Defender's operations, including its crucial engine fuelling systems. The factory settings give the best possible compromise between performance, economy, smoothness and the ability to pass the all-important emissions regulations in many parts of the world and in many different operating conditions, including high and low altitude.

It's a relatively simple matter to establish different parameters, ones that improve performance with or without affecting the economy and emissions while, in all probability, losing some of the versatility built into the original settings, such as the ability to perform acceptably in extreme operating conditions.

However, at the time of writing it's not permissible in the UK to use non-

standard settings, and if an external plug-in electronic 'box' is fitted the vehicle will fail the MoT test. The situation regarding a reprogrammed ECU isn't so clear-cut. If you're considering having your Td5's ECU reprogrammed, you must first satisfy yourself that you'll be acting within the law and regulations in the country or territory where you and your vehicle are based.

1 The ECU is located on a bracket beneath the right-hand seat.

2 On the later, Puma-engined models the ECU is in the engine bay, mounted on the bulkhead behind the engine (arrowed). All Puma-engined ECUs are fitted with flash chips and can be reprogrammed.

3 Early Td5s up to 2002 have a non-flash chip, which means that the settings can't be altered. The solution – for those who know what they're doing – is to remove the original chip and replace it with a flash type that can be reset. This earlier ECU bears the alphanumeric code 'MSB' followed by six numbers.

4 The later Td5 ECU carries the alphanumeric code 'NNN' followed by six numbers. This type contains a flash chip and can be reprogrammed. Some people try to fit 'NNN' ECUs to earlier vehicles, but they don't operate satisfactorily. The Td5 engine fitted until 2002 is substantially different to the 2002-on engine, so the two ECUs are incompatible.

5 Here you can see the difference between the chip in the earlier ECU (left) and the later type (right).

6 One solution is to remove the non-flash chip from an earlier ECU by melting the solder from each connection…

7 …and then solder in its place a mounting socket that allows a new, clip-in, flash-type chip to be fitted.

8 Then, whether it's a replacement square-shaped chip or rectangular flash-type chip, you can connect IRB Developments' reprogramming tool to a computer, insert the flash chip and reprogram it, applying settings from on-road mild to competition wild as required.

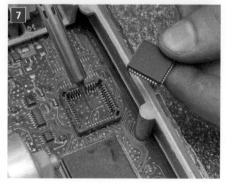

CHAPTER 2

Transmission

Quaife limited slip axle differentials

Those Land Rovers without advanced traction control can suffer from individual wheel slip. Quaife diffs prevent this and provide automatic, full-time 4WD at all times. Here's a pair of Quaife axle diffs being fitted at Ashcroft Transmissions.

There was I, happily reversing a three-tonne trailer load of logs down the garden. The ground was slightly boggy, the grass was slippery, and as soon as I hit a slight incline progress stopped and all drive went through one spinning wheel, courtesy of the standard differentials. So naturally, I locked the centre diff and tried again, this time achieving two spinning wheels instead of one.

This brought home to me the difference between a traditional Land Rover with 'open' diffs and a more modern torque-sensing set-up. I then discovered that a purely mechanical solution can be achieved by fitting Quaife differentials.

As a direct replacement for the standard, factory-fitted 'open' differential, Quaife's Automatic Torque Biasing (ATB) Helical Limited Slip Differential (LSD) automatically directs torque away from a spinning wheel, across the axle to the other wheel. Unlike a conventional limited slip unit, it uses gears

rather than clutch plates for its operation. So it's silent, much smoother (because, unlike a conventional plate-type LSD, it never locks harshly with a set pre-load of wheel slip across the driven axle), works

to a constantly varying degree (depending on requirements) and is fully automatic. Consequently you never need to stop and engage your diff lock, even where you've got one.

1 The heading picture shows the two Quaife axle differentials as delivered to Ashcroft Transmissions. We also fitted a Quaife centre diff in the transfer box, and we'll be covering that later. First DiXie, my Defender, was taken to Autoland 4x4, who removed and refitted the main units for Ashcroft.

2 Autoland's mechanic removed the front half shafts by detaching each front hub complete. There's a bit of work involved, of course, including detaching steering arms.

3 After clamping off the brake hoses, he removed them from the calipers and took off each front hub, complete with caliper assembly and half shaft still fitted at the outer end. On reassembly brake bleeding took a mere two pumps per side, but if you were concerned about it another approach would be to leave the hoses connected to the calipers, unbolt the calipers from the hubs and leave the calipers hanging in the wheel arches, taking care not to put any strain on brake hoses.

4 After detaching the prop shaft, the fixing nuts were removed and the front differential was freed and lifted out ready for Ashcroft Transmissions to take away.

5 At the back the process is somewhat simpler. After removing the dust cap, the circlip is freed and removed...

6 ...and the hub bolts extracted...

7 ...enabling each back axle half shaft to be removed...

8 ...before taking out the back axle differential. Then it was over to Ashcroft Transmissions for the next stage in the process.

9 At Ashcroft, the engineer made witness marks on the bearing caps with a centre punch so they could be refitted on same side and the right way round.

10 Next he drove out the locking pins in the bearing adjusters so that the adjusters can be turned when the diff is reassembled later. The pins are left in place – no need to remove them completely.

11 After unbolting the bearing cap bolts, they're simply lifted off...

12 ...and the bearing side adjustment nuts are removed.

13 The differential crownwheel assembly can now be lifted out of the differential casing.

14 Once out, remove the bolts holding the differential to the crownwheel...

15 ...and, using a mallet, tap evenly around the perimeter of the crownwheel, which is a tight fit, until it's free of the flange...

16 ...and lift away the 'old' open diff. Note that the old bearings are left on the ends of the diff...

17 ...because we'll be fitting new ones to the Quaife diff. It would be madness not to, in view of the amount of dismantling carried out and the cost of fitting the new diffs.

18 Each of the new bearings is pressed on using an hydraulic press and applying pressure only to the centre part of the bearing.

19 Now, with both new bearings fitted, the new Quaife diff (right) is ready to be built back up. Differentials that don't have any torque-sensing or lock-up mechanism are known as 'open' diffs, and the standard diff (left) is quite literally open in the sense that you can see the gears inside, though that's not what's meant by 'open' in this context of course! It means that the diff will allow one wheel on an axle to sit stock still if the other one is spinning freely.

20 The crownwheel is placed over the open jaws of the vice and the Quaife differential is lowered into position.

21 All-new high tensile bolts are used, with thread lock applied. It's not unheard of for bolts inside a differential to come loose, but it's expensive and would potentially be very dangerous if it caused the diff to lock solid. So Ashcroft always fit new bolts.

22 Holes and threads are perfectly aligned and each of the bolts is started off by hand before being tightened across opposite sides, first one side, then the other – though not fully tightened yet. **NB** Don't leave the bolts, between first tightening and torquing them down, because otherwise the thread lock will go off (which it does as soon as air is excluded), and all you'll do is break the thread lock joint, destroying its effectiveness.

23 Final tightening is carried out with a torque wrench. This has to be done according to the torque figures in the workshop manual for the particular differential fitted to your Land Rover.

24 On this particular differential, Ashcroft knew that the height from the top of the pinion should be between 76.1 and 76.2mm. The reading they got was 76.22mm, which was deemed to be perfectly acceptable. If it had been outside the acceptable range the pinion height would have had to be adjusted by adding or removing shims beneath the pinion, as necessary. However, it's rare for a diff that hasn't been badly worn to need any adjustment in this area.

25 The assembled Quaife differential and crownwheel are lowered into position in the casing after first checking that they're going in the right way round. You can't get it wrong because the crownwheel matches the cutaway inside the casing.

26 Note that the adjustment nuts are threaded. It's essential that the threads on the nuts bed fully into the threads in the casing...

27 ...as well as those in the caps. Check that each cap is properly bedded down into its thread before fitting and tightening each cap bolt. If you're not as experienced as Ashcroft's engineers it would be best to tighten each of the bolts with a spanner. Constantly check that the nut turns freely as each bolt is tightened up. The nut must turn freely even after the bearing cap is fully home.

28 The process to be followed here is quite critical, but it's logical when you think about it. The bearing adjuster on the opposite side to the crownwheel is backed off quite a long way, then the adjuster on the same side as the crownwheel...

29 ...is tightened using the correct spanner, pushing the crownwheel against the pinion...

30 ...until you can *just* feel no backlash between the prop shaft flange and the crownwheel when trying to turn one against the other. Then the adjustment nut on the opposite side is tightened up again, in effect pushing the crownwheel *away* from the pinion until you can just feel a little backlash. Admittedly, most of us wouldn't feel confident judging what is and isn't the right amount of backlash, in which case it's best to follow the procedure described in the workshop manual.

31 Another rather technical area is establishing that the crownwheel is in the correct position relative to the pinion. Ashcroft achieve this by applying engineers' blue to four of the teeth on the crownwheel...

32 ...and after turning the crownwheel so that the blued area is in contact with the pinion, work it backwards and forwards several times so that some of the blue is rubbed off. The resultant roughly oval patches are the areas of contact. Once again, it takes a certain degree of engineering experience to ascertain with certainty the actual area of contact.

HOW DO QUAIFE DIFFERENTIALS WORK?

Sets of floating helical gear pinions mesh to provide conventional differential action. If a wheel slips, torque bias is generated by the axial and radial thrusts of the pinions in their pockets. The resultant friction forces enable the differential to transmit a greater proportion of the torque to the appropriate wheel. The effect is progressive and at no stage does the differential lock solid, so you'll never find the steering trying to plough straight ahead, as with other performance differentials.

Quaife claim these diffs are true 'fit and forget' units. Indeed, they come with a lifetime guarantee. This means that unlike a conventional plate-type LSD, the Quaife ATB Helical LSD unit requires no special maintenance or rebuilds. Also, it only needs standard lubrication oil.

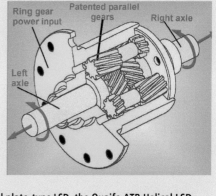

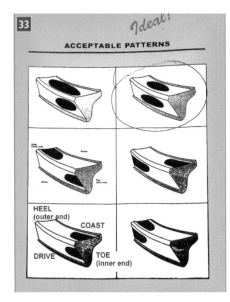

33 This picture from the workbook used by Ashcroft Transmissions shows acceptable patterns on the teeth of the crownwheel. The bottom four are typical faults, where the crownwheel position would need adjustment.

34 Note that the area of contact on the 'backs' of the teeth (correctly described as the 'drive' side) have to be checked as well.

35 With tensions correct, drive in the lock pins to prevent the adjustment nuts from turning.

36 Earlier, Ashcroft had fitted the bearing bolts so that the adjustment nuts could be set. However, it's crucially important that thread lock isn't applied until you're ready to torque each bolt down, as already explained. Now, one at a time, each bearing bolt is removed and cleaned of any old thread lock. New thread lock is applied and the bolt is refitted and tightened down to the recommended torque setting.

37 Ashcroft Transmissions' work was done, and the differentials were returned to Autoland. Their mechanic applied silicone gasket to the diff (no paper gaskets were used on this version)...

38 ...offered up the diff carefully, taking care not to disturb the liquid gasket...

39 ...and placed it on the studs on the axle casing before refitting the nuts that had been removed the previous day.

40 The half shafts *do* have paper gaskets, and new ones were fitted...

41 ...before sliding each half shaft into place. A measure of jiggling is often required to persuade the splines on the half shaft to enter those on the differential.

42 With front and rear axles fully reassembled, the last job is to top up with (in this case) semi-synthetic differential oil. Note that earlier vehicles, those whose oil seals weren't designed for use with synthetic oil, will almost certainly spring a leak if synthetic oil is used.

Quaife limited slip centre differential

Before having these diffs fitted, I envisaged what would happen if you'd fitted Quaife diffs to the axles and were waiting on an icy slope to pull away. You might find that all the drive went to either the front or the rear axle because of the open centre diff in the transfer casing. OK, you could always stop and apply the centre diff lock but that wouldn't be much use if a 20-tonne truck was bearing down on you! It seems to me that it's something of a false economy to fit torque-sensing diffs to the axles but not to the differential. So here's what's involved in fitting a Quaife ATB Helical LSD unit to the differential unit.

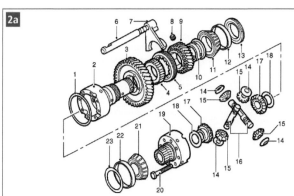

1 The complete transfer gearbox, the unit that sends drive to both axles, was collected from Autoland 4x4, who removed and refitted the main units for Ashcroft Transmissions.

2 It's helpful at this stage to have an idea how the transfer box's parts fit together and what they're called, so:

DIFFERENTIAL COMPONENTS

1 Retaining ring	13 Bearing retaining nut
2 Differential carrier – rear half	14 Dished thrust washers
3 Low range gear	15 Planet gears
4 High/low hub	16 Cross shafts
5 High/low selector sleeve	17 Sun gears
6 High/low selector shaft	18 Selective thrust washers
7 High/low selector fork	19 Differential carrier – front half
8 Setscrew – high/low selector fork	20 Bolt – differential carriers
9 High range gear	21 Differential front bearing
10 High range gear bush	22 Bearing outer track
11 Differential rear bearing	23 Selective shim
12 Bearing outer track	

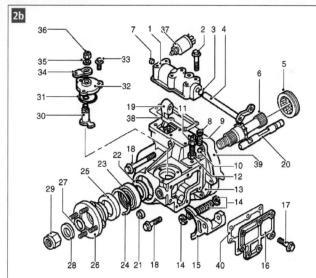

FRONT OUTPUT HOUSING COMPONENTS

1 High/low cross shaft housing	22 Bearing spacer
2 Bolt – high/low cross shaft housing	23 Output shaft bearing
3 'O' ring	24 Circlip
4 High/low cross shaft and lever	25 Oil seal
5 Dog clutch	26 Output shaft flange and mud shield
6 Front output shaft	27 Felt washer
7 Hollow plug	28 Steel washer
8 Detent plug – differential lock	29 Self-locking nut
9 Detent spring – differential lock	30 Differential lock selector finger and shaft
10 Detent ball – differential lock	31 'O' rings
11 Differential lock warning lamp switch	32 Differential lock selector housing
12 Lock nut	33 Bolt – housing
13 Front output housing	34 Selector lever
14 Spring and clips – differential lock	35 Washer
15 Differential lock selector fork	36 Self-locking nut
16 Side cover	37 Neutral warning lamp switch – Range Rover Classic – if fitted
17 Bolt – side cover	38 Gasket – high/low cross shaft housing*
18 Bolt – front output housing	39 Gasket – front output housing*
19 High/low selector finger	40 Gasket – side cover plate*
20 Differential lock selector shaft	*Up to serial no 288709E.*
21 Plug	

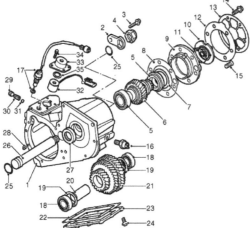

MAIN CASING COMPONENTS

1 Main casing
2 Retaining plate
3 Bolt – retaining plate
4 Stake nut – intermediate shaft
5 Bearings and outer tracks – mainshaft input gear
6 Mainshaft input gear*
7 Selective shim
8 Gasket†
9 Mainshaft input gear bearing housing
10 Oil feed plate‡
11 'O' ring‡
12 Gasket†
13 Cover plate/power take-off cover*
14 Bolt – cover plate
15 Countersunk screw – bearing housing
16 Oil temperature switch‡
17 Neutral warning lamp switch and washer – not Range Rover Classic‡
18 Bearings and outer tracks – intermediate gears
19 Circlips

20 Collapsible spacer
21 Intermediate gears
22 Gasket†
23 Bottom cover plate
24 Bolt – bottom cover plate
25 'O' rings – intermediate shaft
26 Intermediate shaft
27 Mainshaft oil seal
28 Locating dowel
29 Detent plug – high/low selector
30 Detent spring – high/low selector
31 Detent ball – high/low selector
32 Interlock solenoid‡
33 Cover – interlock solenoid‡
34 Bolt – interlock solenoid cover‡
35 Belleville washer‡

*Defender mainshaft input gear and Discovery power take-off cover plate illustrated.
† Up to serial no 288709E.
‡ If fitted.

3 Start by removing the detent plug from the side of the transfer box case. Be sure to hang on to the plug, spring and ball found beneath.

4 Next remove the bolts holding the high/low cross shaft housing in place.

5 Give it several smart raps with a soft-faced mallet to unstick the liquid gasket.

6 Follow the same approach with the intermediate gears' cover plate – ie remove the screws and give it several clouts from different angles to dislodge the plate. Note that it's extremely bad practice to use a lever pushed between the two faces – there's the minor risk of distorting the plate and the very major risk of damaging the mating surfaces and causing an oil leak later.

7 The neutral warning lamp switch and washer (not always fitted) are unscrewed and removed from the side of the casing.

8 A ring of bolts holds the differential casing to the main casing.

9 Once again, the soft-faced tapping stick was used to break the seal. Always hammer on strong points on the case, *never* on the relatively vulnerable smooth areas of the casting.

10 Inside is the standard 'open' differential – 'open' meaning that there's nothing to stop all the drive going to a pair of spinning wheels on an axle, leaving the wheels on the other axle stuck and static. A limited slip diff prevents this.

11 Go round to the other side of the casing and take out the speedometer drive.

12 There are four different speedo drive gears available – the blue (fitted) and red shown here, plus black and yellow. Each has a different number of teeth, and the correct gear has to be selected to suit wheel/tyre size and final drive ratio, if they've been changed from standard. My speedo had been reading about 18% too fast (I'd checked it with a satnav), but the red gear put things absolutely right.

13 The nut holding the intermediate gear pin in place was a swine to remove!

14 After removing it, take off the nut and tap the pin right up to the casing...

15 ...before drifting it right through and out the other side.

16 Thus released, the intermediate gears are withdrawn from the casing.

17 Remove the differential components by turning the assembly on its side and lifting the casing up and away.

18 Remove the selector fork and shaft from the original, open differential.

19 Ashcroft have a special adapter fabricated to sit over the bearing retaining nut, but even with this in place the nut may be difficult to dislodge.

20 With the nut removed, a hydraulic press is used to push the differential and carrier from the low-range gear, the high-range gear and the bearing...

21 ...separating the differential from the components that will be used again. The bearing on the original diff is left in place...

22 ...because new bearings will be fitted to the Quaife diff.

23 After drifting on the new front differential bearing, turn the diff over and slide on the low-range gear – the right way round, of course!

24 It's interesting that Quaife require the use of the earlier, smaller high/low selector hub (left) rather than the one used on later transfer boxes (right). Dave Ashcroft tells me that he has never encountered any wear or reliability issues with the earlier type of hub so it's not obvious why Land Rover made the change, and there doesn't seem to be any disadvantage in going over to the earlier one.

25 The selector hub is followed up with the high/low selector sleeve and the high-range gear.

26 Put on the high range gear bush...

27 ...followed by a new bearing...

28 ...and a new retaining nut.

29 After tightening the nut, drift over the lock tabs.

30 Reinsert the fully assembled Quaife diff into the main casing.

31 Treat the output housing to a bead of non-setting gasket sealant...

32 ...before refitting it. The rebuilt transfer box assembly is then finished off on the bench.

33 Finally, bolt the box back into place, reconnect everything and...

34 ...fill to overflow plug level with semi-synthetic transmission oil. It's worth noting that synthetic oil isn't suitable unless specified in the handbook for your vehicle. Use it in an early vehicle, for which the seals aren't suitable, and it will almost certainly pour out again.

The first time the new diffs were used in anger was when I collected 2.5 tonnes of logs with my one-tonne (unladen) Atlas trailer, pushing the towing weight up to its maximum. All four wheels spun against the huge forces behind it, and my Defender travelled sideways and forwards at the same time until the trailer was pulled clear of the soft, clinging sand.

The addition of three Quaife diffs has completely transformed certain aspects of my Land Rover's behaviour. If I pull away rapidly on a very slippery road, I know that all four tyres will now grip almost instantaneously. On the other hand, normal use on the road shows no difference whatsoever in terms of handling or noise. It seems like a win-win to me!

Converting a Defender to automatic transmission is certainly a big enough job, but world-famous Ashcroft Transmissions have developed the ultimate in conversion kits for all models of Defender from 300 Tdi right up to the later Puma-engined versions. Let's look at how this kit was fitted to my 2006-built Defender.

Ashcroft Transmissions' kits are available for DIY or specialist fitting, or Ashcroft can convert your Defender for you. The majority of vehicles now being converted are, unsurprisingly, Puma-engined types, though the same electronic ZF auto 'box can be fitted to all versions of the Defender.

Alternatively, pre-Td5 models can be fitted with the non-electronic version of the automatic gearbox shown here. Indeed, since the 300 Tdi lacks electronic controls the electronically controlled 'box can only be fitted by using a Compushift electronic control unit, developed by Ashcroft to allow a wide range of user settings.

At the point where we start, the manual transmission assembly has already been removed in the conventional way, as described in the workshop manual. Note that the order in which the work is carried out is that preferred by Ashcroft's mechanic, and isn't necessarily that shown in the workshop manual. That doesn't make either of them right or wrong; there are almost always several alternative ways of doing the same job correctly.

BACKGROUND

Originally, Ashcroft converted Defenders to auto by using a Disco Td5 autobox rebuilt with hydraulic control as opposed to electronic control and fitted with a linkage to the throttle pedal to pull the kickdown cable. With the arrival of the Compushift programmable electronic control unit they're now able to use the stock Disco Td5 autobox, keep it electronic and use the Compushift to control it.

Both routes have their pros and cons. Looking at the hydraulic control option first, the disadvantage is that, as with any other hydraulically controlled autobox, you have a shift pattern that's pretty well fixed. The advantage is lower cost and simplicity.

The disadvantage of the electronic option is that it costs more. But there are quite a few advantages such as:
- You can adjust the Compushift to make the autobox shift exactly as you want it, lock up when you want it, or even operate it with a 'paddle' or switch-shift.
- When set up correctly it drives perfectly, just like a factory vehicle.

- You're now able to use the stock Disco 2 Td5 autobox, so if you're on a budget you can get the autobox, converter, starter ring, cooler etc from a breaker and just buy the Compushift and console from Ashcroft to complete the job.

COMPUSHIFT

The Compushift electronic control gear enables you to run an electronic 'box on a 300 Tdi, which doesn't have electronic controls, as well as on a Td5 or Puma-engined Defender, both of which have. It allows you to select shift patterns, change points, torque converter lock-up points and more, and even to install a sequential paddle shifter if you want one. The centre console is purpose-made for Ashcroft, based on an original Land Rover design, and looks like it's original equipment.

STAGE 1 UPGRADE

A Stage 1 upgrade option to the 4HP22 autobox is available at an additional cost: Ashcroft can fit the centre section of the box with the bigger internals from the ZF 4HP24 'box. This gets rid of one of the gearbox's weak links, the C1/C2 one-way clutch. The one from the 4HP24 gearbox is much stronger.

Another upgrade in the Stage 1 option is the planetary gear set, the solid 4HP24 type being much stronger than that of the '22 gearbox. Only the internals are changed, and the gearbox remains the same externally.

STAGE 2 UPGRADE

In the Stage 2 version the 'box is built with both of the internals described above, plus the 4HP24's front end, which provides the added strength of a larger A-clutch, which is another weak point on the 4HP22 gearbox.

TORQUE CONVERTER UPGRADES

The ZF auto used in Land Rover vehicles uses three different diameters of torque converter:

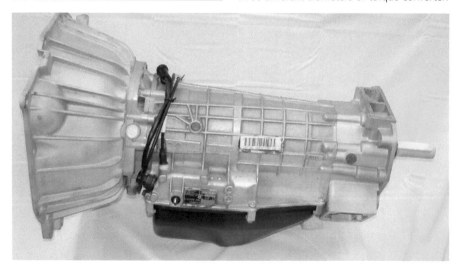

Because DiXie was effectively new when I bought it and we want to keep it 'for ever', I wanted to start with a brand new gearbox rather than a second-hand one. The uprated Ashcroft Stage 2 ZF 'box that we chose came from Bearmach, who were very helpful in supplying the exactly correct ZF 4HP22 electronic unit as specified by Ashcroft Transmissions.

small, medium and large. Small is used on the 300 Tdi, P38 diesel Range Rover and the Td5; medium is used on the 3.9, 4.0 and the later 4.6 P38 Range Rovers; and large is used on the early 4.6-litre P38 Range Rover.

Each converter has a lock-up clutch inside it. According to Dave Ashcroft the smaller one struggles to cope even with a stock engine, never mind a tuned one. If you have a tuned engine, in addition to the Stage 1 or 2 options mentioned above, Ashcroft are able to replace the 'small' diameter torque converter for the 'medium' one. This gives you the benefit of the larger lock-up clutch and the lower stall speed V8 torque converter which will take up drive earlier. This option is recommended for tuned engines or vehicles used to tow. You do have to bear in mind, however, that the power loss through a larger torque converter will always be greater than that through a smaller torque converter – a point worth considering with a standard, untuned 300 Tdi engine, which has significantly less power than a Td5 unit.

I chose the medium variety for my conversion, because several times a year I tow the full 3.5 tonnes and there are some fierce hills around here, so I wanted to be sure the auto transmission would bear up under the strain.

1 The medium torque converter is OK for the Td5 engine's bell housing, but for my 300 Tdi engine it was necessary for Ashcroft to use a V8 engine bell housing, specially converted.

2 There's also a special adapter fitted to the sump to accept the fluid temperature sender unit.

3 This is the heavier-duty 4HP24's front end to provide added strength. The transmission unit now becomes 15mm longer than standard so there may be fitting implications, such as having to adapt or elongate transmission mountings.

4 If you were to use a standard V8 bell housing with this combination of engine and gearbox, it wouldn't be possible to tighten the torque converter bolts when fitting the transmission. A special cut-out has been machined…

5 …and a bolt-on cover plate is fitted later. It's all beautifully accurate and well machined by Motor & Diesel Engineering, from whom I bought the parts via Ashcroft Transmissions.

6 There's also an extra cut-out and welded-on shroud for the starter motor…

7 …and a relief cutaway for the head of one of the bolts that fixes the adapter plate to the block.

8 This is the main engine adapter plate for the automatic gearbox…

9 …this is the engine side of the specially machined flywheel…

10 …and this the transmission side.

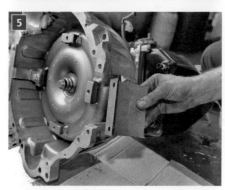

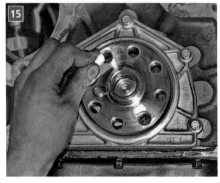

11 This shim and spacer are fitted to the flywheel after fitting it to the engine…

12 …while the adapter and drive plate will be fitted to the torque converter before the gearbox is installed.

13 Assembly began with the removal of the manual transmission's spigot (or first-motion shaft) bearing from the end of the engine crankshaft. Ashcroft's engineer carefully chiselled it out, but I prefer a large dab of grease inserted into the bearing and a drift, the same size as the spigot shaft, hammered in to force the grease in and 'hydraulic' the bearing out.

14 A blade was used to remove any traces of contamination from both the flywheel mounting faces…

15 …and that of the engine crank.

16 Next the starter motor was removed from the 'old' engine housing…

17 …this cleverly curved, steel filler plate was added to the adapter plate…

18 …and the starter motor was temporarily fitted to flatten out the steel plate, friction-fitting it in position on the aluminium adapter plate.

19 The cables were then lifted out of the way and the adapter plate offered up to the end of the engine.

20 The plate must align with the two dowels on the end of the block before tapping the plate home with a mallet and fitting the new retaining bolts.

21 Next the new flywheel was offered up…

22 …followed by the spigot aligner and 2mm thick packing shim. As you can see, holes had to be aligned carefully.

23 The eight M14 x 1.5 pitch capscrews supplied were treated to a dose of thread lock compound before being inserted, hand-tightened, nipped up with a ratchet wrench…

24 …and finally torqued up to 100lb/ft, all before the thread lock had a chance to set. Note that the flywheel has to be jammed with a suitable lever to prevent it from turning as the bolts are tightened.

25 Here's a cunning plan! You can use an old wheel to stand the ZF gearbox upright, enabling you to work on the torque converter in the bell housing. If you look back to the picture in Step 5, you'll see that the torque converter was temporarily held in place with a steel strap.

26 This is the drive plate that will be bolted to the engine via the flywheel and spigot aligner. It's being held up here just for demonstration purposes. When the gearbox is in place, the drive plate is bolted to the torque converter at the four bolt holes indicated.

27 The M10 setscrews and washers supplied with the kit were prepared by adding thread lock.

28 The drive plate and its buttress ring were offered up to the back of the engine and each setscrew inserted by hand before being spun on with an air wrench and tightened to 35lbf/ft with a torque wrench.

29 There was then a bit of a hiatus while we waited for more parts to arrive, but this time was used productively to remove the gearbox mounting studs from the old engine fittings with a stud extractor and screw them into the back of the engine block.

30 This is the standard shifter assembly.

31 For this set-up, the Discovery 200 Tdi diff lock linkage must be used.

32 The existing linkage is removed…

33 …the pivot arm (arrowed) is screwed into the shifter casing and the spacer washers refitted…

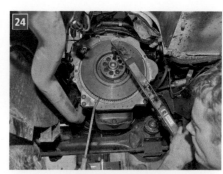

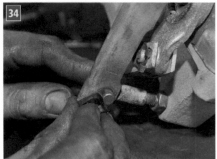

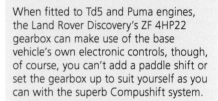

When fitted to Td5 and Puma engines, the Land Rover Discovery's ZF 4HP22 gearbox can make use of the base vehicle's own electronic controls, though, of course, you can't add a paddle shift or set the gearbox up to suit yourself as you can with the superb Compushift system.

What's being fitted here?
- Type 765, electronic ZF 4HP22 autobox with specially adapted Compushift sump.
- 3.9 V8 torque converter.
- Setrab oil cooler and pipes.

34 ...followed by the pivot pin and spring retaining clip.

35 Another preparatory job was to work out where the Setrab oil cooler would be fitted.

36 'Now what's this clutch slave cylinder doing here? Don't need that any more!'

37 The Bearmach-supplied ZF 4HP22 electronic gearbox has been fitted by Ashcroft with their uprated Stage 2 transmission parts: the larger torque converter and the V8 bell housing required to house the extra size of the torque converter while still being able to connect to the 300 Tdi engine.

38 The temporary locating plate fitted by Ashcroft when they built up this gearbox now had to be removed.

39 With the help of the transmission hoist, an extra pair of hands and no little fiddling to obtain the correct alignment, the new auto transmission unit was fitted up to the rear of DiXie's engine.

40 You always need to take care when bolting any engine and transmission unit together. You need to fit bolts on opposite sides of the bell housing but not to pull any of them fully tight until you're certain that the mating faces close easily against each other. Never use bolts to force components together. If they won't fit together easily, find out what's causing the obstruction and put it right.

41 A socket extension is required to reach some of the fixings around the top of the engine/transmission.

42 After first tightening by hand to make sure the bell housing was evenly in place, an air wrench was used to run the bolts in more rapidly.

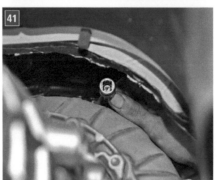

43 Oil cooler pipes supplied with the kit need to be cut to length and fitted to the banjo unions. Here they're crimped using special pliers. An alternative would be to go to an agricultural engineer or someone specialising in digging machines and have them make the connections for you. The pressures that have to be withstood by hydraulic machinery are greatly in excess of those found here.

44 When fitting hydraulic pipework, make sure that the correct washers are used and that there's absolutely no trace of dirt on any of the mating faces. Unless everything is kept perfectly clean you'll end up with a leak.

45 Ashcroft took a commendable amount of trouble to route the oil cooler pipework neatly and well away from any possibility of damage being caused when driving off-road. Each installation is different, depending on engine type and accessories already fitted, and it takes a little care to work out the best route. Large cable ties were used to ensure that the new pipework stayed where it belonged.

46 Now, if you think this is an odd place to site an oil cooler, you'd be right! Later I'm planning to fit a long-nose grille and a full-width intercooler, and a more practical home will be found for the oil cooler, because an oil cooler mounted in front of the grille is all too vulnerable.

47 Once the bell housing bolts were tight, free movement of the torque converter was checked. It should have between 1mm and 3mm clearance between the pads on the converter and the flexplate. If there was more, equal-thickness washers would have to be installed to reduce clearance to within the acceptable range. If there was too little, the transmission would have to be removed and checked to see if the converter was seated properly.

48 A spanner was used on the front of the crank to turn the flywheel...

49 ...so that the holes in the flexplate were aligned with the threaded holes in the torque converter so that each of the four bolts could be added in turn.

50 Before fitting each of the bolts it's important to apply thread lock. It's also important to remember that thread lock only works on threads that have no trace of grease on them, so be sure to meticulously degrease pre-used bolts.

51 A good strong lever was used to prevent rotation while each bolt was tightened in turn.

52 Bear in mind that this is a V8 bell housing that's been adapted by Motor & Diesel for use with this particular set-up. They machined this access hole, without which it wouldn't have been possible to access the torque converter bolts. They also supply this cover plate, which fits snugly inside the machined opening. Later we removed the plate, painted it and gave it a coat of underbody treatment. Unlike the bell housing, it's steel and will rust.

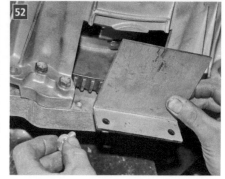

53 Earlier we showed how the Discovery 200 Tdi diff lock mechanism was adapted using parts provided with the kit so that it would work with this gearbox in this vehicle.

54 The mechanism was now fitted to the top of the gearbox.

55 A location dowel was removed from the back of the old manual gearbox…

56 …and tapped evenly into the corresponding location on the auto 'box. Then the transfer box was refitted following conventional workshop manual procedures.

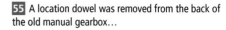

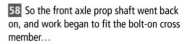

57 This is a good time to fit the chassis mounting to the transfer box, while it's still relatively easy to lift and move around using (in this case) the workshop transmission jack.

58 So the front axle prop shaft went back on, and work began to fit the bolt-on cross member…

59 …the whole transmission unit being lifted with the transmission jack, the cross member being tapped into place – it's a tight fit – and bolted on when the holes lined up, before removing the transmission jack from under the vehicle.

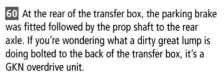
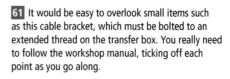

60 At the rear of the transfer box, the parking brake was fitted followed by the prop shaft to the rear axle. If you're wondering what a dirty great lump is doing bolted to the back of the transfer box, it's a GKN overdrive unit.

61 It would be easy to overlook small items such as this cable bracket, which must be bolted to an extended thread on the transfer box. You really need to follow the workshop manual, ticking off each point as you go along.

62 Because this gearbox was never designed for this specific chassis layout, the conversion kit replaces the original chassis mounting bracket (top) with a purpose-made one. The rubber block (right) simply bolts to the new bracket in the same way as to the old one.

63 The trick is to unscrew the stud holding the rubber block to the chassis, to screw the rubber block to the new bracket and then to loosely bolt the new bracket to the gearbox.

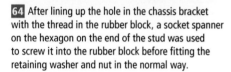

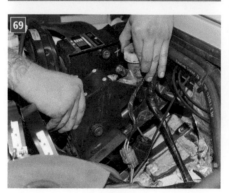

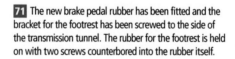

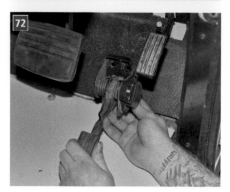

64 After lining up the hole in the chassis bracket with the thread in the rubber block, a socket spanner on the hexagon on the end of the stud was used to screw it into the rubber block before fitting the retaining washer and nut in the normal way.

65 The bolts holding the bracket to the gearbox were then tightened.

66 Everything so far had been plain sailing. The standard of fit of all the adapters, brackets and ancillaries was well nigh perfect, with no need for any adaptation or 'fitting'. So we were due a minor snag. It turned out that the exhaust mounting bracket fouled on the overdrive unit, which, of course, had nothing whatsoever to do with the Ashcroft Transmissions automatic conversion kit. After a little bit of reshaping, all was well again.

67 These are components of the gear selector linkage. They were actually to be fitted during the final stage of installing the automatic conversion kit, back at the Ashcroft Transmissions ranch. The selector lever is on the left and the cable outer will be clamped to the bracket on the right. But as far as installing the hardware was concerned, almost everything was now complete.

68 Earlier we saw the clutch slave cylinder being taken away after the manual transmission had been removed and before the automatic was fitted. These are the bolts that hold the clutch pedal box to the bulkhead, found deep inside the footwell just upstream of the clutch pedal.

69 Taking care not to spill clutch fluid into the engine bay, the now redundant clutch pedal box was lifted out of the way complete with the clutch master cylinder.

70 The brake pedal on an automatic is larger than that on manual transmission vehicles. Part of the kit is this brake pedal adapter plate. It was offered up to the existing pedal, tapping-size holes were drilled in the pedal, and then the pedal plate was tapped to take the four countersunk-head screws provided.

71 The new brake pedal rubber has been fitted and the bracket for the footrest has been screwed to the side of the transmission tunnel. The rubber for the footrest is held on with two screws counterbored into the rubber itself.

72 The Compushift system needs to know how wide open the throttle is at any one time. This is a Td5 throttle pedal with a throttle position sensor (TPS) built on to it. Dave Ashcroft looked at the possibility of fitting this throttle in place of the original 300 Tdi throttle but there's insufficient movement to fully operate the Tdi's injection pump.

SOME USEFUL TORQUE WRENCH SETTINGS

Gear change lever to gearbox	25Nm
Cooler pipe adapter to gearbox	42Nm
Bell housing mounting bolts	46Nm
Control unit mounting bolts	8Nm
Sump plug	10Nm
Mounting screws for sump	8Nm
Drive plate to converter	39Nm*
Gearbox to engine	42Nm

These bolts must have threads coated with Loctite 270 prior to assembly.

73 Ashcroft's preferred solution was to substitute a new TPS, as on the Td5's pedal...

74 ...but positioned at the injector pump using an adapter plate and drive pin, made in-house.

75 The adapter plate has been fitted using the two threaded holes on the pump and countersunk-head screws (a), the drive pin (b) has been used to extend the existing, threaded pivot on the pump, and the new TPS is about to be screwed to the plate, with the top of the pin turning the potentiometer built into the TPS.

76 Inside the vehicle, the seat bases, centre cover plate and transmission tunnel were all removed in order to gain access to the newly fitted auto 'box.

77 It's a good idea to fit these components of the gear selector linkage before connecting the wiring because access will be so much easier. The selector lever is on the left and the cable outer will be clamped to the bracket on the right.

78 Next it was a matter of following the instructions to the letter by first identifying then removing (where necessary) original electrical fittings and installing the Compushift loom.

79 These are the connections that have to be made or remade:

- A socket connected to the gear position indicator. The socket on the original Land Rover unit has been removed and replaced with one that connects to the Compushift loom. The plug that goes into this socket has two wires from it.
- (a) wire soldered to the cable after terminal E has been cut from it – it operates the reversing light.
- F starter inhibitor, which only allows starting in N or P.
- B socket, also from the gear position indicator.
- C from temp sensor on 'box to Compushift.
- D from Compushift control unit, which provides electronic 'instructions' to the gearbox.

80 Incidentally, it's worth pointing out that there's no substitution for soldered joints where a permanent join is needed. Anything else risks an electrical breakdown in future. The engineer bares the end of the cable, slides on a length of shrink-fit insulation tubing, solders the joint and then, when it's cool enough, slides the shrink-fit insulation over the joint. The insulation is heated with a heat gun or the flame of a match and this shrinks it tightly on to the cable. Note that if you try to slide the insulation on to the joint while it's still hot it will grip and bind before you can get it all the way on – most annoying!

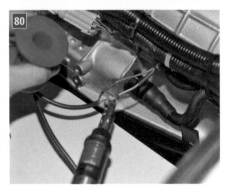

81 With all of the wiring complete, it's tidied up and strapped neatly out of the way alongside the transmission casing.

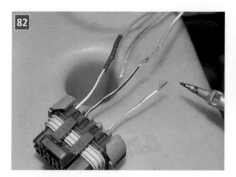

82 Inside the engine bay, these are the three wires on the Compushift loom being soldered to a Land Rover plug to fit the throttle position sensor.

83 Next the kit's gear selector mechanism was installed.

84 The cable outer was passed through the seat box as shown and clamped to the bracket on the right. The inner fits to the selector mechanism on the gearbox (left).

85 Now preparations were made to assemble the partly prefabricated gear selector and ECU support brackets and to fit them to the centre cover plate, the one that would fit beneath the centre seat, if fitted. After drilling suitable holes in the location shown on the template provided, a rivnut gun was used to fix the rivnuts – captive nuts fixed in a similar fashion to pop rivets – into the plate.

86 Here you can see all of the support brackets placed on the centre plate in their correct locations. Note the hole that's been drilled on the left side of the plate to allow cables to pass through.

87 Each support bracket was bolted down in turn. As you can see, it's possible to use conventional nuts and bolts if you don't have access to a rivnut gun where you can get at the back of the plate to which the supports are being mounted.

88 At this point, you can see that the necessary electrical and selector cables have been passed through the base plate, the support brackets are in place, and the gear selector mechanism has been offered up to its mounting bracket.

89 The sealing grommet for the drilled hole allowing the cables through from beneath, and the plate for holding it down.

90 This is typical of the thoroughness that's gone into this conversion kit. It means that the underside of the vehicle is effectively sealed off from the area beneath the centre console.

91 Here's where it would be difficult to fit a bracket without the use of rivnuts. You could do it by deliberately not screwing down the centre plate at this stage, but it would be a fiddle! We'll come back to this bracket in a moment.

92 There's no fixed order for carrying out this part of the work, but it was decided to fit the gear selector indicator at this stage.

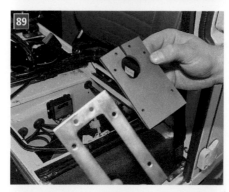

93 This is the Compushift kit before fitting had commenced. Much of the wiring shown here was by now in place, and attention was about to be turned to the ECU (middle bottom).

94 The mounting bracket shown three pictures ago is an ideal place for mounting the ECU, which simply screws down into the threaded holes provided. The ECU is well away from dampness but has air all around it to allow for cooling if necessary.

95 With the hidden assembly all out of the way, attention was turned to the centre console. When used on 110 models, the console is slightly too long and needs the addition of a special bracket provided with the kit. This is simply bolted to the back of the console...

96 ...and slid neatly down on to the back of the seat box as the console is installed, front end first.

97 Pieces of wood were used to ensure the console was evenly spaced between the two front seats...

98 ...before drilling and screwing through the bracket and into the seat base.

99 With the centre console in place, Simon was able to fit the trim around the gear selector. It's important to note that this type of selector, fitted to Range Rovers for example, is, at the time of writing, no longer available brand new in its entirety...

100 ...so if you must have a selector with a centre pull-up knob you'll have to put up with some second-hand parts. These long-nose pliers were used to tweak the nut holding the body of the selector in place. A long socket would be preferable.

101 The release catch was pushed on to the shaft...

102 ...and held on with the spring clip, as shown.

103 If you've got a Compushift system, this part of the job depends on where you want the control unit to be situated. In this instance the cubby trays were removed from the front and rear of the console and control unit's cable was plugged into the ECU before passing the cable through the console...

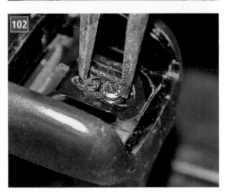

104 ...and through the front, before plugging it into the control unit.

105 Finally, Dave Ashcroft used the comprehensive setting-up instructions supplied with the kit to program the Compushift to match the engine, transmission, gearing and other mechanical factors before taking DiXie for a test drive and fine-tuning some of the settings.

106 In some respects the Compushift is programmed to suit individual preferences. For instance, I was easily able to change it later to give slightly slower but softer shifts so that you can now hardly tell when the gearbox is changing up on a light throttle. I might even change it again later, but that's the beauty of the Compushift system – it's easy to set up the gearbox just however you want it.

The Ashcroft automatic conversion has transformed DiXie. It's still as capable as ever of rugged hard work but is soooo much easier and more relaxing to drive. Manoeuvring in tight spaces and reversing a trailer, for example, are far easier. And I've always been a fan of automatics for the way you can pull out instantly into traffic and be up to speed in less time than you can with a Land Rover manual shift.

This is an expensive modification but it's one that transforms the vehicle entirely.

And if you need or simply prefer having an automatic Defender conversion in any of Tdi, Td5 or Puma versions, an Ashcroft automatic conversion will provide you with a vehicle that's just as good as the factory-fit version. Yes, that's the one that never was available.... Indeed, with Compushift added, it's a whole lot better in terms of adjustability – although I find gear changes to be slightly more noticeable than on an older Discovery with standard 'hydraulic' (non-electronic) 'box!

AUTO TRANSMISSION SWITCH-SHIFTER

Some quite sophisticated transmissions allow a choice between fully automatic and semi-automatic with the use of a sequential switch-shifter. These are usually mounted on the steering column for convenience, and also, one supposes, because they look a bit like the ones fitted to many racing cars.

The Compushift electronic 'box fitted by Ashcroft Transmissions can be adapted to provide the addition of a sequential shifter. When the shifter is in its central position the transmission acts like a normal auto. However, if the shifter is operated up or down (usually the latter) the transmission goes into manual/sequential mode. To return to full automatic mode, the driver has to flick the gearchange momentarily out of 'Drive' and into 'Neutral'.

After installing the shifter switch you have to enter the Compushift's set-up program to tell it that a sequential switch has been installed. The process through the menu system is described in the Compushift manual, available online from the manufacturer's www.hgmelectronics. com website; there are also instructions on the Ashcroft Transmissions website.

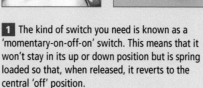
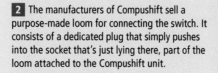

1 The kind of switch you need is known as a 'momentary-on-off-on' switch. This means that it won't stay in its up or down position but is spring loaded so that, when released, it reverts to the central 'off' position.

2 The manufacturers of Compushift sell a purpose-made loom for connecting the switch. It consists of a dedicated plug that simply pushes into the socket that's just lying there, part of the loom attached to the Compushift unit.

3 Ashcroft Transmissions recommend simply cutting off the Compushift auxiliary socket and making fresh wiring connections. We used a Würth Multi-Plug, which not only allows instant connection and disconnection as with the original plug but is also waterproof. Würth Multi-Plugs are simply connected to your existing wiring and are available with two to six terminals.

4 The three cables were then connected to the back of the momentary switch following the colour codes on the original Compushift loom:
White with black trace Top terminal, for downshift
White with red trace Bottom terminal, for upshift
White Centre terminal, common
Note that the switch positions on this particular unit are opposite to what one might have expected. We used a test lamp to determine which terminal did what.

If your Defender has a more powerful engine or considerably larger wheels and tyres, it's best to consider beefing up the drivetrain. The single outstanding choice is the range of world-renowned axle components from Ashcroft Transmissions – and this is how they're fitted.

Ever since the days when Morris Minors ruled the Earth, broken half shafts have been a feature of Land Rover ownership. Half shafts are fitted to each axle and carry the drive from the differentials to the road wheels. Typically they fail at the differential end and can be a pain to replace. Under some operating conditions, broken half shafts are a regular and irritating occurrence, but there's a solution to hand.

Ashcroft's new generation of heavy-duty half shafts are made from '4340' alloy steel and are supplied with a five-year replacement warranty against failure. Ashcroft's own test figures show that a standard half shaft tends to break when twisted through about 42°, whereas their own half shaft will go to an amazing 166° of twist before breaking.

Note that Ashcroft don't supply 10/32 or 24/32 spline half shafts. By replacing the 32 spline CV with a 23 spline Heavy-Duty CV you can use the stronger 24/23 shaft.

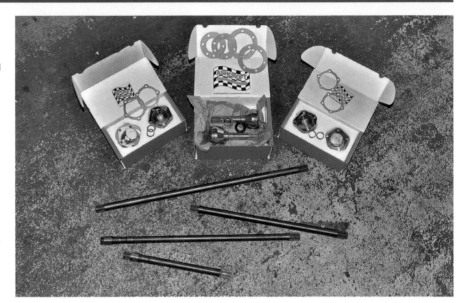

1 Bill, the boss at Autoland, one of Ashcroft's fitting stations, started by removing the rubber cap, the circlip and the washer behind it…

2 …which, once the ring of bolts holding it in place had been removed, allowed the drive flange to be levered free.

3 The brake caliper also had to be removed and suspended carefully out of the way.

4 On these later Defenders, the hub nut is a use-once fitting with a tab that needs opening up before removing and discarding the nut.

5 At least, that was the theory! This nut couldn't be shifted, so careful use was made of the cut-off grinder, stopping before the component beneath was reached. The nut was then sprung free with a hammer and chisel. Later, with the hub removed, we could see that the thread had picked up last time the nut was fitted, probably because old thread lock hadn't been thoroughly removed before refitting it.

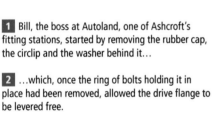

6 The six bolts retaining the stub axle to the swivel housing were removed…

7 …the swivel housing was removed…

8 …and, while catching spilled oil…

9 … the half shaft and universal joint were removed.

10 Then the mud shield was removed…

11 …and the steering arm disconnected.

12 Next the swivel pin housing was unbolted from the end of the axle and removed.

13 Rather than reusing the old seal, it was levered out of its location…

14 …and a new one offered up…

15 …and drifted in evenly and with meticulous care.

16 Remembering what had happened when old thread lock hadn't been removed by a previous mechanic, a tap was run down each female thread.

17 A thin wipe of non-setting gasket sealant helps to hold the new gasket in place when refitting.

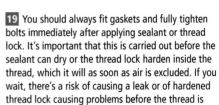

18 All the bolt threads were cleaned to remove all traces of thread lock so that fresh thread lock could be applied before they were reused.

19 You should always fit gaskets and fully tighten bolts immediately after applying sealant or thread lock. It's important that this is carried out before the sealant can dry or the thread lock harden inside the thread, which it will as soon as air is excluded. If you wait, there's a risk of causing a leak or of hardened thread lock causing problems before the thread is properly tightened to the correct torque.

20 The new Ashcroft half shaft comes ready greased and with circlip already in position.

21 This has to be inserted into the end of an Ashcroft CV joint.

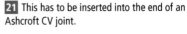

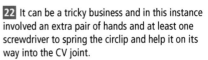

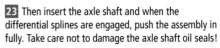

22 It can be a tricky business and in this instance involved an extra pair of hands and at least one screwdriver to spring the circlip and help it on its way into the CV joint.

23 Then insert the axle shaft and when the differential splines are engaged, push the assembly in fully. Take care not to damage the axle shaft oil seals!

24 You have to fit the stub axle with the flat at 12 o'clock position. The stub axle also received a new gasket. Coat the threads of stub axle bolts with Loctite 270.

25 It's important to ensure that the constant velocity joint bearing journal is butted against the thrust ring on the stub axle before the latter is tightened.

26 Back on went the hub and brake disc assembly…

27 …followed by a new lock nut.

28 After tightening to the correct torque, the nut was staked into position.

29 A bolt was temporarily inserted into the threaded hole in the end of the half shaft so that its position could be adjusted before fitting the new circlip.

30 The old rear half shafts have been stripped and removed and the new Ashcroft shaft is being inserted. A good coating of grease was applied to the spline…

31 …before the new heavy-duty drive flange was fitted to the end of the half shaft and fully pushed home.

32 This sealable end cap comes with all of Ashcroft's heavy-duty drive flanges.

33 Tightening the drive flange bolts with a torque wrench completes the job.

WHICH HALF SHAFTS?

Early rear half shafts
There are Ashcroft shafts to fit the earlier thick-style rear-drive flanges fitted to the 'wet'-type hub. Others are made to fit the earlier 'thick' hub driver (18mm), as fitted to the 200 Tdi and earlier vehicles. You'll need a pair of separate outer drive flanges if you don't already have them.

Late rear half shafts
These are made to fit the later 'slim' (15mm) hub driver as fitted to the 300 Tdi. Again you'll need a pair of separate outer drive flanges if you don't already have them. Half shafts for the 90 rear, up to VIN number LA930456, have separate flanges so it won't be necessary to replace the existing flanges unless you wish to upgrade to Ashcroft's heavy-duty versions. Half shafts after this VIN number have integral flanges so it'll be necessary to purchase both the half shafts and the 859 flanges.

Salisbury rear half shafts
Ashcroft are also able to offer both early-style and late-style heavy-duty rear half shafts for the 90/110 Salisbury rear axle. The early style suits all 90/110s up to and including the 200 Tdi Defender. The late style suits the 300 Tdi and early Td5 axles.

Disco II rear half shafts
As the D2 has an 'open knuckle'-type of front axle, Ashcroft are able to put in a much larger diameter CV joint. This increased diameter not only allows a much thicker walled CV bell but also the use of bigger balls, which reduce stresses and allows an increase in the half shaft from the small-stock 32 spline to the much larger 24-spline, the same as the 24-spline at the diff end. Ashcroft use the same proven materials as for their other shafts and CVs, ie '4340' for the shaft and CV outer and 300M for the cage and inner.

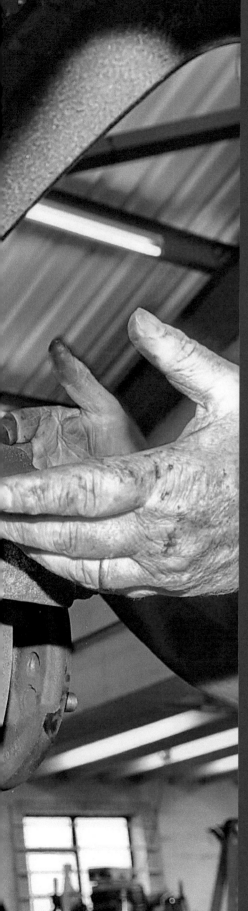

CHAPTER 3

Suspension, steering and brakes

There must be literally thousands of different suspension component permutations available to the Defender owner. But before installing modified suspension parts you should ask yourself two questions. Firstly, what's wrong with the set-up you've already got? And secondly, what do you want to achieve in terms of comfort, roadholding, off-road capability and load-carrying capacity, among other things?

Biggest, highest, meanest, sexiest suspension modifications can look great on a stationary Land Rover and are macho and tempting when seen in bright colours and chrome on display at the Land Rover shows. But you need to be aware that it's all too easy to make a Defender look good but drive and handle horribly, if not downright dangerously, if the wrong modifications are fitted and in clashing combinations.

Manufacturers spend literally millions of pounds developing suspension in which all the different factors work well together. Bear in mind that it's not just a matter of the height and stiffness of springs. Defender springs are designed to do all of the following, and more:

■ Allow for variations in load-carrying capacity.
■ Be able to work differently at different degrees of compression.
■ Work well at different cornering speeds and under different road conditions.
■ Have sufficient movement for off-road work.

Then there's a whole lot more that needs to be taken into consideration. Shock absorbers need to have the right length, the correct degree of damping effect and the ability to work without overheating, which changes their characteristics and could bring about rapid failure.

The amount of unsprung weight (weight of axle and steering gear, wheels and tyres) will have been part of the original manufacturer's calculations, and if they're altered suspension requirements will change too.

Size and height of wheels and tyres will affect roadholding and handling, because the higher a vehicle is the more it will be inclined to roll when cornering or when driven off-road on heavily sloping ground.

Suspension, steering and anti-roll bar bushes will also have an effect on the compliance of the suspension.

The point is that each one of these factors, as well as others we haven't touched on – such as installing uprated (heavy-duty) steering rods – can't be considered in isolation. Every time you change one aspect

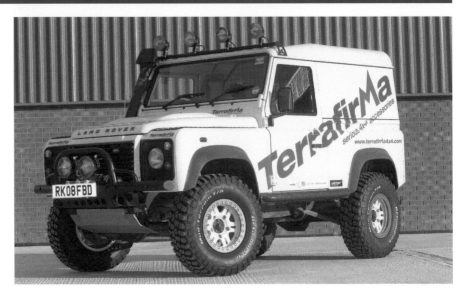

of the suspension, it has a knock-on effect on the others, as well as other parts of the vehicle as we'll see in a moment.

So, are you really sure that you know more than Land Rover's engineers, or do you have special requirements? And are you ready to end up with something that's worse than before you started? Or might you be better off simply overhauling your existing suspension set-up so that it works as it did when it was new?

Most of us can't help but tinker, but if you don't have very special requirements such as extreme load-carrying, on-road performance or off-road needs, you're strongly advised to carry out only one modification at a time, where practicable, so you can judge its effect in isolation, and make minor alterations rather than huge, radical ones.

All of the illustrations in this section are used courtesy of Terrafirma, whose range is even greater than the items shown here.

LIFTING THE SUSPENSION
Many if not most serious off-roaders like to raise the suspension because it provides them with extra ground clearance and can, if longer springs are fitted, increase axle movement. The idea is that on very rough ground a vehicle may have one or even two wheels off the ground, which means the wheels will spin but the vehicle won't go anywhere. Locking or limited-slip differentials will overcome most of the problem, but having more tyres in contact with the ground will help even more. Downsides? You won't be able to get into multi-storey car parks; you might have difficulty getting in and out of the vehicle;

on-road handling will be worse, and if the job is done badly the vehicle could even be dangerous. The main options are to use purpose-made longer springs…

…or to fit spring spacers or packers to the spring base mounting. But whichever approach you follow you'll also have to modify other items to match.

SHOCK ABSORBERS

If you were to raise your ride height by 50mm (2in), your shock absorbers would either need to be longer – or mounted lower – by the same amount, because otherwise they'll bottom-out before the suspension has reached its full extent of travel.

However, what will happen if you fit lower shock absorber chassis mounts (these are rears)…

…or reduced-height front turrets (below)? Although the shock absorber will reach its fully extended length of suspension travel, it will now bottom out when the suspension is fully compressed.

You could fit larger bump stops…

…or bump stop spacers…

…or lower top shock absorber mounts (rears shown), but these modifications all prevent the axle from rising as far as it might need to. In other words, ride height is increased but axle articulation remains the same.

Some people will tell you that they've left the shock absorbers and their mounts alone after increasing the ride height by 50mm and that everything was fine. It could be that they haven't fully explored suspension travel length; it could be that they haven't noticed there's anything wrong; it could be that their particular shock absorbers have got a little bit extra built into them, but how are you going to know?

Purpose-made longer shock absorbers are the only acceptable solution. But even then there's another problem. Longer shocks, and especially those designed for 100mm (4in) lift, now move in an arc that's outside the manufacturer's design limits which puts

strain on the shock absorber mountings and bushes as well as on the absorbers themselves. You won't be surprised to learn that there's another solution to hand: it's to fit swivelling shock absorber mounts.

Alternatively, rear, top shock absorber mounts…

…allow for a different location point.

DISLOCATION

Longer springs and shock absorbers will increase axle articulation when driving off-road, but the length of the spring…

…if fixed in position top and bottom (these are coil spring retaining plates), will still be a limiting factor.

One popular modification is to allow the springs to dislocate from their seats, allowing the axle to drop further away from the body when required. However, there needs to be a device to relocate the springs when the axle comes back up and this takes the form of cones or spikes…

…these are fronts…

…and these are rears.

Alternatively you could fit supplementary, lightweight, helper springs set inside the existing ones. As the axle moves past the length of the main spring, the helper spring remains in place and provides some downward pressure for traction. However, helper springs are bound to have an effect on non-road handling, while the amount of pressure they apply to assist traction must be minimal.

Extreme axle dislocation reaches its limits when suspension linkages and bushes call a halt. In order to solve the problem, you're looking at spending even more serious money on all-new links with spherical-type joints in them to replace the standard bushed links and purpose-made mounting plates. Huge amounts of articulation also require that the prop shafts are modified to cope with the extreme angles at the universal joints.

This could take the form of UJs machined to allow more movement, or those with larger yokes to achieve the same effect.

You also have to remember that radius arms will try to drop below their design limits, and this will destroy the lower part of the chassis bushes, as well as restricting movement.

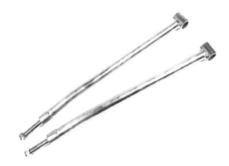

One option is to fit kinked radius arms while another is to fit the more expensive jointed radius arms. And at the rear you need to look at lateral movement of the A-frame joint.

SPRINGS

If you fit springs that are too heavy-duty they'll provide an uncomfortable and possibly even dangerous ride and might not compress enough for off-road purposes. On the other hand, a spring that's too soft can be dangerous on-road and could start to bend sideways under compression and catch on other components when driven hard or off-road.

If you feel your springs could do with extra help when your Defender is under very heavy load or when towing up to the limit, another option might be to fit spring assisters, such as these Air-Lift 1000 units. These American air bags are designed to

be fitted and left in place, and only inflated when required to support a heavy load and perhaps maintain ride height.

The bag is inserted into the spring – it's soft enough to be compressed and slid in through the top – and the red and black pads can also be inserted into the spring coils, to fit above and below the air bag. You could inflate with a vehicle tyre pump as and when required, but a more sophisticated approach would be to fit one of the high-quality, onboard 12v pumps available from Air-Lift's UK suppliers, Air-Lift.co.uk.

ANTI-ROLL BARS

If you want to improve on-road performance, standard anti-roll bars are often the best option and will make a significant difference to what is, after all, a top-heavy vehicle. A very thick front anti-roll bar combined with a much thinner rear anti-roll bar will give quite distinct understeer, where the front end of the vehicle drifts out

on a bend instead of following the line that you're steering. Obviously, this can be very dangerous. A very thick rear anti-roll bar combined with a much thinner front one will, under more extreme circumstances, makes the rear end whip round, which is also pretty damned dangerous! Remembering the millions manufacturers spend on these things, standard anti-roll bars are probably the best way to go.

For playful off-road or competition use, however, anti-roll bars will restrict axle articulation quite notably. Some enthusiasts take them off completely, while others fit detachable axle or chassis mountings so they can be disconnected when required. For less demanding off-road circumstances, use of standard anti-roll bars will still be fine.

WHEELS AND TYRES

When it comes to wheels and tyres, it's tempting to go for the visually most appealing wheels and tyres on the market. However, while appearance is undoubtedly important to the eye of the beholder, it must take a far lower priority than both road safety and usability.

First, bear in mind that wider tyres aren't necessarily better when it comes to grip and roadholding. In fact they can increase the

risk of aquaplaning and tram-lining, where the steering tends to follow undulations and markings in the road.

Larger wheels may look sexy but can have some dire side-effects. Extra weight on the ends of the axles can lead to suspension hop – potentially dangerous when cornering. The vehicle's gearing will also be changed, as will the speedometer and odometer readings.

One solution to the axle hop caused by an increase in unsprung weight is the use of uprated and/or twin-shock absorbers.

These are rear twin shock absorber mounts…

…while this is a front twin shock absorber mounting kit.

There's a lot more to be said about wheels and tyres than there's space for here, but one crucial point to bear in mind is that whatever you fit, you must make sure that they're rated for the weight and carrying capacity of the vehicle, otherwise you might not be covered by insurance in the event of accident.

Of course, for the really determined there's nothing to stop them going really wild with wheels and tyres, provided that they stay legal, that the Defender is still safe to drive and that any other ancillary components are changed or adapted to suit. But most users are recommended to stay mild rather than go wild.

Sixteen-inch wheels with slightly lower profile tyres than normal (check with your supplier first) can give you the same circumference as standard tyres and thus unchanged speedometer readings. Wheels with a slightly greater offset can increase the track of the vehicle, providing an improvement in roadholding but with an increase in the amount of mud splashed up the sides of the vehicle.

Seventeen-inch wheels can look better and will allow room for larger brakes but you'll have to use even lower profile tyres and you're starting to get to the point where you'll experience a noticeable increase in harshness when driving.

STEERING

If a coil-sprung Defender's suspension is raised the castor angle is automatically changed, which makes the steering feel less precise and may make the vehicle more difficult to drive in a straight line. Some specialists recommend that vehicles with 50mm (2in) of suspension lift should have the castor angle corrected by 3° in order to return the steering to the correct geometry, while Defenders with over 50mm of suspension lift might need 6° of castor correction.

Incidentally, for a vehicle with standard ride height, changing the castor angle by 3° will simply provide better self-centring and sharper steering at the cost of very slightly increased steering weight.

Castor correction can be carried out by fitting modified swivels, radius arms (shown here) or – the least expensive approach – radius arm bushes.

Finally, don't buy suspension modifications based on looks, either of the finished vehicle or the parts themselves. Ask yourself specifically what's wrong with the set-up that you've got and decide whether it can't be corrected by simply fitting new parts to replace worn-out ones. Then, when you've decided what the actual problems are that you want to solve, keep things as simple as possible and make small-step changes, reviewing progress before making the next modification.

And don't forget that the standard Defender has a wonderful and well-deserved reputation for driving performance, both on- and off-road, to start off with.

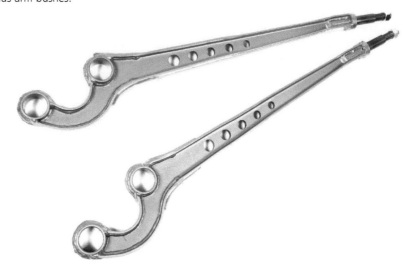

Two vehicles are the main subjects of this section, and this is an outline of the work we carried out on them. The modifications shown aren't specific to the vehicles featured – they can be fitted to almost any Defender, as can a whole lot of different components, of course. Consult your supplier for compatibility details.

Td5 110

ARB's 'Old Man Emu' Nitrocharger shock absorbers were originally designed with Australian driving conditions in mind, where heavily loaded vehicles are often driven on harsh, Outback roads for prolonged periods. Old Man Emu's engineers specialise in 4WD suspension systems, and it's this experience that differentiates their Nitrocharger from its competitors. And while OME Nitrochargers will improve overall performance when fitted with standard springs, more substantial benefits can be achieved, it's said, when fitted in conjunction with OME springs.

So, on this vehicle, Old Man Emu variable-rate coil springs were fitted to the rear while standard springs were left on the front. That's because most OME springs have a notably raised ride height, which I didn't want. However, Old Man Emu produce a range of both constant- and variable-rate coil springs, and I like their stated emphasis on ride control improvements.

200 Tdi

Stuart Harrison, following the plan laid down by Britpart's manager, Paul Myers, fitted the company's performance front springs and 'Super Gaz' shock absorbers, which came with Britpart's own-brand polyurethane bushes. These shockers are said to offer a vast improvement in ride quality and damping performance while the springs will provide a slight increase in ride height.

FRONT END

Td5 110

1 IRB's Ian Baughan used axle stands before undoing the bottom mounting nut; note that the body has first been supported with the suspension fully extended. It's worth paying attention to how the bushes and retaining washers fit together as you remove them, so that the new ones can be correctly fitted.

2 After removing the coolant reservoir from this side of the engine bay and the rubber cover on the inner wing top, a ratchet extension was used to remove the four nuts...

3 ...holding the suspension tower in place. The axle being supported with the suspension fully extended meant there was no pressure on the spring as these nuts were undone.

4 An air-driven ratchet gun made short work of removing the top shock absorber nut without having to lock the shock absorber to prevent it from turning. Once again, it pays to take note of the correct orientation of the bushes and washers as they're removed.

5 Remembering the correct order of fitting, the washers and bushes supplied with the OME kit were fitted to the top of the new shock absorber after it had been pushed into the tower.

6 After a wipe of copper grease, the smaller washer and lock nut were fitted...

7 ...before offering up the Nitrocharger shocker with its tower and with the upper washer and bush fitted to the bottom so that it could be pushed down into its locating hole.

200 Tdi

8 To fit new suspension turrets, the top shock absorber nuts are unscrewed and the axle lowered.

9 As you can see, getting the bottom bush, washers and lock nut into the mounting on the axle is quite a fiddly business.

10 This is where one of those ratchet ring spanners looked as if it ought to be a godsend. However, we found that though you can tighten the nut on the bottom of the shock absorber you can't get the spanner off again afterwards! The reason is that the shaft on the bottom of the shock moves downwards as you tighten the nut, leaving no space between the bottom of the shaft and the axle. So you have to use a ring spanner for as long as you can and then switch to an open ender to finish the job off.

11 The new radius arm being prepared to be fitted.

12 A Clarke Strong Arm Vehicle Lift (maximum load 1,800kg) had earlier been used to raise the vehicle. The axle needed to be supported separately from the vehicle, and the way to do it with the Clarke hoist is to raise the whole vehicle, place the axle stand in position and then slowly and carefully lower the vehicle until the axle weight is supported on the stand.

13 Two large sets of nuts, bolts and washers hold the front end of the radius arm in place. You'll invariably need a breaker bar to start them off.

14 A single nut attaches the rear end to the chassis bracket.

15 With everything slackened off, the front bolts can be tapped free. If you intend reusing them make sure that the nut is spun most of the way on before hammering the end of the bolt, otherwise the thread will be damaged.

16 In order to remove the radius arm, the steering link arm needed to be detached from the driver's side of the vehicle. Here the engineer springs the tapered hole in the eye by hitting it with a large hammer to free the matching tapered pin on the ball joint.

17 Freed off, the arm can simply be slid out of its bearing and left to dangle loose.

18 It's best to lever the rubber bush from the end of the radius arm before trying to remove it from the front end because the bush will tend to hold it in position.

19 The front end can then be hammered down and free.

20 The old radius arm was removed.

21 The new polyurethane bushes are a tight fit in their housings. Unlike rubber bushes, however, polyurethane bushes can be given a smear of grease without any harm coming to them.

22 The jaws of a vice or a woodworker's G-cramp can be used to encourage them to go all the way in. And all the way in they must go, if they're going to fit back into the chassis.

23 The steel centre bush will certainly be a tight fit and a squirt of releasing fluid or other lubricant will be a big help…

24 …as you drive it in. A socket was used to make sure the bush was recessed equidistantly on both sides.

25 It may help to tap the lobes of the mounting bracket very slightly open with a hammer before refitting the radius arm. Don't tap them too far, however, otherwise the holes will be badly angled and the pin won't go back in level. You'll definitely find it helpful to sand off any corrosion from the insides of the bracket and to grease them liberally.

26 The inner bush was fitted to the rear end of the new radius arm, which was then slid into the bracket on the chassis.

27 The front end of the radius arm was an extremely tight fit in the bracket. However, don't make the mistake that we made! If you hammer the radius arm into position – as you might with a standard one without any finishing on it – the plastic coating will chip and break off, which will allow corrosion to occur. We're going to have to paint the damaged areas so as not to negate the value of the plastic coating.

28 The last-but-one job was to fit the new bolts and nut assemblies to the front end of the radius arm.

29 Only then can the rear bush, washer and lock nut be fitted.

REAR END

Td5 110

30 Once my Defender was off the ground the suspension hoist was used to support the weight of the rear axle. You'll see why later.

31 The nut holding the rear shock absorber top mounting in place was slackened...

32 ...and removed along with the backing washer.

33 Next, attention was turned to the bottom nut. You'll need to grip the shock absorber to prevent it from turning as you undo this nut. Invariably the shaft will have a flat on it, but while this is enough to stop it turning while you're tightening the nut on a brand new unit, you won't stand a chance of locking it when it's been on a while. If marking the shock absorber body doesn't matter you could use a Stillson's wrench (left), but if you don't want to damage it try using an oil filter removing tool with rubber strap.

34 Here you can see the shock absorber body being gripped while the bottom nut is removed.

35 The rear shock absorber can now be removed, but you have to take care that the flexible brake hose (inset) isn't stretched as the axle is allowed to drop. This is why the suspension hoist was fitted!

36 Because the rear springs were also to be replaced, a long extension was used on the ratchet to loosen the spring clamp nuts and bolts. Note that you need a second spanner to prevent the bolt from turning.

37 Without fully removing the clamp plate, the spring was rotated to 'unscrew' it, making sure the axle was low enough to allow the spring to clear the top of the housing.

38 This is how the spring plate should look if corrosion isn't too bad. Sometimes components will need replacing.

39 The spring seat and clamp were removed, cleaned off and loosely refitted.

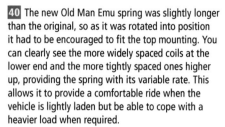

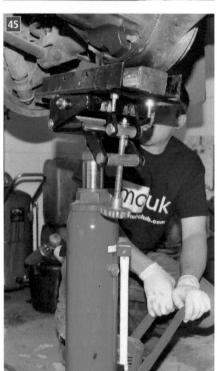

40 The new Old Man Emu spring was slightly longer than the original, so as it was rotated into position it had to be encouraged to fit the top mounting. You can clearly see the more widely spaced coils at the lower end and the more tightly spaced ones higher up, providing the spring with its variable rate. This allows it to provide a comfortable ride when the vehicle is lightly laden but be able to cope with a heavier load when required.

41 You mustn't use grease on rubber bushes but it's OK to do so with polyurethane. These bushes were wiped with silicone grease, but even so couldn't be pushed in by hand. A hydraulic press was consequently used, but a vice or woodworker's clamp would be almost as good.

42 The top end of the OME shock absorber is pushed on to its mounting pin and the retaining washer and lock nut are loosely fitted.

43 This is the arrangement of bushes and upper and lower washers you'll need in all cases. Whether or not you use the dished washers will depend on whether your Defender has them built into the bracket on the axle. Ours, being a 2006 model, has them, so the supplied washers weren't needed.

44 With the upper large washer and upper bush in place, the bottom of the shock absorber was lined up with the hole in the bracket...

45 ...and the axle was raised until it became possible...

46 ...to fit the lower bush, plus large and small washers followed by the lock nut. The inset shows the original bush and the way it appears not to have been correctly seated when the vehicle was manufactured.

47 After fully tightening the bottom nut (you need to just compress the bushes, but not so much that they become flattened or heavily distorted)...

48 ...the top nut was fitted too.

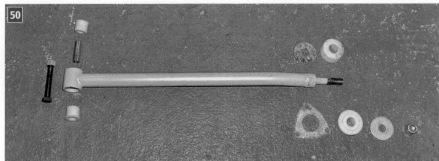

200 Tdi

49 A Britpart performance spring and 'Super Gaz' shock absorber being held up like a pair of prize fish. The springs will give us a slightly higher ride height. Various lengths are available. These powder-coated springs handle off-road terrain and provide a good ride on road, while the shockers are said to offer a vast improvement in ride quality and damping performance.

50 'Super Gaz' shock absorbers come with Britpart's own-brand polyurethane bushes, as does the radius arm kit shown here. This is cranked to allow for an increase in ride height – though if it affects the castor angle, it shouldn't be used with standard height.

51 Installation commenced with removal of the nut holding the top of the shock absorber to its mounting. You should apply releasing fluid plentifully, preferably a day before starting work. Don't use heat from a flame because of the risk of setting fire to the bushes, which can create a chemical that's extremely dangerous to the skin. If the mounting shears off, don't despair (see later).

52 Since the old shock absorber was to be scrapped, it was decided that instead of trying to grip the shock absorber to prevent it from turning while undoing its lower nut, a cutting blade on the angle grinder would be used to cut vertically through the bottom of the shaft and the nut – taking care not to damage the mounting, of course.

53 This accomplished, the bottom of the shock absorber was simply lifted away from its mounting.

54 The old shocker was now free to be slung into the recycling bin.

55 The body of our Defender was supported on the Clarke hoist which, with the shock absorber removed, allows the axle to fall, taking the tension out of the coil spring. You'll need to keep an eye on the brake flexible hose and, if it looks like being stretched, disconnect it. An alternative to removing it would be to use a pair of spring compressors, which would mean that the axle wouldn't have to be lowered so far. You may also wish to control the descent of the axle using a trolley jack.

56 Having slackened the two bolts holding the bottom spring retainer in place, the retainer can be removed...

57 ...followed by the coil spring itself.

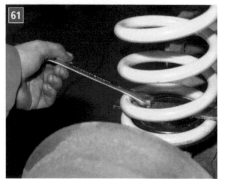

58 The locating plate is removed from beneath the spring. These always become very rusty and a new one was obtained from the Britpart inventory.

59 The new locating plate and spring are offered up after cleaning up all traces of rust from the axle and coating it with copper grease where the locating plate would sit.

60 Next the new retainer was offered up...

61 ...and bolted down.

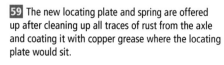

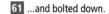

62 The top mounting bracket was usable but tatty so it was decided to fit a new one. The heads were ground off each of the three through-bolts...

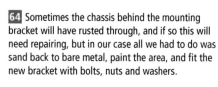

63 ...the bracket removed, and the bolt remnants – still with their nuts on the far end – drifted out.

64 Sometimes the chassis behind the mounting bracket will have rusted through, and if so this will need repairing, but in our case all we had to do was sand back to bare metal, paint the area, and fit the new bracket with bolts, nuts and washers.

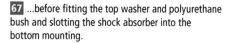

65 It was now time to fit the new backing washer and polyurethane bush to the bracket, followed by the outer bush, washer and lock nut.

66 The top nut was then tightened...

67 ...before fitting the top washer and polyurethane bush and slotting the shock absorber into the bottom mounting.

68 The bottom shock absorber mountings were then assembled in a similar way to those of the top. The correct torque setting for both top and bottom nuts is 37Nm (27lb/ft).

69 A breaker bar was used to undo the large nut on the end of the old radius arm. A combination of tightness and rust mean that an ordinary ratchet spanner will rarely do the job.

70 Three more smaller bolts hold the bush mounting in place. These must also be removed.

71 At the other end of the radius arm there's a through bolt with lock nut that must also be removed. Once again, you'll probably need a breaker bar to start the nut moving. Then the bolt can be drifted out and removed from the bracket.

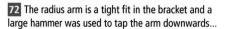

72 The radius arm is a tight fit in the bracket and a large hammer was used to tap the arm downwards...

73 ...enabling the radius arm and the large bush from its front end to be removed.

74 The new radius arm kit was shown on page 73. Here the two polyurethane bushes have been inserted, one from each side, before tapping in the steel centre bush.

75 The rear-most polyurethane bush and washers having been fitted to the front end of the radius arm, it was inserted loosely into the bracket on the chassis.

76 It's important that the rear end of the radius arm is fitted first. If it's difficult to push the bushes into the space between the sides of the bracket it's a good idea to tap each side outwards slightly with a hammer, before lubricating them with copper grease.

77 Even so, our radius arm still needed to be tapped into place with a soft-faced mallet. If you're concerned about the risk of damaging the powder coating, place a few layers of masking tape over the end of the bush and interpose a piece of softwood between the hammer and the radius arm.

78 After aligning all the holes, the pivot pin was inserted, the washer and lock nut fitted, and the nut tightened to 176Nm (130lb/ft).

79 With the vehicle in the air, the large nut can be fitted to the front end of the radius arm...

80 ...and the three sets of nuts and bolts and washers fitted in place. They mustn't be fully tightened at this stage but should only be pulled tight when the vehicle is on the ground and after you've 'bounced' the suspension a few times. The large nut is tightened to 176Nm (130lb/ft).

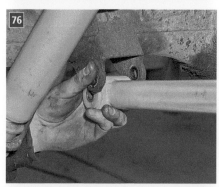

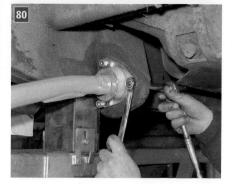

Polyurethane suspension bushes

Ian Baughan of IRB was convinced he could improve DiXie the Defender's roadholding and handling with a few relatively inexpensive tweaks. The plan was threefold:

- Fit a set of SuperPro polyurethane bushes all round.
- Fit SuperPro's castor-angle adjustment bushes to the radius arms to improve steering self-centring effect.
- Fit a pair of standard Land Rover anti-roll bars.

This is how it was done.

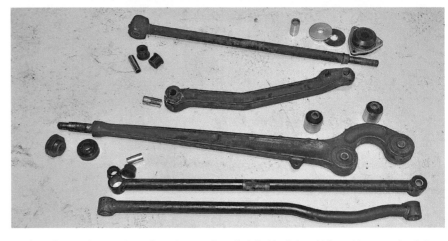

Here's a selection of suspension and steering arms from the left side of the vehicle, waiting to receive their new castor angle change bushes. In the foreground is a pair of Panhard rods. They're there because, when my Defender was converted from left-hand drive to right, the LHD Panhard rod (at bottom with the kink in it) was left in place because it's exactly the same length as the RHD one. However, Ian decided to swap it for the straight RHD rod.

CASTOR ANGLE

It's easy to get your head round the idea of castor angle if you stop thinking about cars and start thinking about castors on shopping trolleys. The pin, or swivel, on any castor is not in line with its axle; it's to one side of it. That's so that as you start to push the trolley, the castor swivels and its wheel follows the line in which you're pushing. If you've ever tried pushing a shopping trolley where the castor has jammed you'll know how difficult it is to follow the direction you want to go in.

Similarly, the kingpin on a vehicle (the equivalent of the pin on your shopping trolley) is ahead of the centre line of the wheel, so that the steering tends to swing the front wheels straight-ahead if you take your hands off the steering wheel.

To add to the effect, the kingpin on a vehicle isn't only 'ahead' of the wheel, it's also angled, adding to the self-centring effect on the steering. Steering without (or with insufficient) self-centring feels vague, especially when driving on a straight stretch of road, and can have a lack of 'sharpness' about it when cornering.

If a coil-sprung Defender's suspension is raised, the castor angle is changed. Some specialists recommend that vehicles with 50mm of suspension lift should have the castor angle corrected by 3° in order to return the steering to the correct geometry, while Defenders with over 50mm of lift might need 6° of castor correction.

For a vehicle with standard ride height, changing the castor angle by 3° will simply provide better self-centring and sharper steering at the cost of very slightly increased steering weight.

RADIUS ARM

1 Off came the steering arm, to allow the radius arm to be detached from the vehicle.

2 The front of the radius arm was detached by removing the two bolts, one each side of the axle.

3 At its rear end, the radius arm passes through part of the chassis. Its threaded end has bushes, washers and a large lock nut holding it in place while cushioning shocks from the front axle.

4 The radius arm was removed.

5 At the front-end of the radius arm is a pair of bushes, and at the rear an arrangement of washers and bushes. All of these bushes will be replaced by polyurethane versions. Theoretically they should last a lot longer and give slightly firmer steering and suspension control.

6 Two sets of front-end radius arm bushes – on the left, a pair of standard SuperPro polyurethane bushes with steel inserts shown separately; on the right, a pair of castor change bushes with the steel inserts offset from the centre line.

7 A SuperPro polyurethane castor change bush is compared with a regular Land Rover Defender bush.

8 As a general rule, bushes at the chassis ends can be pulled off by hand, whereas those at the axle ends need pressing out. So here an hydraulic press is being pumped to remove the front radius arm bushes. They can take a lot of pressure to remove and even Polybush's Bushwaka – a very strong threaded bar with the correct size inserts to pull the bushes in and out – can sometimes struggle. If you don't own an hydraulic press you'll invariably save yourself a lot of time and grief by taking the bushes to an agricultural or mechanical engineer's garage with a suitable press.

9 SuperPro polyurethane castor change bushes come with a template and instructions that state 'Lay the trailing arm on this template and mark the bush positions as indicated.'

10 Ian also marked the bushes themselves to indicate their centre line.

11 The instructions next say 'Press in the bush with the hole closest to the mark.' So the bushes were placed in position ready for being pressed, but before doing so we checked that the distance between hole centres was 164±1mm, as stated in the instructions. Note that when measuring centres between holes of the same size, an edge-to-edge measurement is identical to the measurement between the centres – and is far easier to measure.

12 Using lots of the lube supplied with the kit, a press was used to insert the bush…

13 …making sure that the outer part of the bush was fitted centrally in the radius arm. The centre tube can be centred separately later.

14 The bushes at the axle-end are a simple push-on fit.

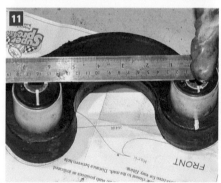

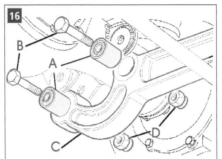

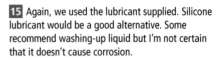

15 Again, we used the lubricant supplied. Silicone lubricant would be a good alternative. Some recommend washing-up liquid but I'm not certain that it doesn't cause corrosion.

16 On our example the bushes were already in, but this is a reminder about which way round the bolts (B) should fit, according to the manual.

17 However, it can't possibly matter which way round they go and you'll find you can push them in more easily from this side. A fair bit of levering will be required in most cases. This is especially true of castor angle adjustment bushes where the angle of the axle is being changed.

18 An air tool was used to spin nut and bolt together. They'll be tightened later with a torque wrench.

REAR SUSPENSION LINK ARM

19 It's best to slacken the large nut holding the link arm to its mounting while it's on the vehicle so that it's held firmly and can't turn. Next the three sets of nuts and bolts holding the mounting to the chassis were slackened and removed.

20 At the other end, the nut was removed from the pin…

21 …and after a battle to get the pin out of the mounting bracket the link arm dropped free.

22 At the rear of the link arm, the old bush has been pressed out in the hydraulic press and the new bushes are ready to go in. Sure enough, the bushes will go into the end of the arm by hand, but the centre tube proved trickier and the hydraulic press was used, though a vice or woodworker's cramp would certainly do the job.

23 The new mounting was fitted and the lock nut finger-tightened…

24 …before being offered up to the vehicle, and the three nuts and bolts holding it in place were loosely fitted. Always use lots of copper grease on bolt shanks and threads.

25 At this point, the axle won't want to play the game. You'll need to use a ratchet strap to pull it in whichever direction it needs to go…

26 …until the rebushed arm slides easily into its mounting position.

27 After fitting the axle-end, the three chassis mounting bolts were tightened followed by the large lock nut.

PANHARD ROD

28 The Panhard rod prevents excessive lateral movement of the front axle. First the pins were removed…

29 …and the rod levered out ready to be rebushed with new SuperPro polyurethane bushes as before.

30 Anti-roll bars, when fitted, are also located with rubber-type bushes as standard.

31 New SuperPro polyurethane bushes, lubricated as before, are simply pushed over the anti-roll bar and retained in the normal way using the standard brackets.

32 At the axle end there are more SuperPro bushes at the anti-roll bar links.

33 This, incidentally, is one of two standard anti-roll bars Ian fitted to my vehicle. He later used a torque wrench on these and all other mounting bolts to ensure they were tightened correctly.

34 Following top engineering practice, each nut or bolt was marked with a paint pen after being checked and tightened. You then go around the whole vehicle after you've finished and make sure that each threaded connection is marked.

WAS IT WORTH IT?
It's impossible to completely separate out each modification from the others, but I've done a fair bit of this sort of thing and I've got a good idea by now of what does what…

Anti-roll bars
As you'd expect from factory-developed equipment, DiXie handles pretty much as it did before, except that body roll is reduced. In other words, there's no notable extra under- or over-steer, although I suspect that the anti-roll bars have made the suspension very slightly stiffer.

Polyurethane bushes
If they haven't made the suspension any stiffer they have, I think, added to a general feeling of tautness. Whether it's the anti-roll bars or the bushes that have caused it, the extra stiffness isn't enough to be at all uncomfortable. At the very least I'm certain that these bushes will outlast the original ones many times over.

Camber adjustment bushes
Ian forewarned me that the steering might feel a little heavier, but happily the difference is negligible. Steering is a lot more stable at speed, such as on the motorway, and has a greater tendency to return to the straight-ahead position if you experimentally lift your hands from the wheel.

SUMMARY
These are the sort of modifications I really like – nothing dramatic or cursed with unfortunate side-effects, while the whole package makes driving my Defender a noticeably more pleasant and secure experience.

Even if your Land Rover was fitted with anti-roll bars from new, you can change its handling characteristics by upgrading them. And if it was never fitted with them in the first place, you might want to improve its on-road performance by adding a pair.

Anti-roll bars do just what it says on the tin. When, as your vehicle is cornering, it tries to roll to one side, the anti-roll bars transmit some of the rolling effect away from the wheel on the outside of the corner to the wheel on the inside. This makes the suspension compress more evenly, keeping the vehicle on a more even keel.

In theory, anti-roll bars have no effect on suspension stiffness. On a perfectly level road surface that would certainly be true. However, undulating road surfaces cause each wheel to rise and fall in opposition to the wheel on the other end of the axle. When this happens the anti-roll bar tries to keep the vehicle level, and this has the effect of causing more suspension stiffness. It's worth bearing that in mind when specifying the fitting of thicker anti-roll bars than standard. It's also worth remembering that anti-roll bars will be detrimental to more extreme off-road work because they won't allow the axles to 'twist' as much as they otherwise would.

Another even more important consideration is that if you fit a much thicker anti-roll bar to one end of the vehicle, that end could slide dangerously under hard cornering as the suspension stiffens up more at one end of the vehicle than at the other.

If, after purchasing an Extreme kit, you're unsure about any of the procedures described here, you're welcome to phone Extreme 4x4 Ltd and ask for technical advice.

CHOICE OF ANTI-ROLL BARS

1 Several different anti-roll bar kits are available from Extreme 4x4 and IRB Developments, comprising various thicknesses of bar to produce different handling characteristics. Both IRB and Extreme will be happy to advise regarding your particular needs. The parts listed here relate to the drawing below:

2 My Defender came with anti-roll bar brackets already welded to the chassis. This makes it particularly easy to fit anti-roll bars where none have been fitted before. You can carry out this work without removing the wheels.

3 For earlier Defenders without anti-roll bar mounting brackets, Extreme can supply new brackets for fitting to the bare chassis. The chassis bracket set seen here is for a 90/D1/ RR Classic, for example. The 110 rear is the only one with the four-bolt fixing.

4 The new brackets come folded and drilled ready to be fitted.

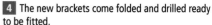

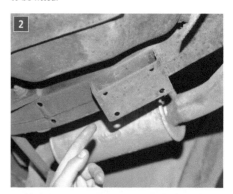

No Description and quantity
(per bar unless otherwise stated)
1   19mm anti-roll bar front (1)
1   25.4mm anti-roll bar rear (1)
2   Urethane anti-roll bar bush kit (2 pieces) (1)
2   Urethane anti-roll bar bush kit 25.4mm bar (2)
3   Bracket strap anti-roll bar (per bar) (2)
4   M10 Nyloc nut (4)
5   M10X x 30mm bolt (4)
6   M10A washer (8)
7   Ball joint assembly (2)
8   M16 Nyloc nut (2)
9   Urethane anti-roll bar bush kit for ball joints (4 pieces) (1)
10 M18 washer (2)
11 M18 pin M16 thread (2)

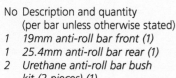
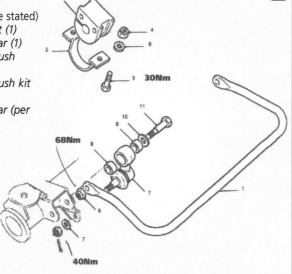

30Nm
68Nm
40Nm

5 Extreme can advise on the correct location for the brackets. You can then drill holes in the chassis before inserting the rivnuts to provide captive nuts. Rivnuts are supplied with the kit and Extreme also sell a tool to set the M10 rivnuts into the chassis.

6 The axle mountings consist of a pair of brackets for the end of each axle. You can see the welded-on variety already fitted to my axle (arrow).

7 The back of the bracket is self-locating on the Panhard rod bracket.

REPLACING EXISTING ANTI-ROLL BARS

- Undo the two M16 nuts and bolts that connect the ball joint to the existing anti-roll bar (if fitted) and remove the split bushes.
- Remove the split pins from the existing ball joints and undo the castellated nuts.
- Tap the body of the ball joints firmly to release the tapered shaft from the axle brackets and remove.
- Undo the two anti-roll bar clamp nuts and bolts.

REAR ANTI-ROLL BAR

8 The orange Extreme anti-roll bar in the size recommended by them is compared by Ian Baughan with the thickness of an original Land Rover anti-roll bar. The effect of a thicker rear bar is to increase oversteer which may, or may not, be what you're looking for.

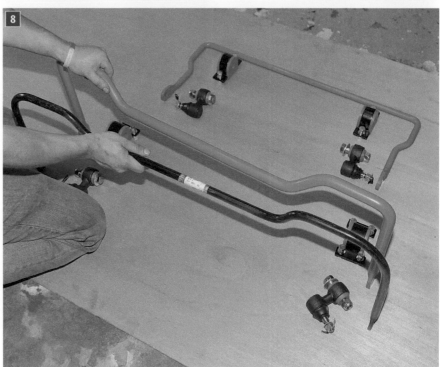

9 Assembly starts by fitting the polyurethane bushes on to the bar, followed by the two mounting brackets. The brackets must be fitted the right way up – the dog leg (if bent into the bar) must face down to clear rear-mounted fuel tanks.

10 Copper grease should be brushed into the threads of every mounting bolt before fitting them, and Würth aerosol wax applied where the steel of the mounting brackets would be in contact.

11 The heavy rear anti-roll bar was held in place for the polyurethane bushes to be slid into their correct locations...

12 ...only to find that Land Rover had made the welded-on mounting bracket with two different sizes of hole, 10mm and 8mm. Of course, you don't notice this until you start to fit the bolts! So the 8mm holes had to be carefully drilled out and the bare metal treated with Würth Protection Spray...

13 ...before the remaining 10mm bolts could be fitted.

14 Before fitting the tapered ball joint to the axle bracket, make sure that the tapered hole is clear and clean. If it's not, the taper won't seat correctly.

15 The tapered pin was pushed into position and the castellated nut plus washer loosely fitted.

16 You can partly tighten the castellated nut at this stage (though not fully), but you must turn the tapered pin so that you'll be able to insert the split pin later on.

17 The shouldered pin for connecting to the end of the anti-roll bar got the copper grease treatment before being used to attach the bar to the ball joint assembly. Note that the large washer goes between the head on the pin and the polyurethane bush.

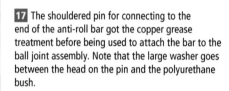

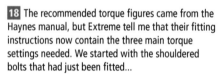

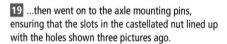

18 The recommended torque figures came from the Haynes manual, but Extreme tell me that their fitting instructions now contain the three main torque settings needed. We started with the shouldered bolts that had just been fitted...

19 ...then went on to the axle mounting pins, ensuring that the slots in the castellated nut lined up with the holes shown three pictures ago.

20 Note that the chassis mounting bolts were left loose so that the anti-roll bar centred itself correctly inside the polyurethane bush. Each of the bolts was now nipped up before being tightened to the correct torque.

21 A tip from Ian Baughan of IRB is don't push the split pin fully home so that its head disappears

into the castellated nut. If you do, and you need to remove it later, you'll have nothing to grab hold of. Position the split pin head as shown here and then use pliers to fold the legs of the pin in opposite directions to each other.

FRONT ANTI-ROLL BAR

22 Extreme recommended and supplied a front anti-roll bar (orange) that's thinner than the standard one (black), to increase the effect of oversteer mentioned earlier.

23 The front anti-roll bar was offered and loosely fitted up in the same way as the rear had been, with the chassis mountings left deliberately loose so that the bar could slide sideways as the ends were fitted.

24 The ball joint assemblies were installed in the brackets on the axle.

25 Then the ends of the anti-roll bars were bolted to the ball joint assemblies before everything was tightened and torqued, as before.

26 On the front axle, it doesn't matter how the hole for the split pin is orientated because there are no obstructions.

27 As with the rear anti-roll bar, the axle mounting bolts are tightened last of all. Ensure that all nuts, bolts and fixings are tightened to the manufacturer's torque specifications.

Do be careful to specify the type of roadholding you want to achieve *before* purchasing your anti-roll bars. After fitting the very heavy rear anti-roll bar, I had a close encounter with a homicidal school bus driver on a greasy, wet, narrow country lane and ended up going sideways before taking a trip into the undergrowth. Later, I fitted standard

'bars front and rear, and now, even in similar extreme on-road circumstances, the Defender feels quite controllable.

IRB and Extreme tell me that if a customer has a winch bumper and winch on the front, a roof tent or spare wheel and tyre on the bonnet, or a combination of these, they'll often advise that the standard

anti-roll bar is retained or a 25.4mm diameter unit is fitted.

Extreme 4x4 advise that any suspension modification or upgrade can change the handling characteristics of your vehicle, and you should road-test it with care to become accustomed to any changes before using it to its full potential.

Steering damper

The steering stabiliser, sometimes called the steering damper, is another integral component of Old Man Emu's 4WD suspension range. It's designed to reduce the effect of wheel vibration and improve the feel, handling and control of the vehicle, while at the same time, reducing kickback of the steering wheel over rough roads.

The OME unit has nine-stage, coil-spring valving; a 15mm piston rod; a steel stone-guard to protect the piston rod against damage; 35mm piston and bore, providing increased oil volume; twin-tube construction to protect the internal components against stone damage, and a multi-lip seal to prevent oil loss.

1 Once in situ, the lower bush and washer were fitted and all of the fixings fully tightened.

2 It was a simple matter to remove the nut and lock nut on the end of the old steering damper, though severely rusted components might take a bit longer.

3 Copper grease was applied to the steering damper threads. Here you can clearly see the extra capacity of the OME damper compared with the original. You can also see the inner bush already fitted.

4 The outer bush and shaped washer go on once the damper has been inserted into the hole in the bracket.

5 The inner nut is then tightened sufficiently to put the bush under the right amount of tension (without squashing it too much). Then, gripping the inner nut with one spanner, you fit and tighten the outer lock nut.

Diff guards

Your Land Rover could become incapacitated from a leaking housing or a broken ring gear, and all it would take would be a split-second miscalculation in your normally superb driving skills! That's because, in extreme off-road conditions, one of the most exposed components on your entire vehicle – the lowest point on your Land

Rover, and therefore the most prone to being smashed by rocks or stumps – is the axle differential casing.

1 This is a Britpart diff guard being fitted to one of their project vehicles. As you can see, fitting is simple and self-explanatory.

2 Under normal circumstances the differential pan is prone to corroding out and that tendency will be made much worse from mud and water trapped between axle and diff guard.

3 It pays to liberally coat the axle with wax-based rustproofer before fitting the axle guard. This is the Extreme 4x4 galvanised version.

If your Land Rover brakes are notably poor under normal driving circumstances, they'll undoubtedly be a lot better if you simply overhaul them. Make sure that all the brake components – discs, pads, calipers, lines/hoses, master cylinder and fluid – are in good order. But then, if you're going to replace discs and pads, you might want to go the extra mile and actually fit upgraded brake components, as shown here.

There's no point in expecting good brake performance from worn discs and pads, but old brake fluid can be even more dangerous. Brake fluid becomes hot as it's compressed. This is nothing to do with the heat generated by the brakes, though of course this can also be conducted into the brake fluid. It's because whenever fluid (or gas) is compressed it heats up.

Even a few fast stops on the motorway can be enough to fade the brakes when using standard components, especially if they're in poor condition. Worn or glazed parts can fade especially quickly. However, tyres are generally the limiting factor in most emergency braking situations.

But for a single stop, standard brakes can generally lock the wheels, so in theory 'wonder' brakes won't be able to stop the vehicle any quicker. However, braking when pulling a trailer or caravan on a long downhill stretch or several, repeated hard stops will almost certainly see the brakes becoming harder and harder to use as brake fade sets in. This is because brakes work by turning energy (reducing the progress of the vehicle) into heat, but when the point comes that the brakes can't dissipate heat faster than it's being created they become less and less efficient (they 'fade') until the point comes when they virtually stop working altogether.

TAKING THE HEAT OUT OF THINGS

So the main purpose of carrying out braking upgrades is in improving heat dissipation. MM 4x4's 'upgrade' brakes have vented front discs (which later Defenders have as standard), plus cross-drilling to improve heat dissipation still further, and grooving to improve water dispersion. Then there are the EBC pads which, unlike standard pads, are OK to use on cross-drilled discs and won't fade as quickly in extreme circumstances, plus stainless steel braided brake hoses that resist the swelling suffered by standard brake hoses when you brake hard.

You'll also need new gaskets (or liquid gaskets) for the drive members and new nuts for later models with one-shot hub nuts (as shown here), as well as things like split pins. When you're ordering the parts,

talk to the people at MM 4x4, who'll be able to advise on the ancillaries you'll need depending on the age and model of your Land Rover.

My Defender is a 2006 model with Td5 running gear, and there are detailed differences between this and earlier models.

1 MM 4x4's mechanic removed the dust cap, followed by the circlip (using circlip pliers), and retrieved the shims fitted underneath, ready for later reuse.

2 Look at the rust already forming on the driveshaft splines – which is why it was a struggle to get the driven member off the end of the driveshaft. It's best to raise one side of the vehicle at a time, so the axle oil runs to the other end of the axle, minimising oil leakage.

3 After removing the split pins from the inner ends of the brake pad retaining pins, each pin can be slid out. Make sure you retrieve the springs fitted to them.

4 You might need to lever the pistons back in, especially if the old discs have a wear ridge around the outer edge, before sliding out the pads.

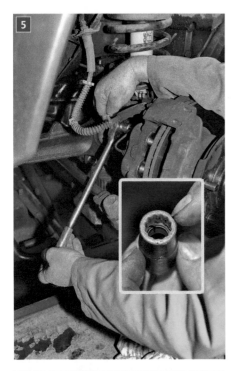

5 You'll need a long breaker bar and 12-point socket to remove the two bolts holding the caliper in place.

6 If you're removing the caliper but not replacing the flexible hose, you must hang the caliper so that it's not dangling on its hose, potentially causing it damage.

7 Inset you can see the hub nut we're dealing with here, while the annotated illustration shows the components of the very common earlier layout.

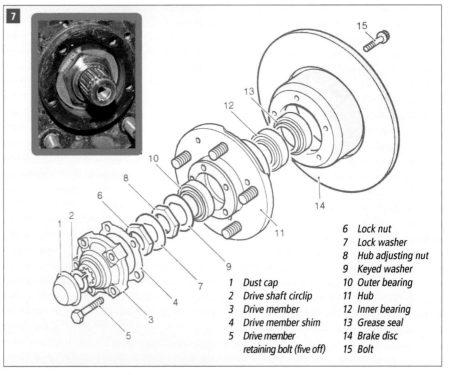

1 Dust cap	6 Lock nut
2 Drive shaft circlip	7 Lock washer
3 Drive member	8 Hub adjusting nut
4 Drive member shim	9 Keyed washer
5 Drive member	10 Outer bearing
retaining bolt (five off)	11 Hub
	12 Inner bearing
	13 Grease seal
	14 Brake disc
	15 Bolt

8 The large nut is quite difficult to start off because of the retaining system you'll see later.

9 Unlike the earlier model, this one has a taper bearing assembly. After removing it...

10 ...the hub and disc assembly can be lifted away.

11 Half a dozen bolts hold the disc to the hub.

12 After ensuring that the mating surfaces are perfectly clean, the new MM 4x4 brake disc is placed in position.

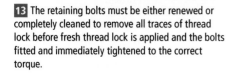

13 The retaining bolts must be either renewed or completely cleaned to remove all traces of thread lock before fresh thread lock is applied and the bolts fitted and immediately tightened to the correct torque.

14 Note that it's possible to fit each brake disc the wrong way round. The slots in the disc must be aligned so that they throw water out as the disc rotates when the vehicle is travelling forward.

15 The bearing and washer are refitted and a new lock nut applied. The lock nut must be tightened to the recommended torque.

16 There's a flat against which the lip on the lock nut has to be hammered, locking it in place.

17 Next, although it doesn't need to be done at this stage, the caliper was refitted.

18 The old gasket was thoroughly cleaned off the drive member, any rust removed from the splines and a new gasket fitted.

19 Here's how to lock the hub to prevent it from turning while tightening the drive member bolts to the correct torque.

20 Invariably, the caliper pistons will need pushing back in before new pads can be fitted.

21 The 'correct' way of doing it is with a special tool but, provided you're careful, there's no reason why you shouldn't be able to do this with a screwdriver. If the pistons are too stiff to move easily there's probably some corrosion going on, and you should consider changing calipers.

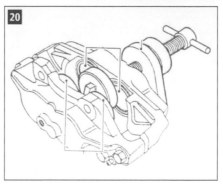

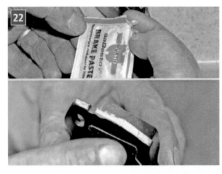

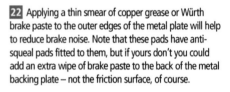

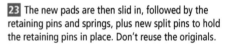

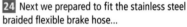

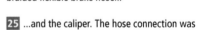

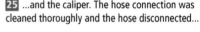

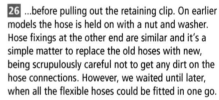

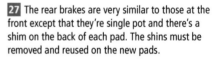

22 Applying a thin smear of copper grease or Würth brake paste to the outer edges of the metal plate will help to reduce brake noise. Note that these pads have anti-squeal pads fitted to them, but if yours don't you could add an extra wipe of brake paste to the back of the metal backing plate – not the friction surface, of course.

23 The new pads are then slid in, followed by the retaining pins and springs, plus new split pins to hold the retaining pins in place. Don't reuse the originals.

24 Next we prepared to fit the stainless steel braided flexible brake hose...

25 ...and the caliper. The hose connection was cleaned thoroughly and the hose disconnected...

26 ...before pulling out the retaining clip. On earlier models the hose is held on with a nut and washer. Hose fixings at the other end are similar and it's a simple matter to replace the old hoses with new, being scrupulously careful not to get any dirt on the hose connections. However, we waited until later, when all the flexible hoses could be fitted in one go.

27 The rear brakes are very similar to those at the front except that they're single pot and there's a shim on the back of each pad. The shins must be removed and reused on the new pads.

28 Because there's no steering at the back, the brake pipe is rigid. The pipe can be left connected to the caliper but has to be detached from its fixing clips on the axle.

29 The caliper is removed, though this bolt required the use of a ring spanner, there not being enough room for a socket.

30 The caliper was removed over as short a distance as possible so as not to strain the rigid pipe, and suspended carefully out of the way.

31 The new MM 4x4 rear disc isn't vented but is thicker than some standard discs, and is cross-drilled and grooved like the fronts.

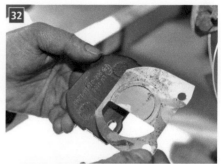

32 The retrieved shims were fitted to the new pads before installing.

33 The top end of the front flexible hose is detached. The clip was removed before separating the hose joint.

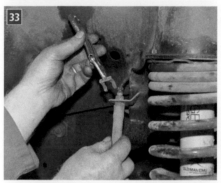

34 However, when refitting the hoses it's best to at least start the threads without the clip in place because it's then much easier to line up the threads and make sure they're not crossed.

35 You could then either refit the clip before tightening the two halves of the hose, or fully tighten the two halves before fitting the retaining clip – the choice is yours.

36 The MM 4x4 braided hose kit comes with two alternative hoses for the rear axle. You simply fit whichever type is appropriate to your Defender and discard the other.

37 Although it's more fiddly because of the more restricted space, the process of swapping the rear axle hose is essentially the same.

The new brakes will, of course, need to be bled thoroughly and with great care. We used Automec silicone brake fluid because, unlike conventional brake fluid, it doesn't cause corrosion inside the braking system and never needs replacing, only topping-up. Be aware that the new pads are notorious for being very noisy for the first couple of days until they bed in, when they quieten down.

My Defender's braking efficiency is now much improved, with a noticeable decrease in fade when towing my fully laden three-tonne trailer up and down steep hills.

WARNING: Brakes are one of the most important safety items on a vehicle and you should only work on them if you're fully competent to do so.

For those with 18in wheels or larger, IRB Developments has designed a bolt-on brake conversion developed in conjunction with brake specialists Alcon. There's a huge six-pot caliper and a 343mm, two-piece vented disc and bell assembly. It works with both ABS and non-ABS Defenders. At the time of writing Alcon four-pot rear calipers and vented discs are also said to be on the way. They're very expensive!

CHAPTER 4

Bodywork and body electrics

If those with evil intent can't actually see into your Land Rover's load area because the windows are tinted, they're much less likely to want to break in. And if they're physically prevented from smashing the glass you'll have a useful extra layer of security. Here's how Pentagon Reading apply Supaglass security film and tint.

Note that in the UK (though not in every European country) you can have any tint, as dark as you like, from the rear of the front doors back; but front side windows are, when manufactured, already virtually at the required legal limit of 70% VLT (visible light transmitted), while a windscreen's maximum permissible tint is even less, as 75% of light must pass through it.

1 Here, one of the rear side glasses is removed...

2 ...before liquid is sprayed on to the piece of tint we'll be using.

3 The template is then placed on it, which the tint is meticulously cut to match.

4 The redundant material is removed and the piece of tint marked so that we know which glass it's for.

5 Next the template is peeled off the film, ready to be used for the rear glass from the other side.

6 Pentagon Reading have developed a special cleaning material that helps the tint to stick to the glass. It's sprayed on, then wiped to produce an even coating. This particular piece of film is now ready to be fitted.

THE SECURITY FILM

7 Before we move on to the other rear glass, let's look at how the Supaglass security film is applied. Here a piece of door glass is fitted to a special holding frame.

8 There's nothing special about the cleaning material used, but an impressive amount of time was spent rubbing the entire surface with a coarse material (though one that won't scratch glass), followed by a squeegee to remove all traces and a much finer, non-scouring pad to remove every last blemish.

9 A final wash-off removes all traces of dirt and abrasive material. It's essential that no contaminants are left on the glass, or the protective film will show a noticeable bubble.

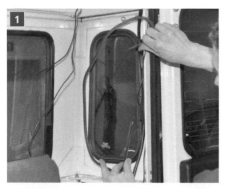

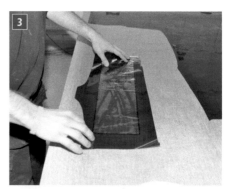

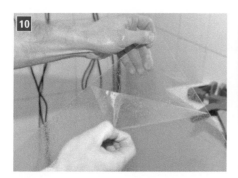

10 The protective backing is then peeled from the piece of Supaglass film to be fitted, exposing the film's adhesive surface.

11 The next liquid to be sprayed on is a special solution to assist the bonding process...

12 ...then a slippery solution is sprayed on to the glass to prevent the adhesive from sticking, before offering up the film.

13 The film is aligned before trimming off excess.

14 All traces of air were squeegeed out, a special adhesive was applied to the film edges (this ensures there's no risk of the film lifting or shifting in future), and finally a heat gun was used to help bond the Supaglass in place by starting to dry the solution applied earlier. The glass was then removed from the frame.

After fitting, you're advised to not open or close door windows for three full days so that enough of the solution has evaporated to remove any risk of the film sliding on the glass. To help things along, Supaglassed and tinted windows are heated and dried out some more in the workshop before refitting.

THE TINT FILM

15 Now we return to the rear side glass that we saw security film being applied to earlier. This was now fitted to the support frame and sprayed with what Pentagon called 'special bonding fluid'.

16 The piece of tint film we saw being cutting was sprayed with slippery solution as the backing sheet was peeled away...

17 ...and the film skilfully applied to the glass.

18 Once again a squeegee or spatula was used to push out excess solution and remove air pockets...

19 ...and the tint film trimmed to precisely match the shape of the glass.

20 After the glass had been heated for a while it was ready for refitting. Here the finished rear side door glass is slid into its runners.

When tinting, film can be added without removing the windows. Some alternatives to Supaglass even add film to the glass while it's in situ. However, a thief can then shatter the glass by smashing it near the edge. The *only* way to do the job properly is to remove the glass and Supaglass it right up the edges.

Most van-bodied Land Rovers are made that way because of tax implications. If a vehicle is a 'car' (as defined by UK's HM Revenue and Customs), a business can't reclaim the VAT. If it's a commercial vehicle, it can. Though the regulations have changed in recent years, meaning that the absence of side windows isn't necessary for 'vehicles with a payload of more than one tonne' to be classed as commercial vehicles, many Land Rovers with van rear-ends are still in use and are still being bought new.

Wilfred, our project 200 Tdi Defender, was a one-owner workhorse until we bought it. Driving a van can be a right pain though, especially when pulling out from angled junctions and reversing into spaces. Having side windows makes it much more user-friendly.

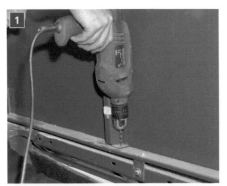

1 Wilfred's side panels were in superb condition. You must make sure yours are free from distortion or damage, otherwise the new side windows won't seal properly. On earlier Land Rovers, there's a vertical line of rivets passing through the side panel but on later ones the reinforcing strut shown here is only attached at the bottom and the top. Drill through the head of each pop rivet.

2 The reinforcing channel is bonded to the side window. In winter, it would help if you applied a hairdryer or heat gun to soften the adhesive. Lever from the bottom and press the panel outwards as you go, freeing the channel section slowly and carefully rather than trying to force it away. You'll also need to carefully use an angle grinder or power file to clean up the remnants of the pop rivets. Fit new pop rivets and sealant to the holes left at the top.

3 The box that the side windows came in is used to make a template, drawing all the way around the inner lip on the side window and then cutting along the lines with a razor sharp knife and a straight edge.

4 You need to check inside the vehicle to make sure the windows will miss the seat belt mountings. In our instance a position 26cm back from the edge of the doorframe was about right.

5 After putting a strip of masking tape on the outside of the body, the measurement we'd taken was transferred to the outside of the panel.

6 The horizontal position was also marked on a strip of masking tape...

7 ...and this allowed the template to be temporarily taped in place so that it could be drawn around in order to make the relevant cut marks. As you'll see later, the final cut marks were also made on strips of masking tape.

8 We weren't confident about the shapes of the corners so a fresh template was made from paper, making sure that the shape of the curve was just right...

9 ...and transferring it to the cut marks on the vehicle.

IMPORTANT NOTE: It pays to not simply trust your template! You should hold the window assembly up to the marks you've made on the vehicle to check that everything's in the correct place before you actually start cutting!

10 Drilling starts with a hole inboard of the cut line. The drill bit is large enough to accommodate the size of the jigsaw blade.

11 As well as putting masking tape all the way around the perimeter of the body, we also taped the foot of the jigsaw. If you don't do any of this the jigsaw will most certainly cause paint damage as it cuts.

12 With a standard width of jigsaw blade you can cut slow curves, although you might need to backtrack and widen the curves slightly as you go along. You can purchase narrower blades but they're less robust. Starting in the hole drilled earlier, a narrow curve was cut to meet the line drawn on the masking tape.

13 Cutting was done along the bottom of the cut line, first in one direction and then in the other. The amount of swarf that flies around means it's very important to wear goggles.

14 The sides are cut 'uphill', and then the top from one end towards the middle and then from the other. Don't cut the top line first or the panel will droop and bind on the blade!

15 Even so, you have to be alert or preferably get someone to support the panel as you make the final cut. It's best to wear gloves, although aluminium doesn't tend to be as sharp as freshly cut steel.

16 The window is test fitted without removing the masking tape.

17 As expected, the aperture was slightly too tight (better than making it too big!) and was opened out with a hand file. It's best not to use an angle grinder on soft aluminium sheet because there's the risk of it digging in and taking off far more metal than you want.

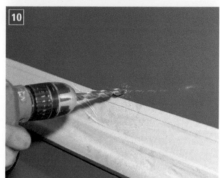

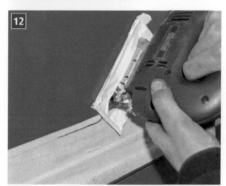

18 The window should slide in nicely without having to be forced.

19 When you install the windows make sure the drain holes are at the bottom and the opening section at the front – it's not unknown for them to be incorrectly marked 'near-side' and 'off-side' by the manufacturers.

20 You now need to hold the window temporarily in place, preferably with masking tape, while you drill four holes – one towards each corner – and push a pop rivet into each hole as you go. But don't tighten them up. Alternatively you could use small nuts and bolts of the same diameter as the pop rivets. You should then drill all the remaining holes through the body panel using the window as a guide.

21 You can now remove the window and strip all the masking tape off the side panel. We used panel wipe to ensure that the meeting faces of the window and the panel were completely clean and grease-free.

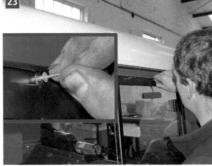

22 The correct way of sealing the window to the roof is by following current Land Rover practice and using butyl tape. It's used extensively in the caravan and van body building industries, and while it doesn't have much in the way of bonding properties it's excellent at preventing leaks because it never sets.

23 With the window back in place, push each rivet through the butyl tape and fully into position. (You can see now why it was important to drill the holes earlier – if you'd drilled them after fitting the tape, swarf would have adhered to the tape and prevented a proper seal.) Ensure that the window is fully bedded in all the way round and pushed tight against the butyl tape.

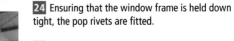

24 Ensuring that the window frame is held down tight, the pop rivets are fitted.

25 The final step was to ease the rubber covering strip into the channel around the window frame, hiding the pop rivets. As with the butyl tape, the joint should be at the bottom of the window so that any water will run out rather than in.

26 It was surprising how much the side windows lifted the appearance of the vehicle. The improved all-round visibility provided by this relatively inexpensive modification will also make Wilfred safer to drive.

TRUE OR FALSE? ANSWERS
Actually, there are so many grey areas it's like trying to walk through a minefield in thick fog, but technically all the statements are true except the last one. In practice, HM Revenue & Customs aren't a bit interested in older vehicles and Wilfred was built in 1992. In practice, however, it's a different matter, and anyone reclaiming the VAT on a new vehicle then immediately fitting side windows would probably end up paying the VAT and a fine.

You are allowed to do 70mph in a Land Rover van on a motorway, by the way.

Interior window guards

Station Wagon sliding windows were pop-riveted in on earlier Defenders, making them a real security weak point since all you have to do is remove the trim, drill out the pop rivets and in you go! Later versions have bonded-in side windows and are much more secure, although a whack with a hammer would soon sort that.

On all versions the glasses each side of the rear door and the door glass itself can easily and quickly be removed with nothing much more than a craft knife. A third problem, for dog owners, is that sliding windows certainly let the air in but they'll also let your dog out. Here's what you can do about it.

1 This is a set of Mantec interior window guards. Interior guards are intrinsically more secure than those fitted on the outside; it's also easier to keep the outside of your Defender clean.

2 Extreme 4x4 sell exterior stainless steel window guards such as these in black. They have the advantage of protecting the glass from mild collision damage but you do have to drill the vehicle's bodywork.

3 The Extreme 4x4 exterior guard for the rearmost windows is available in unpainted stainless steel.

SIDE WINDOW GUARDS

4 If you're working on a Station Wagon you'll need to start by removing the interior trim. That includes the side trim where there are blanking grommets, best removed with a trim removal tool.

5 The upper seatbelt mountings have to be removed too...

6 ...and if there are rear seats they'll also have to be taken out. Note you don't have to completely detach the seatbelt, just swing the trim out of harm's way.

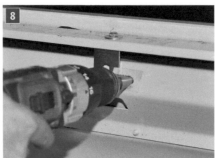

7 Here's a rivnut that can be tightened with a bolt and washer…

8 …after drilling an appropriate-sized hole in the panel to which it's to be attached.

9 Unusually, these particular rivnuts have a hexagonal body. Also unusually, there's access to the back of the panel, so the rivnut could be gripped with a spanner while tightening the bolt in order to spread the rivnut, fixing it in place, rather like squashing a pop-rivet with a pop-rivet gun.

10 With the lower rivnuts in place, the side trim is temporarily refitted and the window guard loosely fitted using the bottom bolts.

11 The hole positions are marked on a piece of masking tape over the plastic trim.

12 A pilot hole was then drilled in the trim followed by a bolt clearance hole.

13 The idea is that this threaded nut plate goes behind the trim, allowing you to bolt the top of the window guard in place.

14 The manufacturers suggest that the plate is held to the back of the trim with double-sided tape so that it doesn't drop off whenever you remove the guard for cleaning.

15 Double-sided tape is likely to come away in time, especially when stuck to plastic, so, although we used double-sided tape, we also measured out locations and drilled holes for self-tapping screws to fix the plate to the back of the trim.

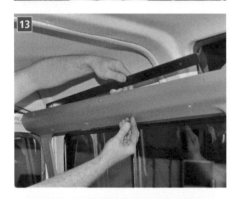

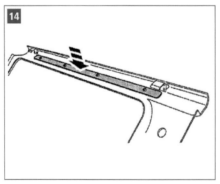

16 We could then lift the window guard into position, loosely insert the screws into the nut plate concealed behind the trim…

17 …and add the bottom screws, before tightening them all up.

REAR WINDOW GUARDS

18 The back panel window guards are somewhat easier to fit and simply involve removing two roof bolts…

19 …before temporarily fitting the window guard in place. You can then mark the positions for the bottom bolts…

20 …before centre punching them, drilling a couple of pilot holes and fitting a couple of self-tapping screws.

21 It only remains to refit and fully tighten the top bolts and replace the rear trim.

REAR DOOR GUARD

22 When fitting the door guard you need to take extra care to ensure that the guard is properly aligned and not fitted askew. The first job is to put pieces of masking tape on the doorframe at the approximate position for each fixing screw. Then, with someone holding the guard in place, mark the position of each hole on the tape.

23 Take the guard away and carefully centre-punch just two, approximately diagonally-opposite hole positions. Centre-punching very thin steel is quite tricky. Though you want enough of a depression to stop your drill running away it's important not to dent the steel.

24 After drilling the two pilot holes the guard is fitted in place using two self-tapping screws.

25 The guard itself is then used as a guide to ensure the remaining holes are drilled in exactly the right place…

26 …before fitting all of the fixing screws supplied with the kit.

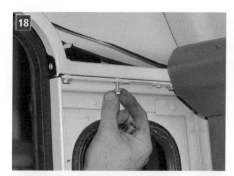
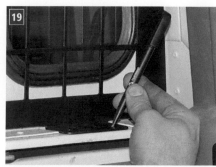

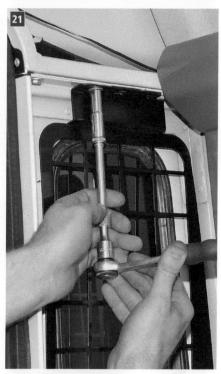
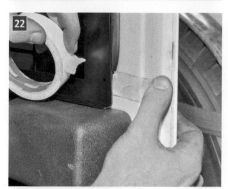

WINDOW CLEANING
- Using a power screwdriver, the threaded studs holding the side windows in place can be spun out in a matter of seconds, making these the easiest windows to clean.
- The rearmost windows can only be removed after first detaching the trim on Station Wagons. However, self-tapping screws aren't made for putting in and taking out several times – their heads tend to round off and threads will strip. The best solution is to fit rivnuts.
- The guard for the rear door window is more easily accessed but the same problem arises with regarding self-tapping screws, and it might be best to fit smaller, conventional rivnuts to the door frame.
- For all of them, screws with Allen key or Torx heads will be quicker and simpler to remove without the risk of causing damage around a hexagonal bolt head.

The idea of wind deflectors is to let fresh air in while keeping rain, snow and excessive wind out. They also allow air to pass through the vehicle without the howling wind noise you experience without them. Another advantage, for dog owners, is that when you leave your dogs in the car you can safely leave the windows open quite a bit further than you'd otherwise be able to without fear of their getting out.

Using wind deflectors can also reduce the amount of time you use air conditioning (when fitted), thus saving fuel.

These German-made ClimAir wind deflectors are the best you can get and are fitted by some manufacturers (such as Volkswagen) as OE accessories. They're all vehicle-specific and custom manufactured to fit your vehicle. They have milled, rounded edges for safety, don't cause damage to window seals, don't interfere with electric window anti-trap systems and are impossible to remove when the windows are shut. Don't be lured by cheaper versions that just stick on the outside of your vehicle, as they'll almost certainly not stay on for very long.

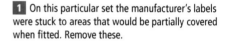

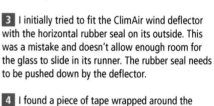

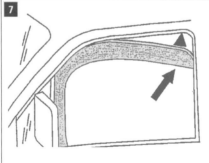

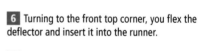

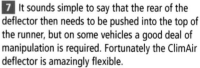

1 On this particular set the manufacturer's labels were stuck to areas that would be partially covered when fitted. Remove these.

2 You have to wind the window fully down, but take note of the positions of the rubber and runner while doing so.

3 I initially tried to fit the ClimAir wind deflector with the horizontal rubber seal on its outside. This was a mistake and doesn't allow enough room for the glass to slide in its runner. The rubber seal needs to be pushed down by the deflector.

4 I found a piece of tape wrapped around the front edge of each deflector. This might be there for a good reason, but it had the effect of once again limiting the amount of space in which the glass could slide, so I removed it.

5 Insert the front bottom corner of the deflector and push it fully home. On the Defender, the front bottom edge is pushed down on to the rubber seal so that the lip of the seal runs inside the deflector.

6 Turning to the front top corner, you flex the deflector and insert it into the runner.

7 It sounds simple to say that the rear of the deflector then needs to be pushed into the top of the runner, but on some vehicles a good deal of manipulation is required. Fortunately the ClimAir deflector is amazingly flexible.

8 Fortunately it's less difficult on the Defender and you can insert the rear lip part-way down the runner and simply push up from there. The manufacturers suggest that you now check the fitting of the wind deflector by wobbling it. A correctly fitted deflector won't change its position during 'wobbling' because it's held by its own tension.

9 Wind the window up slowly, checking that the glass is able to slide smoothly against the edges of the deflector.

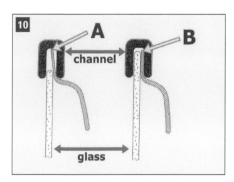

10 A common problem is for the wind deflector not to be seated tight against the edge of the channel (A). If this is the case, go all the way round seating it properly to leave room for the glass to slide against it (B).

ELECTRIC WINDOWS

Close the window in several small steps, then open it again and repeat the procedure at least five times.

- While closing the window, ask another person to help the window up by squeezing it – gripping it from each side with both hands – while pushing upwards. At the same time, use the electric window button to close the window completely.
- While doing this, pull the deflector towards the outside of the car so the door window has room to slide.
- You'll need to keep the door window closed for 24 hours so that the deflector is pressed into the rubber by the permanent pressure of the glass, after which the electric windows should work smoothly.

11 The wind deflectors for the rear windows are much simpler affairs. Because there's no angled upright as on the front deflector, there's a piece of self-adhesive tape from which the backing has to be removed.

12 Once again, the manufacturer's labels had to be removed. The last traces of adhesive didn't come off easily so were wiped away with the same Würth Silicon Remover I used to wipe the edge of the channel against which the self-adhesive strip would sit. You could use methylated spirit – but don't use thinners, because of the risk of damage, and white spirit is too oily.

13 Take great care to keep your fingers off the self-adhesive strip, otherwise it will lose its stickiness; and when inserting the front edge of the draft excluder, push away from you so that the self-adhesive strip doesn't yet touch the surface…

14 …to which it will become attached.

15 Still pushing away from the front edge, slide the draft excluder right up to the top of the runner…

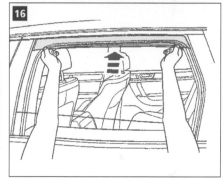

16 …and pull it tight towards you when it's fully at the top.

17 Work all the way along to encourage the self-adhesive strip to stick to the outer edge of the runner. Then open the door and check that the lower part of the ClimAir draft excluder is seated tight against the runner as described earlier.

18 Here you can see just how much further down you can leave your windows when parked up with wind deflectors fitted.

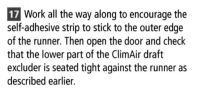

TOP TIP

- Door glass can be stiff to wind up and down after you've first fitted wind deflectors. ClimAir deflectors need 24 hours with the windows closed to bed in against the rubbers, after which things should return to normal.
- Window glass glides more easily if you apply washing up liquid or silicone to the tapered edge of the deflector.

Have you ever wanted to pull out at an angle at a road junction but not been able to see through your Defender door mirror because it's misted up or frozen over? So have I. Have you ever parked too close to a wall or struck a branch and broken your Defender mirror? Me too.

So I got a pair of Bearmach unbreakable mirrors with polycarbonate lenses and polypropylene cases and bought a pair of heated mirror elements from eBay shop 'Bolt On Bits'. Though intended for fitting to standard mirrors, they suit Bearmach's unbreakable mirrors just as well.

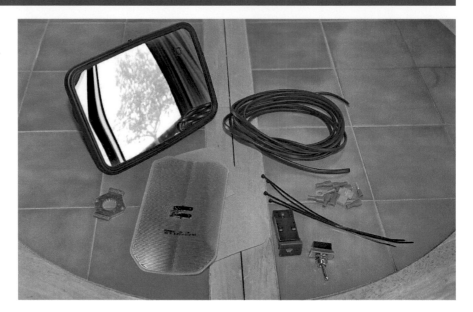

FITTING AN UNBREAKABLE MIRROR HEAD

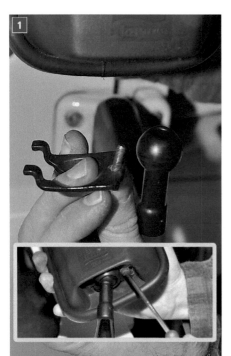

1 The original mirror head is removed by undoing the retaining bolt (inset), removing the clamp and lifting the mirror head from the ball on the end of the arm.

2 The replacement mirror head is prepared by removing the two stainless steel screws holding the cover in place.

3 The correct adapter plate is supplied with the kit and has to be placed in the bracket on the back of the mirror head with the lugs facing downwards. Note that the adapter plate as supplied has a yellow, passivated protective finish. As you'll see later, there's a large hole in the top of the mounting bracket and the yellow bracket shouts out a little bit! So I used U-Pol aerosol etch primer so that paint would stick to the passivated finish, followed by their satin black aerosol paint. It makes a surprising difference to the appearance.

4 You place the mirror head complete with adapter plate on the ball then slide the cover back on and reattach the two screws. There's some adjustment between the mirror head and the bracket but not enough to compensate for folding the arm out when towing. Instead you use the two long screws to adjust the pressure between bracket and ball, allowing you to adjust the mirror in the same way as the original.

5 These mirrors aren't handsome but they do the job they're built for supremely well. They feature larger areas than standard Defender mirrors; optical quality polycarbonate lenses; a hard lacquer lens coating that repels condensation and surface water; and a strong, flexible polypropylene casing.

FITTING MIRROR HEATERS

6 With the door closed, remove the top door hinge and mirror arm by taking out the four screws holding the hinge in place. Note that the screws into the door have nuts on the back and you'll therefore need to detach at least the top corner of the door trim to get at them.

7 Lever off the plastic cap from the bottom of the mirror swivel...

8 ...and use something like a screwdriver to push out the top cap from beneath. If you try to lever the cap with a small screwdriver from above you'll very likely damage it.

9 The aluminium is marked smack in the middle with a centre punch...

10 ...before being drilled with a pilot hole followed by a 7mm drill. The webs on the bottom of the arm had been protected with masking tape so that the drill chuck won't damage the arm. We found it perfectly acceptable to drill at this slight angle – if you want to drill at exactly 90° to the swivel you'll need a bit at least 145mm long.

11 Also drill a hole in the side of the arm, near the ball end, making sure the hole's far enough along the arm to break into the hollow section on the underside. Take care that you drill the hole in the *rear-facing* side of each mirror arm.

12 Insert a suitable length of cable into the hole at the inner end of the arm (arrowed) and push it down into the swivel tube via the access point made by removing the top cap shown earlier. The end of the cable that will later find its way into the mirror head is passed through the hole in the side of the arm.

13 After drilling a similar hole in the bottom cap and passing the wire through it the cap is simply pushed back on.

Although this is quite a fiddly job to carry out, in this day and age you really miss not having heated mirrors, and it's a day's work well spent.

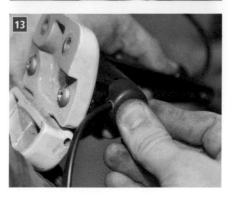

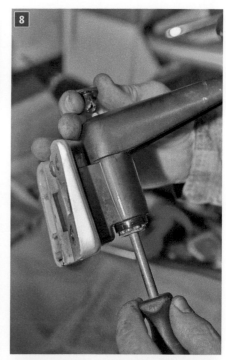

14 To ensure that the cable couldn't get trapped in the hinge, remove one of the screws holding the hinge to the mirror, place a cable clip over the wire and then screw it down with the mirror fixing screw. Check that there's sufficient clearance between the wire, clip, screwhead and bodywork when the hinge is refitted.

15 Next, remove the glass from the mirror head. With the original Land Rover-type mirror, heat the seal if it's cold, to make it flexible, ease it away and you'll have the glass as a separate item. The glass may well be lightly bonded into the back in which case you'll have to carefully work it free.

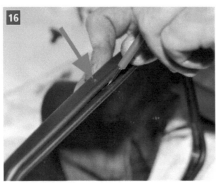

16 Remove the screws (arrowed) on each side of the mirror head and use a small screwdriver to lever the glass out of its casing, working around the periphery.

17 Remove any stuck-on labels and clean and degrease the surface of the back of the glass using something like Würth Silicone Remover. Don't touch the surface with your fingers after degreasing it.

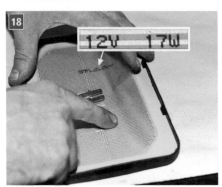

18 Remove the backing paper from one of the heater elements. Take great care not to touch the self-adhesive surface with your fingers. Gripping it by the edges, curve the element downwards so that the centre part makes contact with the mirror back first. Push the element down with the forefinger of the other hand, starting at the centre and working outwards to remove all air bubbles.

If you aren't 100% successful avoiding air bubbles prick each bubble with a pin – between the element traces, of course, otherwise you could easily break the circuit – before pushing the plastic down and removing the air. Lack of contact between the element and the glass back would certainly make the heater less efficient and might even make the element prone to burning out where it isn't in contact with the mirror back.

Incidentally, note the current rating shown on the back of each element. Their low load is the reason why these elements can be connected without having to use a relay. For the same reason they could even be connected into the heated front screen circuit (if fitted) or the rear screen heater circuit if required.

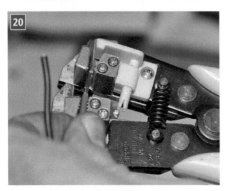

19 Drill a 6.5mm hole near the base of the mirror back. Once the wire's in place this hole (and all others) can be sealed with Würth Bond & Seal PU sealant.

20 Push the end of the wire through the hole and strip a few millimetres of insulation from the end of each cable.

21 Then use a crimping tool to crimp the female connectors supplied with the kit on to the cable ends.

22 The male connectors on the elements look a bit vulnerable so I folded each one up a little. Hold each connector firmly down while its female connector is pushed on.

23 The original screws holding the mirror glasses in place were discarded and replaced by small stainless steel ones (I always keep a box of Screwfix self-tapping screws handy).

24 Next it's a matter of finding an access point through to the interior of the Land Rover. On my vehicle, at about the point indicated here by the drill, the double skin on to which the rubber door seal is pushed has a small area cut away on one of the skins. This was an ideal point at which to drill a 7.5mm hole. A piece of steel was used to protect the dashboard in case the drill broke through.

25 After painting the bare metal with primer, push the cable through the hole, using Würth Bond & Seal in place of a grommet, and offer up the hinge/mirror assembly. Apply aerosol body wax to the hole as well as the hinge mounting positions before refitting.

26 The wiring for this installation is quite straight-forward. If no heated rear screen is fitted you could use the supply for that as a feed, or you could take a new supply from the fuse box. Alternatively – especially on the latest vehicles – you could use a redundant supply such as that for the heated front screen.

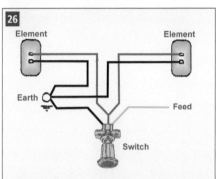

27 There are going to be differences between different models of Defender but essentially you need to gain access to the dashboard if that's where your switch is going. To remove the cover on the driver's side, the tiny screws holding the heater control knobs in place have to be removed and the knobs taken off.

28 Then you need to take out the plethora of screws holding the end cover in place, ease it out from the main dash panel and remove it.

29 On the passenger side, the grab-handle end is also unscrewed and removed after easing the dash top out of the way.

30 We used a length of plastic rod as a fishwire, which had the advantage that we didn't yet need to disconnect the battery because nothing conductive was used. The wire from the left-hand side had already been passed through at this stage and you can see it sticking through the switch hole in the dash panel.

31 In order to secure the cable and keep the cable run tidy we utilised existing dash screws to hold cable clips in place before drawing the cable all the way through the back of the dash.

32 I decided to use a Land Rover heated rear screen switch from Bearmach, the downside of which is that you have to make up connectors for the back of the switch as well as work out, using the wiring diagram from the Land Rover manual, which pin does what. It's not difficult, though. Every wire identification on the wiring diagram ends in a number and that's the pin number (inset) seen inside the switch connector housing.

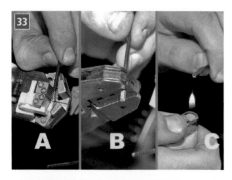

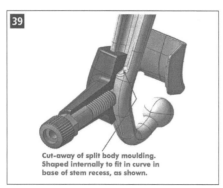

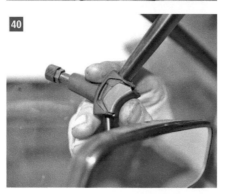

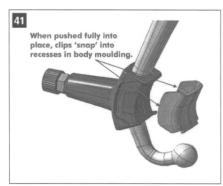

Cut-away of split body moulding. Shaped internally to fit in curve in base of stem recess, as shown.

When pushed fully into place, clips 'snap' into recesses in body moulding.

33 We stripped the wire ends (A), crimped on electrical connectors (B) and insulated them with shrink-fit tubing (C).

34 My original plan had been to use a heated front screen switch because it looks slightly different to that for the heated rear screen. Unfortunately, however, the front screen switch is a non-latching type. After it's pressed it operates a timer built into the heated front screen circuit, so you can't use this type as a conventional on-off switch. However, the rear screen switch mounted upside-down looks slightly different to its (genuine) rear screen neighbour. This switch has a tell-tale light so you know when the mirror heaters are on and the dashboard illumination light – the one that comes on with the sidelights – was fed from the same circuit as the other switches.

'Bolt On Bits' suggest that the switch they supply with their kit could be used in the hole to the right of the steering column. It's still there on diesel Defenders, even though it was originally put there by Land Rover for the manual choke on petrol models.

35 In case you're wondering about the wisdom of using a heater element on a polycarbonate mirror, so did I! So we tested the mirror heater and my infrared thermometer showed that the surface reached no more than 35°C. Happily, this isn't enough to soften the plastic, but will melt frost on the mirror in seconds and evaporate misting-up in a couple of minutes.

ANTI-VIBRATION INTERIOR MIRROR MOUNT

The standard Defender rear-view mirror arrangement has a long stem and sprung mounting, both of which cause considerable vibration. However, Ian Baughan of IRB developments sells this simple-looking little kit which solves the problem.

36 It's not essential to remove the mirror, but if you want to, twist to the left (anticlockwise) and pull away. Refitting is usually a lot trickier!

37 This is it: the mirror anti-vibration kit, as delivered by IRB.

38 Making sure you get it the right way up, push the body of the anti-vibration unit on to the stem of the mirror, ensuring the lips of the body moulding are folded around the edge of the mirror stem that's nearest you...

39 ...and that the rubber moulding is slid down the mirror stem until it locates in the position shown in this cutaway.

40 Now take the clip and push it on to the moulding from the front...

41 ...until it's properly located, when it will stay permanently in place and cause the rubber moulding to grip tightly on the mirror stem.

42 As you can see, this clip hasn't been properly located. Once it is, all you have to do is unscrew the plunger until it provides just enough tension between the windscreen and the mirror stem to remove any risk of vibration.

Roll cages

Some people think roll cages just look cool, but there's a good deal more to it than that!

Probably the best-known supplier of roll cages, Safety Devices produce cages for just about every model of Defender. Properly made and fitted roll cages have a vitally important safety function in protecting your vehicle in the event of a roll-over. Consequently the only reliable roll cage is one that's been designed and built by people who know what they're doing.

1 When you get your Safety Devices kit the materials will be of the correct strength, the fixing points will have been properly calculated in order to add strength to the original vehicle body or chassis and the cage will have been designed so that it can actually be fitted. It's not a simple matter and there's quite a lot of work involved, so the last thing you want to be doing is cutting holes in your Defender on a hit-or-miss basis.

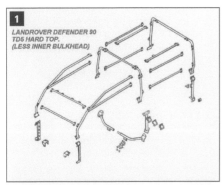

2 The instructions supplied are unusually comprehensive, and for that reason – as well as the fact that there are so many different models – we provide only a brief outline of what's involved. In order that the cage can bolt through to structural components, holes have to be cut in the bodywork.

3 Templates and detailed instructions are supplied with each kit showing the correct positioning and measurements for all the holes. These instructions state: 'Masking tape body at places where plates are to go. Mark plate positions. Position template plate on body side and mark the four 13mm diameter holes. Drill 12mm holes then cut out centre as shown in sketch.'

4 In this instance a reinforcement plate is bolted both inside and outside the vehicle and...

5 ...there's a reinforcing strut inside the front wing.

6 This particular fixing takes advantage of the fuel filler mounting. The instructions state: 'The original fuel filter mounting has to be re-drilled so that the mounting can be lifted up, onto the chassis, as follows:

- Remove fuel filler lid.
- Undo filler from chassis.
- Remove back plate from chassis.
- Re-drill backplate following drawing.
- Pop rivet nut plate provided to the filter mounting holes on the backplate, using 3mm pop rivets provided.
- Refit backplate in higher position using M 8 x 20mm bolts and washers provided.
- Refit filler lid.'

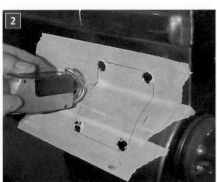

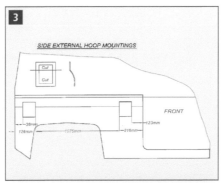

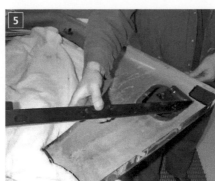

As everyone knows, an open Land Rover bonnet acts like a magnet, drawing spectators from far and wide. And what do they do when they get there? They lean on the wing top to see what's going on in the murky depths and put all the weight on the points of their elbows, leaving neat craters in the tops of the wings. Add to that the more serious business of those with working Land Rovers who actually need to stand on their wing tops and you've got two sound reasons for fitting chequer plate wing top protectors.

Most of the work in this section was carried out at Nene Overland where more major work was being done on my Defender at the same time. For that reason you'll see parts on and off the vehicle that you wouldn't normally see when carrying out this job.

1 Nene Overland's mechanic started by removing the air inlet and blanking plate from the top of each wing.

2 The wing top protectors come with sheets of thin, closed-cell foam to act as gaskets between the chequer plate and wing tops. Because it's closed-cell this foam can't absorb water and is much better than simply screwing or riveting to the paintwork.

3 After wiping the lower face of the chequer plate with panel wipe to remove all traces of grease, some of the protective paper is peeled back and sticking the foam down commences at the front of the protector.

4 The foam is smoothed it out as it goes on to ensure there are no air bubbles and that pre-punched holes in the foam line up with those in the chequer plate.

5 Because there's nothing sticky on the other side of the foam it's possible to line up the chequer plate with the ventilator hole in the wing. It's also essential that the outer edge of the chequer plate aligns accurately with that of the wing.

6 It's sometimes easier to check the inner edge where the wing's edge is more clearly defined.

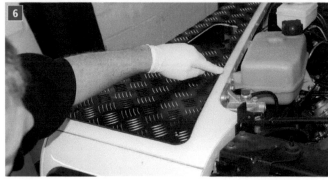

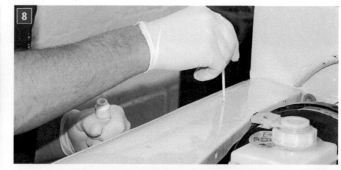

7 With the protector precisely in place the first hole is drilled, using the hole in the chequer plate as a guide. Before drilling the second hole it makes sense to pop the first bolt in place and bolt the plate firmly down so that it can't move out of position.

8 It's essential to protect all raw edges with paint to prevent corrosion.

9 Contact with mild steel also causes corrosion in aluminium. The problem is solved by using stainless steel screws.

10 The hole in the wing top is used to hold a spanner on the lock nut while tightening the screw with an Allen key.

11 With the other wing being off the vehicle already it all became much easier!

12 If you had to remove the ventilation pipes in order to fit the chequer plate, now would be the time to replace them.

13 It can be quite a fiddle reconnecting the pipes and you may need to reach through the access hole on the side of the wing after removing the cover plate.

14 You may have to drill a hole in the chequer plate to take the aerial. Because we weren't fitting a standard aerial (top), a smaller hole than normal was drilled in the plate to receive a whippy aerial (bottom).

15 If you fit the chequer plate accurately there should be plenty of clearance for refitting the grille and blanking plate.

16 Later on I selected a pair of Hi-Force wing-top air intakes from KBX Upgrades. Once again, stainless steel screws were used to prevent corrosion occurring.

Wider wheel arches

In the UK at least, it's a legal requirement that your tyres don't stick out further than the outsides of your wheel arches. So if you fit wheel spacers or extra-wide wheels you'll need to add wider wheel arches. Fortunately these are widely available and come in different widths and materials. Fibreglass wheel arches are among the cheapest but they're also among the least forgiving if you give them a thump. Not only will fibreglass shatter, but its rigidity may well transfer damage into the wing itself. Flexible plastic wheel arches are greatly preferable.

1 These Britpart wider wheel arches are made as direct replacements for the originals.

2 After removing the standard wheel arches, the new ones are simply held in place using the same fixing holes...

3 ...and new fixing rivets supplied with the kit.

4 These wider wheel arches from Extreme 4x4 are designed to be screwed or bolted direct to the wing from the outside.

Rear step and tow bracket

Land Rover's North American Specification (NAS) rear step and tow bracket is an elegant piece of kit and it appears that there are several aftermarket versions of Land Rover's original accessory.

According to Ian Baughan of IRB the Extreme 4x4 NAS step shown being fitted here is indistinguishable from the original Land Rover part, and it certainly fits like an OE component.

Before starting to fit the new step, Defenders with existing tow brackets must have the assembly removed and the wiring sockets disconnected, at least temporarily.

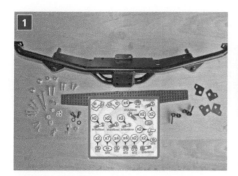

1 The kit of parts supplied by Extreme is comprehensive and the quality is excellent. It pays to set out all the parts before starting and compare them with those listed on the instruction sheet.

2 There are several detailed differences between different years of Defender. In all cases the bolt or bolts in this location have to be removed...

3 ...and there are nuts and washers on the inside of the cross member.

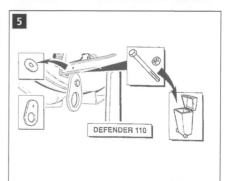

4 To help prevent future corrosion Würth aerosol cavity protection wax was used in the rear cross member in places where the new rear step will sit.

5 On 110 models the bolts holding the towing eyes to the chassis are removed and, as the instructions demonstrate, junked, to be replaced by the longer bolts and nuts included in the kit.

DEFENDER 110

6 If you were to tighten the outer mounting bolts through the hollow cross member it would bend inwards and the bolts wouldn't be tight. Some cross members already have distanced pieces inside them, but for those – the majority – that don't a set of tubular distance pieces has to be inserted into each of the cross member ends. We worked out that inserting them this way was the easiest way in.

7 The new step is offered up and checked for fit. You slide the NAS step into the locating holes in the back of the cross member. The step was temporarily secured in place using two M16 x 30mm socket-head bolts at the central location.

8 Viewed from beneath the vehicle, looking backwards, this steel strip fits between the bottom of the cross member and this mounting plate on the step. Insert the flat plate at the rear underside of the NAS step, sliding it between the vehicle underside and the right-angled plate of the NAS step.

9 Every bolt was given the copper grease treatment. As mentioned earlier, these two centre mounting bolts were loosely fitted by hand.

10 It's unlikely that the brackets on the outer ends of the step will lie flush against the cross member so a selection of packing shims is included with the kit.

11 In our particular installation we chose to use the original mounting bolts at the ends of the cross member...

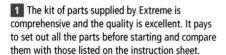

12 ...but as we tried to tighten the bolts we found there was a problem, so the step had to come off again. The problem was a number of fixing points that protruded slightly at the bottom of the cross member. Each of the fixings had to be tapped, slightly denting-in the cross member steel, so that the NAS step would fit flush.

13 Before final fitting the bolts and fixings supplied were methodically checked against the instruction sheet. This sort of preparation can save a lot of time and hassle when you're putting something together.

14 Each threaded bolt was given the copper grease treatment, as were the tapering, self-centralising washers used at the fixing points roughly under each side of the door opening. These two bolts are tightened from inside the cross member...

15 ...seen here from beneath the vehicle.

16 Not forgetting the spacer we saw earlier, the three bolts are inserted into the bottom of the cross member. No bolts are to be fully tightened at this stage.

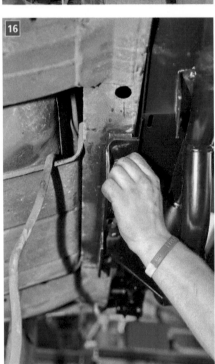

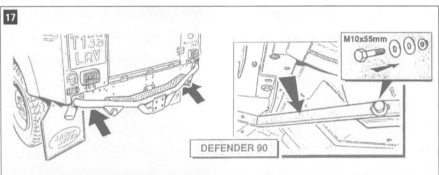

17 On Defender 90 models these two support arms are fitted as shown.

18 On the 110 there's a dirty great fuel tank in the way, so the support arms are heavier and of a different shape.

19 The rear ends of the support arms are loosely bolted to the step.

20 The chassis holes seen in an earlier picture were used for bolting the front ends of the support arms. With the nice new NAS step and

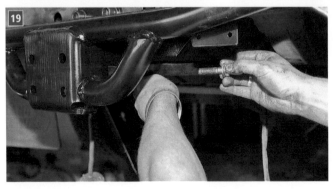

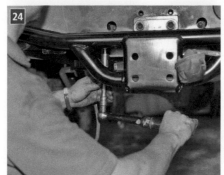

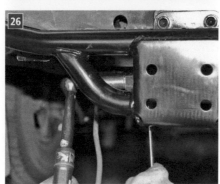

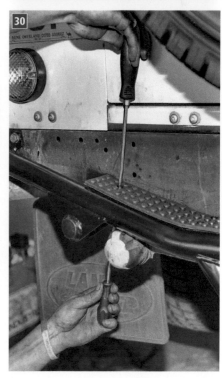

tow bracket in place we couldn't see the need to refit the towing eyes. On the 110 the new bolts, passing right through the chassis, are M10 x 120mm, whereas on the 90 the bolts are M10 x 55mm.

21 Here you can see the rear ends of the support arms loosely bolted to the underside of the NAS step.

22 According to the instructions the first bolts to tighten are the centre cap ones, which go up to a torquing great 240Nm.

23 Then there are the inner bolts with the self-centring washers, found beneath this plug (arrowed) if, as in this case, it's already been fitted. These are tightened to 58Nm. With these four bolts tightened you can double-check the number of shims required before tightening the end bolts to 45Nm. Use as many spacer plates as required to ensure correct alignment. These are fitted at either end of the NAS step where it joins the vehicle.

24 Next turn your attention to the underside, where the three bolts that pass up into the cross member are tightened to 45Nm...

25 ...as are the front ends of the support arms where they bolt through the chassis on both 90 and 110 models.

26 The support arm bolts beneath the step are also tightened to 45Nm.

27 The step has a rubber tread plate held down with nuts and bolts. There's nothing to stop water getting between steel and rubber so the top of the step was well coated with Würth cavity wax.

28 When we started to fit the rubber tread plate it was found that the gap between the step and the two centre cap bolts was insufficient. (At least this explained why conventional hexagonal bolts, with their larger heads, weren't used here.)

29 The simplest solution was to cut off some of the knobbles off the rubber, allowing it to slide beneath the bolt heads. Cutting rubber can be really difficult unless you use soap and water (or even just plain water), which enables the blade to slide easily through.

30 Each bolt has a plastic washer beneath it, and a nut is added and tightened from underneath.

The appeal of the Witter bracket is that two-pin height adjustment is available, and since I find myself towing all sorts of different things I need to be able to adjust for the correct towing height.

Just so's you know you don't have to spot the deliberate mistake, the sequence shown here isn't exactly what happened in reality. Because of the availability of parts at the time, the wiring was fitted first and then the tow bracket afterwards. Normally the steel work would be bolted on first and the wiring run up to it. In practice it made no difference.

1 The Witter components are all protected with plastic coating. The first one to fit is the piece of angle, which bolts beneath the cross member. All the fixing bolts are supplied. Remember that it pays to coat each thread generously in copper grease to prevent rusting and seizing in future.

2 Next the main mounting plate is fitted. None of the mounting bolts must be tightened at this stage, including those fitted earlier to the underside of the cross member.

3 The top two bolts screw into threads in the cross member while the bottom two pass through the angle plate you just added.

4 Next the lashing-down eye on each side of the chassis has to be unbolted…

5 …and the eye and its fixings removed, leaving this bushed hole in the chassis.

6 I know everything's plastic-coated, but before fitting the reinforcing arms each of the ends was coated in Würth wax body protection, as was the chassis where they'd be mounted.

7 The original bolts were long enough to be reused while (at this stage) loosely attaching each of the reinforcing arms to the chassis…

8 …followed by their attachment to the main tow bracket plate.

9 Only when all the bolts have been fitted should they be tightened to the torque figures recommended in the instructions. You must also follow the correct tightening sequence. The angle

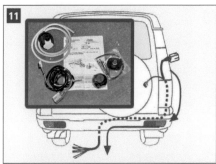

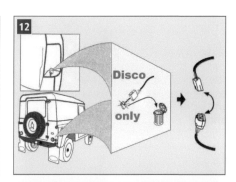

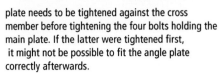

plate needs to be tightened against the cross member before tightening the four bolts holding the main plate. If the latter were tightened first, it might not be possible to fit the angle plate correctly afterwards.

10 Towcraft have several different types of tow ball available, but I'd recommend the AL-KO type, which has a greater distance between the ball and it's mounting than conventional ones, so that caravans and trailers with the widely-used AL-KO anti-snake tow hitch can be towed. It doesn't stop you using conventional tow hitches too if your caravan doesn't have an AL-KO set-up.

11 Now we come to the wiring, which because of the increasing use of electronic controls on vehicles isn't as simple as it used to be but is easier to fit.

12 You can't just tap into the wiring like you used to because it will, at the very least, upset warning systems on more modern vehicles and could even adversely affect the ECU. Instead, Towcraft fit the well-known Ryder wiring kit. It detects signals to tail lights, brake lights and indicators and provides a separate power source to the trailer.

13 As an aside, bear in mind that if you tow a caravan you'll need a separate wiring arrangement for the 12S socket that carries power to the caravan's living quarters.

14 On the Defender, the right-hand rear light cover is removed and a hole drilled for access.

15 The Towcraft wiring was pushed up from beneath and through the hole, which was fitted with a grommet.

16 Next the clever little power sensor was fitted in this location…

17 …and the relevant wiring socket connected beneath the vehicle.

18 The separate power supply was taken direct from the battery…

19 …and connected to the positive terminal. Yes, it's OK to connect at this stage because, as you can see, the fuse holder is free of its fuse.

20 The power supply was then connected into the system.

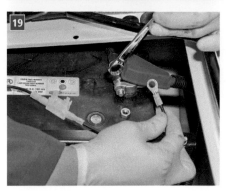

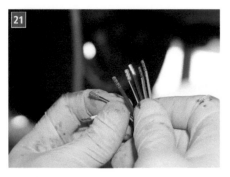

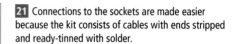

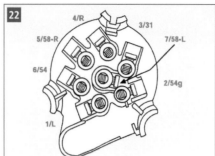

21 Connections to the sockets are made easier because the kit consists of cables with ends stripped and ready-tinned with solder.

22 Connections to seven-pin sockets are universal.

23 Sometimes there are brass screws, and it's then especially important to use a screwdriver with a fresh, square end to prevent damage to the screw head.

24 We fitted an identification label to the wire in the battery compartment.

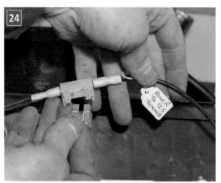

25 Towcraft use their own test device on each socket to make sure all the wiring is correct. If you're doing this work at home you'll need a trailer board or the trailer itself to carry out your own checks.

26 Now for a few useful tips: I always spray the inside of trailer sockets with battery terminal spray. Once damp gets in electrical contacts tend to break down, and this prevents that from happening.

27 With a pre-wired socket it can take ages to disconnect the cable in order to pass it through the mounting bracket. Some brackets come with a cutaway. Otherwise a pair of tin snips and a spot of touch-up paint can save quite some time!

28 By the time wiring sockets break or damp gets in, the mild steel fixing grooves and nuts invariably used can rust solid. Stainless steel 6mm screws and lock nuts from Screwfix Direct are cheap as chips and allow you to remove and refit sockets whenever you like. Incidentally, it's easier to fit the socket to the bracket before fitting the bracket to the vehicle.

29 We had to do a bit of creative thinking and use a pair of mounting brackets in order to fit the twin-socket set-up we wanted.

30 Later the Witter height adjustment plate was bolted to the tow bracket…

31 …which allows the height-adjustable plate to be used.

32 At the time of writing this tow bracket has been on for a few months and has been used for everything from a small trailer to a 3.5-tonner and a vehicle-towing dolly.

Spare wheel carrier: earlier, aluminium doors

a Carrier
b Slider piston and rod
c Steel plate
d Slider cylinder/tube
e Top hinge nut plate
f Top hinge
g Bottom hinge nut plate
h Bottom hinge
i Nylon washers

The main advantage of a spare wheel carrier is that it takes the weight of the spare off the doorframe and the door hinges. Latest Defenders (from around '06 Model Year onwards) have stronger rear doors, designed to take the weight of spare wheels (they can be identified by the rounded window aperture shape). Squared-off-window Defender rear doors are known to suffer from hinge wear and vertical stress cracks near the mid-point of the cross-rail beneath the rear screen. This isn't surprising when you think of the weight of a spare wheel – it's probably heavier than the door itself.

The answer is to fit a spare wheel carrier – but not just any spare wheel carrier. Some of them swing right away, independently of the door, and I'm not at all sure about those. For one thing, after closing the rear door and then, separately, the spare wheel carrier you have to remember to close the catch on the carrier. If you forget, you'll have a spare-wheel slingshot on the loose. For another thing, you have to watch that the spare wheel doesn't swing out dangerously into the path of traffic or against the car parked next to you every time you open the rear door.

The Britpart carrier fitted here attaches to the rear door in such a way that it opens and closes with the door, needing no separate catch and being prevented from swinging open by the door and its stop.

1 This is the drawing we had to work from. It's better than nothing and, in fact, an excellent guide to where all the washers and spacers are fitted, but it doesn't tell the full story.

2 Very often Defender rear doors are fitted with strengthening plates on the inside of the door and on the outer face. Here the plates have been removed and you can see the three larger holes where the wheel support bars were bolted.

3 A new plate had to be fitted to the outside of the door using the seven nuts, bolts and large plain washers provided. Here's how to fit it:
■ Measure out the position for the plate if its dimensions are provided with the kit.
■ If they're not, you'll have to fit the carrier first, temporarily fit the slider in place and work out from that where the reinforcing plate has to be fitted to the door.
■ Mark out the position for one of the holes with a scriber, remove the plate, lightly centre-punch the hole position and drill the first hole.
■ Fit the plate with one bolt, double checking its position.
■ Centre-punch and drill another hole; insert and tighten a second bolt.
■ With the plate now held in its correct position, the other holes in the plate can be used as guides for drilling the remaining five holes in the door.
■ Remove the plate one last time, run a bead of sealant all the way around the perimeter to seal it, then bolt it back on again.

4 This component is what allows the spare wheel carrier to remain attached to the door despite the fact that the door hinges and the hinges on the carrier are in different planes. There's a piston inside the horizontal cylinder. The outer end of the piston is bolted to the hinged carrier frame and slides in and out as the rear door is opened and closed.

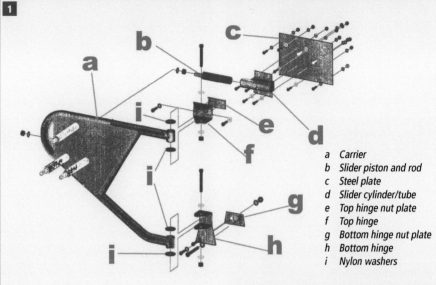
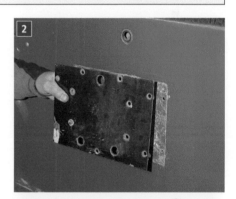

5 The slide is next bolted to the door plate, but not fully tightened, allowing for some adjustment in the mounting bolts. The vertical slots in the slider and the horizontal slots in the door plate provided quite a lot of adjustment in the slider's final position. You have to extend the holes in the door skin to match the slots in the door plate, of course.

6 Just above the centre door hinge, the capping is held in place by two pop rivets with their heads drilled off.

7 Next the hinge was fitted, as follows:
- A hole was drilled right through one of the pop rivet holes for just ONE of the bolts holding the top swivel hinge in place.
- The hinge plate was fitted and then the second hole was drilled. All right, the pop rivets should be in the same positions as the holes in the hinge plate, but if they're not doing it this way will ensure that your drilled holes are properly aligned.
- Then bolt the hinge in place.

8 This reinforcing plate is provided to fit inside the body. It's pushed over the two mounting bolts before the nuts are fitted to the retaining bolts. I'd recommend using Nyloc nuts, or plain washers followed by spring washers.

9 The bottom hinge comes complete with a mounting plate that attaches to the rear cross member. Two of the bolts pass into a threaded plate that's held against the inside of the cross member while the bolts are pushed into position and tightened.

10 It was found that while the holes are already there in the cross member (they're there on all Defenders for mounting the right-hand grab handle), they weren't big enough. As everyone who works on Land Rovers knows, this doesn't mean that the holes in your own vehicle won't be big enough – if someone has fitted a replacement cross member at some time anything could have happened!

11 We held the plate through the open access at the rear of the cross member and fitted the bolts, tightening them once both were in place.

12 The third bolt passes through a kind of double-skinned section of the cross member. This tube is fitted to the third bolt but, of course, inserted behind the back plate of the cross member. The piece of 'flat' is just there so that the tube can be more easily manoeuvred into position.

13 As the nut fitted to the inside of the bolt is tightened, the inner plate on the cross member is tightened securely against the tube. Although the bolts were tightened enough to stop free movement, none of them were fully tightened yet. We'd need to be able to move the hinges later until everything aligned.

14 The frame was then held up to the hinges, the bottom of the frame slid into place and the swivel bolt lowered into position...

15 ...followed by the top swivel bolt in the top hinge.

16 Each hinge has 'slippery' nylon washers (supplied with the kit) inserted both above and below the swivel tube.

17 At this stage the dropped clanger was spotted! It hadn't been possible to tell from the drawing, but the top hinge plate needs to be fitted with its sloping edges facing the outside of the vehicle. The pivot hole isn't central and it needs to be the right way round to line up with the bottom hinge.

18 We next 'folded' the carrier inwards...

19 ...so that the slider could be united with the hole in the back of the carrier.

20 Ideally, you need very long fingers to push the thread through the slotted hole and add the washer and nut! The lock nut was screwed on to the thread before it was offered up to the carrier.

21 Grease nipples on the hinges! Isn't that a nice sight on something you want to last? We tightened the hinge bolts enough to remove play but not by so much as to make the carrier too stiff.

22 They're not provided with the carrier but you'll need to fit spare wheel nuts so that the wheel rim has something to butt up against when it's fitted.

23 Then the spare wheel was fitted, and, with the weight on the carrier, final checks for alignment were made and all the hinge and slider mounting bolts freed off as necessary, aligned and retightened.

24 Then it was a matter of opening and closing the door to make sure that everything lined up correctly throughout its full travel. It's now that you'll probably find that the slider needs adjusting. It either won't allow the door to open fully or will pop out and you'll have to disconnect, reinsert and refit it. Use the slots in the mounting bracket to adjust bracket position.

25 The fitted spare wheel carrier looks unobtrusive, works well and is especially well constructed. Perhaps a locking wheel nut on an expensive alloy wheel would be wise!

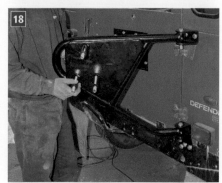

Spare wheel carrier: later, steel doors

The Extreme 4x4 carrier opens and closes along with the rear door and is suitable for a large range of wheels and tyres. It's extremely (so to speak) well built and comes with grease nipples on each of the hinge points.

It's good to see that this particular carrier utilises the Defender's strong body mounting brackets and is therefore suitable for use in conjunction with the NAS rear step. It's also available with a high lift jack mount.

The wheel carrier shown here is for the Station Wagon. There are versions for almost all models of Defender and the principles of fitting them will be similar.

1 These are the components of the Extreme 4x4 swing-away spare wheel carrier.

2 In order to fit the carrier the interior trim of the rear door must be removed. A trim removal tool enables you to do so without damaging the trim. Aim the fork for the centre of each clip but take care not to break them.

3 On models with steel rear doors six nuts, bolts and washers are detached from the inside of the door...

4 ...in order to remove the original door-mounted carrier.

5 The reflector from the offside rear also has to be removed and has to be remounted higher than its previous position. In our case that would be above the indicator, mounted vertically.

6 The bracket marked No1 in the Extreme instructions is mounted first. The two bolts on the offside that hold the back body to the chassis are removed.

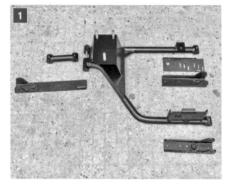

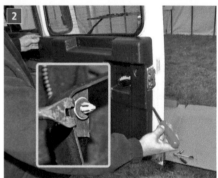

VEHICLES IN GERMANY AND OTHER COUNTRIES

In order to meet some European (such as German) regulations, the upper and lower body brackets should be offset (using the holes marked in the Extreme 4x4 fitting instructions), which moves the carrier to the nearside by approximately 9.7cm.

7 The bolts and washers supplied with the kit were given a liberal dose of Würth copper grease, after which...

8 ...the bracket was mounted through the two inner holes. Note that there are two more holes in this bracket, at the outer ends, but we'll deal with them later.

9 According to the Extreme instructions, the top body bracket is mounted approximately 47.7cm above the lower bracket and bridges the rear wing and back body capping. A plate is provided which fits inside the vehicle behind the top body bracket to strengthen the bodywork. It may be necessary, if prolonged off-road use is envisaged, to rivet this plate to the inside rear body. Holes have been provided in the backing plate to allow this bracket to be moved and strengthened as required. Note that because ours is a later-model Defender we decided to follow a slightly different approach, as you'll see later.

EARLIER DEFENDERS WITHOUT THE DOOR-MOUNTED WHEEL CARRIER SHOWN ABOVE

To fit the upper body bracket:
1 On the right-hand side of the wing top are three rivets. The central rivet should approximately correspond to the central hole in the bracket.
2 Drill out the rivet using a 9mm bit. If necessary, enlarge this hole.
3 Loosely fit the top bracket using just this one hole.
4 Temporarily mount the main body of the carrier using the nylon discs and bolts provided.
5 Adjust the brackets until the top of the carrier is horizontal with the back body of the vehicle.
6 Then the two further holes in the upper bracket can be drilled and bolted through.

To fit the door bracket:
1 Unscrew and remove the rubber bump stop from the door bracket.

2 With the door closed, offer the carrier up to the door until the top bar of the carrier is an equal distance (approximately 3cm) away from it along its length. This will require some pressure, as the carrier is pressing against a rubber bump stop on the lower body bracket. (To make this easier, it may be necessary to remove the bump stop.)
3 Offer up the door bracket so the carrier arm is in the centre of the bracket's arms. Mark the door through the holes. Swing the carrier out of the way and drill two holes with a 9mm bit.
4 Before replacing the rubber bump stops, attach the carrier to the door bracket. If on closing the door excessive resistance is met, adjust the bracket accordingly. If you're now satisfied that the carrier closed correctly, remove the main body from the vehicle and replace the rubber bump stops.

LATER MODEL DEFENDERS

10 We agreed that because the door-mounted bracket and the bracket already mounted to the lower body both had a fixed position, we'd attach the carrier to them and use that to determine the height of the upper body-mounted bracket. So the door-mounted bracket was fitted to the door using the two top sets of fittings from the original spare-wheel carrier.

11 The carrier was temporarily bolted to the bottom bracket, using the nylon washers to establish the correct height...

12 ...and the link arm was attached to the door bracket...

13 ...and to the inner end of the main carrier section.

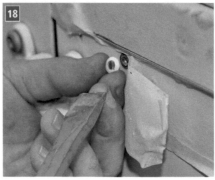

14 At the outer end, the top body bracket was attached.

15 There was no need to tighten the fixing nuts, of course, the bolts alone giving the correct height for the upper body bracket.

16 Masking tape was used both to make it easier to make marks through the bracket and to protect the paintwork. We marked all around the outside of the bracket to establish its position. It was clear which pop rivet heads had to be removed...

17 ...so a rechargeable Makita was used to drill through the rivet heads...

18 ...before carefully chiselling off any that stayed put.

19 Hole positions were carefully marked and centre-punched...

20 ...before 9mm holes were drilled.

21 When drilling steel, it's essential to use plenty of lubricant to prevent the drill tip from overheating. You should even use lubricant when drilling aluminium, because it stops aluminium from picking up on the cutting edge of the drill bit. You can see excess heat being dissipated in the form of smoke from the lubricating oil. The holes were painted to prevent corrosion.

22 Earlier, we mentioned the top reinforcement plate. While this was held in position inside the vehicle we marked one of the holes, for which there wasn't an existing hole in the reinforcement plate.

23 The position was centre-punched then drilled out.

24 The bolts were inserted from the outside...

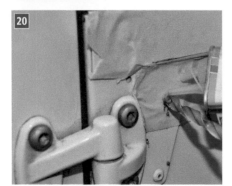

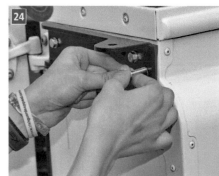

25 ...the nuts tightened from the inside, and we were ready to permanently fit the carrier.

26 A generous helping of copper grease was applied, and the nylon washers aligned so that the bolt could be pushed right through.

27 More copper grease was applied to the bolt and washers holding the outer end of the link arm.

28 The inner end proved slightly difficult to align, being the last of the pivot points, and light use was made of a hammer.

29 It's important to note that if the bolt really doesn't want to go through you'll need to slacken the attachments to the body until all the pivot point bolts are in before carrying out the final tightening – a two-man job in the many places where a locking spanner is needed.

30 To check the correct positioning of the carrier, *close the door slowly*. Approximately 10cm before the door is closed, resistance should be met from the rubber bump stops. This is to allow the carrier to close solidly, removing excessive vibration. If the carrier doesn't open freely with the door, check that the top bar of the carrier is horizontal and adjust accordingly. The carrier is designed to be a tight fit. However, if there's excessive flexing at the offside wing top the carrier is too tight, in which case the door bracket will have to be slackened and moved sideways to reduce pressure. The rear door interior trim can then be replaced.

31 At this late stage we decided we'd use the two extra bolt-mounting points on the bottom bracket. In each case there's room to get at the back of the body for fitting the necessary washers and nuts. Note that in order to fit the outer bolt, the carrier pivot point has to be disconnected.

32 The threaded pins on which the spare wheel is mounted are good and long to enable the fitting of much wider wheels than the standard one I carry.

Light-emitting diode lights are expensive in the short-term, but they last 'forever' and are, in my opinion, superior to any other lights whose use in the UK has been approved by the relevant Vehicle Approval Authority. NB: Latest MoT regulations suggest auto-levelling (of lights or suspension) plus headlamp washers are required.

ADVANTAGE LED!

Some people criticise LEDs because of their directional property, and for domestic room lighting that is a problem. However it's a huge advantage with LED headlights.

A conventional halogen H4 bulb creates around 1,500 lumens of light. Its bulb is mounted into a headlamp and the light is reflected from the mirrored bowl, which loses a large amount of the light created. The remaining light then passes through the lens at the front of the headlight. But because the optics have to collect light coming in from the wide area of the reflector, much of it is wasted. This indirect method is only around 35% efficient, so the great majority of light you started with is lost.

By contrast an LED headlamp produces a sharp beam of light, tightly focused directly through a single optic on to the road, giving efficiency in the region of 60%, so there's minimal light wastage. The results are much more light on the road and a far brighter and sharper headlight beam than is possible with halogen.

1 Before removing the old halogen headlights we placed a board in front of the vehicle. Its position was measured to make sure it was parallel with both headlights and there was some masking tape on the floor so its position could be reset accurately later on.

2 To get at the Defender headlight, you have first to remove the sidelights...

3 ...and then the trim. This applies both to the standard trim and the KBX Upgrades trims I've got fitted.

4 Remove the screws (one shown) holding the headlight to the vehicle but not the headlamp ring screws, shown later.

5 The halogen unit, complete with bulb, unplugs from the trailing lead inside the housing.

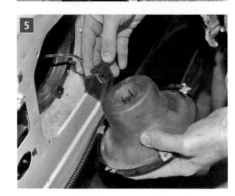

6 Next there are three screws into three clips...

7 ...that hold the headlamp rings to the glass bowls. Remove all three and keep them somewhere safe. Defender headlamp rings are notoriously rust-prone, and you'll want to clean them up and rust-proof them or even fit new ones if necessary. I recommend a smear of copper slip on the inside faces.

8 Land Rover headlamp rings are a tight fit on the Speaker LED headlights so you'll need to ensure there's no rust or high spots on the inner face of the ring. You'll also probably need to expand the ring by heating it with a heat gun or hair dryer...

9 ...so that the ring can be pushed over the front of the LED headlight.

10 You need to ensure that the ring is all the way home.

11 With the clips seen earlier held against the back of the LED headlight surrounds, the retaining screws can be refitted.

12 There's no what-goes-whering required because there's no external wiring. The existing headlight socket simply pushes on to the three terminals mounted on the back of the new headlight unit.

TOUGH AND STRONG

- You'd normally think that using a mallet on a piece of delicate lighting or electrical equipment would be bad news, and normally you'd be right. But Tim Consolante of MobileCentre, the UK importers of Speaker LED lights, assured us that there's no risk of damage whatsoever in using a mallet on these headlights.

- They're approved for military use, not only because of their low power consumption and high output but also because they're extremely strong.
- Each of the lights contained within the housing is individually sealed, and on top of that the glass domed cover provides an extra layer of protection.

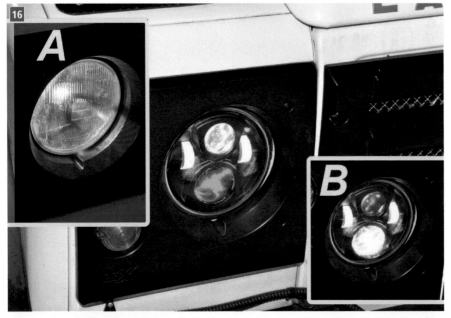

13 The new headlights simply screw back in the same way as the old ones came out.

14 Before refitting the trim, it makes sense to check that the headlight is functioning as it should. Straight away, you notice the extreme whiteness of the light and you also notice how, when you're not looking straight at it, the light isn't at all dazzling. This is because an LED beam is very sharp and directional, which is, of course, highly desirable in a vehicle headlight.

15 Finally, it's simply a matter of replacing the trim and sidelights, as before.

16 In the main picture the LED headlight is on low beam. The two D-shaped lights, one on each side, have the job of creating the correct spread of light, bearing in mind what we just said about the directional quality of LED lights. B is the headlight on high beam, while A is the old, more yellow halogen light.

17 In case the previous picture didn't make it absolutely clear, this is an un-doctored photograph taken with the halogen lamp on the left side and the new Speaker LED lamp on the right side of the vehicle. The picture speaks for itself.

18 It was easy to check the position of the headlight beams against the felt pen marks made earlier on the board while the halogen lights were still in place.

19 The height adjustment screw isn't in the cutaway at the bottom of the trim but at the top, as seen in the previous shot. The side-to-side adjuster is shown here.

In summary, it's fair to say that these headlights are a sensational improvement on anything that's come before. They'll last well beyond the lifetime of the vehicle without ever needing to be changed. They're built for the very harshest and most demanding of environments – the battlefield – and the quality of the light is, one might say, light years away from anything I've ever experienced before, on a Land Rover Defender or any other vehicle. It's a massive leap from normal Defender headlights, which are notoriously poor, to headlights that are among the best on the road. And not one driver coming the opposite way has flashed me to complain of dazzle.

LED DRLs, side lights, brake lights and indicator lights

Here's how you can be bright and highly visible to other road users in your Defender using (almost) everlasting, low power consumption LED side lights.

LED lighting technology has transformed car lighting and it won't be long, I reckon, before all new vehicle lights are LED-only. They're capable of lasting the life of the vehicle without needing new bulbs (though I wouldn't bank on the cheap'n'nasty Chinese versions), and they're sealed against water ingress, so you won't suffer from corrosion inside the unit. As explained in the previous section, their light output is clearer, brighter and more 'directional' and focused than that from old-fashioned incandescent bulbs.

In this section we'll look at changing a Defender's side lights, indicators and stop lights to MobileCentre LED units; and converting the side lights to include MobileCentre daytime running lamps (DRLs).

All new cars sold within the EU from 2011 on must have DRLs fitted to them (trucks too, from 2012). They can also be retrofitted to existing vehicles. Drivers in the UK will be advised but not compelled to use them when fitted, though in some countries they'll be compulsory.

Of course, DRLs should be mounted so that they don't shine directly into the eyes of oncoming drivers, so be sure to angle them accordingly if you're fitting them to your vehicle.

1 Ian Baughan, the man behind IRB Developments, demonstrates the full LED lighting kit. This kit enables you to plug straight in to existing Land Rover wiring without modification.

2 This picture demonstrates just how good these Speaker LED lights are when compared with the originals. Even if you didn't recognise the different shape, you'd have no problem spotting which is which!

3 There are cheaper units around but, for one thing they probably won't be legal (look for the E-mark) and for another they almost certainly won't last very long. I've bought cheap Chinese LED lights in the past and they've done everything from explode to conk out after a few days or grow dim after just a few weeks. They might have been cheaper but they were an expensive mistake.

4 This is the slightly less expensive kit that MobileCentre can also supply, with generic wires to which you have to fit Land Rover-compatible connectors. The more expensive units are plug'n'go.

5 All the kits come with fixing screws and gaskets. These seal any road dirt behind the wing but also mean that the light unit can be tightened down, even against a surface that isn't perfectly flat, without causing damage.

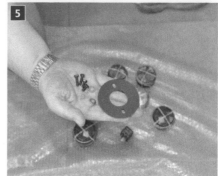

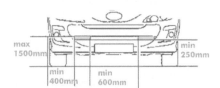

LET FITTING COMMENCE

6 Coming back to DRLs (as opposed to side lights – or 'position' lights as they're correctly known), they must be fitted within specific dimensions which are, in practice, surprisingly generous, especially with regard to height.

7 At IRB Developments, Ian removed the headlight surrounds and popped out the plastic 'nuts' into which the old lights were screwed.

8 He also removed the fixings from the wheel arch liners (it can be a struggle!) to leave the front end of each liner dangling free and providing access to the rears of the front lights.

9 This is the adapter cable supplied with the full-fitting kit.

10 One end of the adapter simply fits onto the plug on the end of the cable – the one that previously went into the back of the light unit.

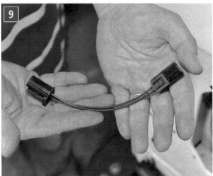

DRL WIRING
- Daytime running lamps have to be wired in a specific way to make them legal.
- They must come on with the ignition switch or when the engine is running and go off again when it's turned off.
- They must go off when the vehicle side (position) lights are turned on, which means they can't be on with the headlights, of course.

11 The kit comes with an electronic control box that automatically and correctly operates DRLs, when fitted. Here a cable is run from the control unit to the socket on one of the new adapter cables. This cable allows the control unit to disable the DRLs when side lights are turned on. This cable isn't supplied already fitted, so any access holes that need to be drilled only need to be big enough for...

12 ...the small terminal already fitted to the end of the cable. Note the spare slot in the socket.

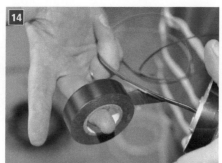

13 The terminal is pushed into the back of the socket until it locates parallel with the two terminals already in there. If you're fitting straight LED side lights without DRLs, neither this cable nor the control unit are required.

14 If you purchase the basic kit without wiring adapters you'll be fitting your own connectors. You should wrap insulation tape around the wires to the same extent as those on the lights you took off.

15 Wire strippers are used to strip off the wire ends...

16 ...before suitable connectors are crimped on. Shielded connectors MUST go on the power side of the connection; the unshielded connector thus goes on the light side.

17 Give each connector a tug after fitting it. If it's loose you want to find out now!

INSIDE INFORMATION

Tim Consolante of MobileCentre always ensures the lights he supplies are fully legal for use. MobileCentre's units are consequently built with the following requirements in mind:

- Front indicators have to be brighter than rears. Legal fronts are marked with a '2a' compared with the '2' marking on rears.
- The legal flash rate is between 70 and 120 flashes per minute. You need a new relay, matched to the resistance of the LED lights, to provide this.

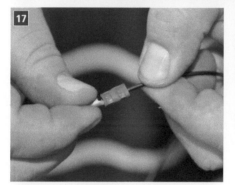

18 Here's how the gasket, fixing screws and washers fit to the backs of the light units.

19 Remember to slide the gasket on before plugging the light unit into the adapter.

20 On goes the side light, with a helper holding the screw inside the wing. Note that this is the version of the MobileCentre side light with built-in DRLs. When turned off it looks almost identical to the side light-only unit.

21 The light is offered up on the other side of the vehicle while the screws are twirled on from inside the wing.

22 Once fitted, this is how the back of the lamp appears from inside the wing. It's worth giving the screw heads a dose of rust-prevention spray.

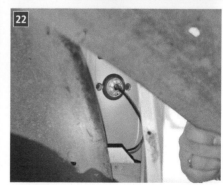

DEFENDER REAR LIGHTS

23 You have to remove the protective plates over the rear lights, starting with the single external screw on each side...

24 ...and continuing to those each side of the rear door. Ignore the grey box – it's for my reversing sensors.

25 As you can see (inset) power consumption is amazingly low with LED lamps, despite their being brighter. The rear lights are just straight plug-ins...

26 ...but have to be screwed in from inside the vehicle. It's a two-man job on the door-hinge side – one on the outside to hold the LED light unit, one on the inside to insert the screws.

27 The rear indicators are trickier to fit than the fronts on Station Wagons, but only because the seat belt support bars have to be negotiated.

28 LED indicators consume so little power that standard flasher units won't work. We removed the screws...

29 ...and lifted away the dash panel, exposing the indicator unit beneath (later models).

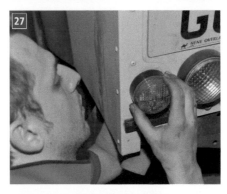

30 The MobileCentre replacement is a direct fit in the socket where the old one went.

31 On earlier models you have to disconnect the battery, remove the fuse box cover and unscrew the carrier plate beneath.

32 The flasher unit is found behind it.

33 Finally, if you're fitting MobileCentre DRLs you'll need a means of telling the control unit that the engine is running. You could run a wire to the battery, but with the battery under the passenger seat the MobileCentre approach is to take a connection to the 12v positive feed terminal (the biggest one on the back of the Tdi's alternator) that goes back to the battery. In other words, not the one to the charge light and not the 'W' terminal on the back of the alternator. Check your manual to make sure you select the correct terminal. Non-Tdis will be different. Here, the shield was removed...

34 ...followed by the cable.

35 The ring terminal on the cable for the control unit was fitted to the alternator when the cable removed earlier was refitted.

36 This is the MobileCentre control unit. It's a hefty, sealed aluminium unit that's ideal for vehicles that might find themselves in the wet.

37 The LED rear side lights are far brighter and clearer than the old incandescent bulb units and should never need attention ever again.

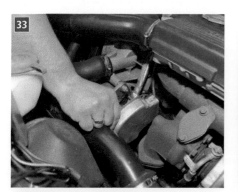

FOG AND REVERSING LIGHT

Here we give DiXie superior-performance LED fog and reversing lights that MCL source from Land Rover's own lighting supplier.

38 One of the great things about MCL's fog and reversing lights is that they come complete with standard Land Rover plugs, enabling them to be simply plugged into the existing wiring.

39 After unscrewing and detaching the existing fog light unit, the wiring plugs and sockets were unlatched and separated.

40 New sealing rings come with the MCL lights and the first job is to remove the surplus material from the inside of the ring. Next, use something like surgical spirit or panel wipe to clean the edge of the mount on to which the light is fitted.

41 Then remove the backing paper, pass the wiring through the sealing ring and use the self-adhesive surface to stick it in place.

42 Provided no repairs are required to the existing wiring or socket (which can deteriorate over time), you simply plug in the new light…

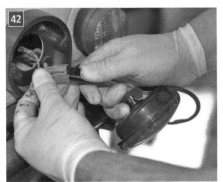

43 …and screw it into place, using the original fixing screws.

44 The light is slightly more directional than that emitted by an incandescent bulb fitting, but that's OK because fog lights are for warning traffic that's following behind. You can see from this shot taken in daylight that the brightness of these LED lights is far better than that from conventional lights. And when you bear in mind that you're never going to get a blown bulb and that the lights are completely sealed against the elements, and thus against internal corrosion, LED lights are a real no-brainer.

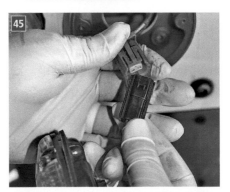

45 The process for fitting the reversing light is exactly the same.

46 This time, the benefits if anything are even greater…

47 …because you'll have a perfectly legal but much brighter reversing light with far greater longevity than a standard unit, making sense of the greater cost of these light units compared with the old-fashioned incandescent sort.

I'm really pleased with my new LED side lights. The daytime running lamps are a great extra too, in my view. The new lights aren't only brighter and vastly longer-lasting, they also consume much less power. What's more, they're also almost completely water-resistant, much stronger and look pretty cool even when turned off. What's not to like?

Central locking

One day I got tired of walking round my Station Wagon with key in hand and decided to go for central locking. Here's how to fit an inexpensive kit from Maplin.

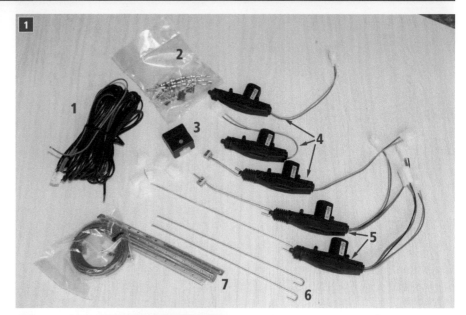

1 The Maplin Central Door Locking System comes complete and comprises the following:
1 Sufficient wiring.
2 Terminals, insulation and screws.
3 Control box.
4 Solenoids with two wires for rear doors.
5 Solenoids with five wires for front doors.
6 Operating rods.
7 Mounting strips.

2 We started by using the template supplied to work out where the solenoid for one of the front doors would go. You'll see later the principles behind correct solenoid positioning.

3 Each solenoid has two mounting holes, as shown here.

4 In this case we were able to mount the solenoid on the actual door frame. It needs to be mounted in a place where it can be held quite rigid.

5 After drilling the mounting holes but before offering up the solenoid we fitted the operating rod, because access is so much easier off the vehicle.

6 The solenoid is offered into the space inside the door panel, then the screws provided are tapped right into its plastic casing.

7 This is one of the rear doors but it helps to illustrate the principle of where the solenoid must be positioned. From the locking button on the door, a steel rod originally passed into the locking mechanism.

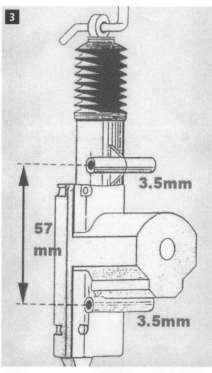

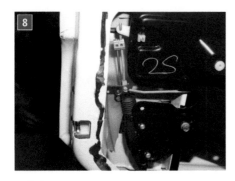

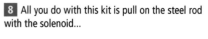

8 All you do with this kit is pull on the steel rod with the solenoid...

9 ...cut the rod supplied with the kit to an appropriate length, and use the clamp supplied to piggyback on to the original operating rod.

10 This diagram illustrates the recommended angle of pull. In other words, the rod from the solenoid must run parallel to the original rod where it joins the clamp.

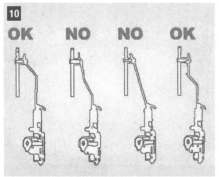

11 The clamp has a plain hole where it pushes on to the central locking rod and a slot where it pushes over the original rod.

12 This bit doesn't apply to Land Rovers with conventional rear door locks, but antiquated-style Defender rear door locks are a different matter! We started by drilling out the rivets on the original lock...

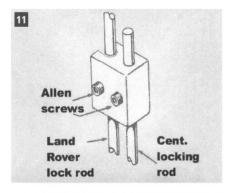

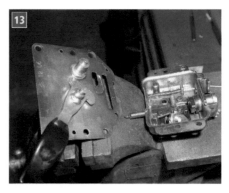

13 ...and opening it up to see if we could add an operating lever to the mechanism. Well, it's possible but very, very difficult, and I wasn't confident that it would last. The lock was reassembled using countersunk machine screws and passed on to a new owner.

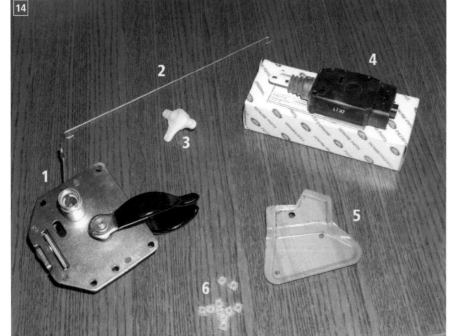

14 Instead, I decided on a new plan of action. After looking at the parts book, I got hold of the following new Land Rover items, made for Defenders with central locking, from Bearmach:

1   Rear door lock with operating rod (it sticks out over the top of the assembly).
2   Operating rod.
3   Quadrant.
4   Solenoid.
5   Mounting plate.
6   Plastic thread inserts.

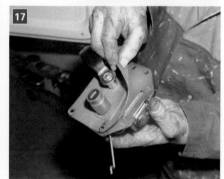

15 The first job was to remove the lock barrel from the old lock assembly. With key inserted into barrel, you push a piece of wire into a hole in the casing, which enables the barrel to slide out.

16 Fitting it into the new assembly is simply a matter of pushing it in complete with key, as shown. Naturally, we lubricated it first with waterproof grease.

17 Before fitting the assembly to the door, the gasket is offered up.

18 I confess that we bottled out of the complexities of wiring the Land Rover solenoid because we didn't have the correct plug for connecting it. Instead, the fifth Maplin solenoid was fitted to the Land Rover mounting bracket.

19 My door had nowhere to mount the thing so we used existing bolts in the door frame.

20 The new locking mechanism was refitted in the normal way...

21 ...and hooked to the plastic quadrant with its built-in operating rod.

22 A screw and washer have to be inserted into the centre of the quadrant...

23 ...which is then screwed to the door after fitting one of the plastic thread inserts into the press hole in the door frame.

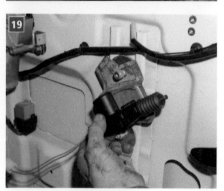

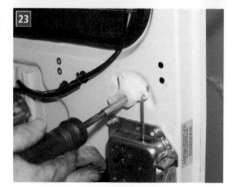

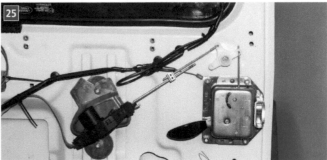

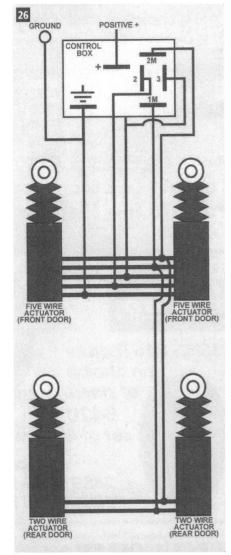

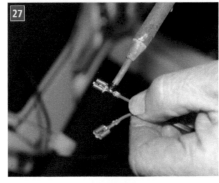

24 A little fiddling and experimentation is required to establish correct rod lengths (you also need to establish whether the lock is on or off and which way the solenoid will go when activated). Then you can tighten the grub screws on the clamp.

25 It's as well to leave a reasonable amount of overlap on the rods to give yourself room for any adjustments you may need later.

26 Wires are connected to the actuators by matching the wires colour to colour, using the wiring diagram supplied. To avoid any risk of short-circuiting, connect the positive wire last.

27 The only reliable way of attaching spade terminals is to crimp them on to the plastic insulation then solder them on to the cable.

28 The spade terminals are then pushed into the housing supplied...

29 ...and male and female blocks can then be plugged together.

30 Since the insides of doors can be damp, the terminals were thoroughly treated with Würth battery terminal spray.

31 Connecting the positive wires last was easy since the control box was the last item to be connected to the fuse box. The central locking unit's control box is small enough to fit inside the fuse box.

The Maplin central locking system ties in well if you have a key-fob operated alarm, and my Defender Station Wagon now has full central locking operated from a key fob. If you don't have such a system, either of the front door locks, when operated by key or internal pushbutton, will operate all of the locks.

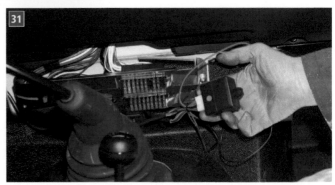

Front electric windows

Defender window winder designs changed with the advent of steel doors in the mid-noughties, and with them came a new sort of electric window winder mechanism. Both fit to a bolt-on subframe, but while the later type of subframe is the same for both manual and electric windows, the earlier type isn't. So if you're converting the earlier variety you'll also need replacement subframes. However, I'm told it's possible to get away with a bit of cutting and fabrication work with these earlier vehicles, though it's not something I've tried or seen done.

Whichever type you're fitting, you'll also need a pair of window switches. In those cases where the dash has provision for them you'll be able to use genuine Land Rover switches. You'll need the wiring loom or else be prepared to make up your own from the correct grade of cable, and you'll need the correct door-to-A-post grommets where the cable passes from one to t'other.

The best way of identifying what's needed for your particular Landy is by visiting your Land Rover dealer or specialist so that they can consult a Land Rover Parts Catalogue and an official workshop manual.

1 When removing the door card we took great care not to damage trim clips. Using a proper trim removal tool helps considerably whereas a screwdriver is almost certain to cause damage.

2 The winder and door pull handles as well as the door lock surround were removed first. It's always a slightly delicate business removing the door card itself, just in case any trim catches are hanging in there.

3 The waterproof seal is designed to keep moisture inside the door where it can (in theory) drain away safely, but it's a pig to remove without damaging it.

4 Using cardboard to protect the paintwork from its adhesive, we wrapped duct tape over the top of the door with the window wound up, so that later the glass would be held in place without dropping.

5 The screws holding the door latch in place were removed…

6 …then the bolts holding the winder mechanism to the door frame.

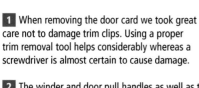

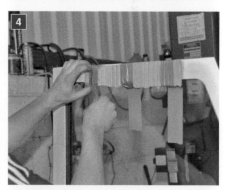

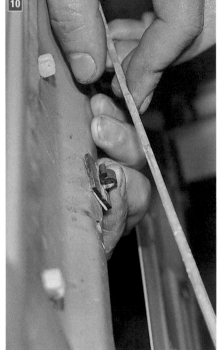

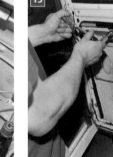

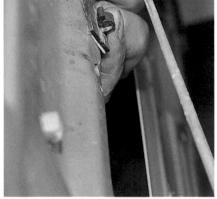

7 My doors have aftermarket central locking solenoids (fitted in a similar way to factory ones). These were unscrewed from the door frame…

8 …before starting to unscrew the frame fixing bolts, working all around the frame until all were removed.

9 The frame was then eased forward to gain access to…

10 …the door latch operating rod, which fits in a clip on the inside of the frame.

11 After fiddling the latch handle free…

12 …it was passed through the hole in the frame, allowing the frame to come free while the latch operating rod and latch handle stayed attached to the door.

13 Next, we slackened the bolts holding the winder mechanism to the channel bonded to the bottom of the window glass. Now you can see why the glass was taped up earlier!

14 And here's why you only need to slacken, not remove the screws: keyhole slots enable you to slide the mechanism free from the glass channel.

15 In its place the electric window mechanism I'd bought previously was offered up…

16 …and slotted on to the screws on the glass channel, which were then tightened up.

17 In its delivered state, the electrically operated mechanism is almost certainly going to be aligned

incorrectly, and the only way of moving it is by powering the motor.

18 A power probe connected to the vehicle battery was used to wind the mechanism…

19 …until it reached this position, which would enable it to be fitted to the door subframe. It's easy enough to offer up the subframe, and if you don't get the location right the first time simply power up the motor to adjust the position of the mechanism.

20 As the subframe and winder mechanism are bolted together it's easy to see how the later subframe was designed to accept both types of winder. We bolted the mechanism to the subframe after lightly hanging the latter in place on a couple of its bolts...

21 …then fitted the remaining bolts without tightening them up.

22 That's because of this little lad, which is fitted with a nut and washer and isn't tightened yet because it's not just a fixing point – it's a glass angle adjuster....

23 ...which you slide up and down to adjust the angle of the glass until its top edge is parallel with the top of the door. Then you tighten the adjuster nut, followed by all of the mechanism fixing bolts.

24 Meanwhile, Tim Consolante from MCL had been working on the switch wiring. Among his range of Land Rover electrical goodies he supplies Carling switches and connector blocks that enable the wiring to be simply plugged in.

25 The Carling electric window switches were mounted with others on my centre console via a Raptor Dash switch mounting plate that can be made to your chosen dimensions.

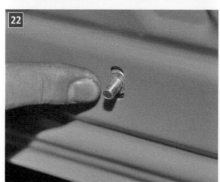

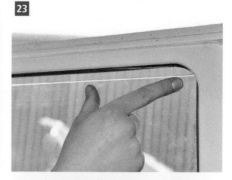

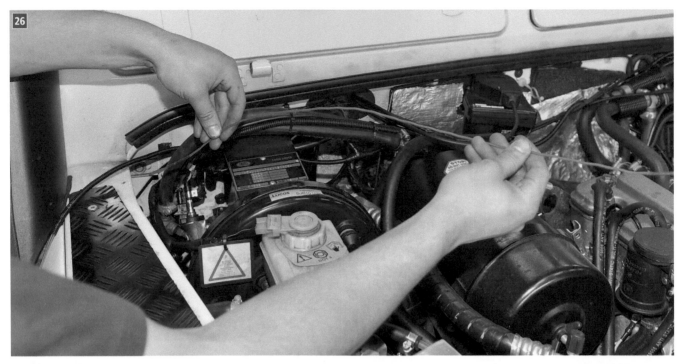

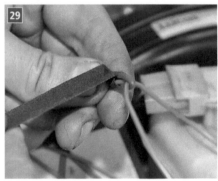

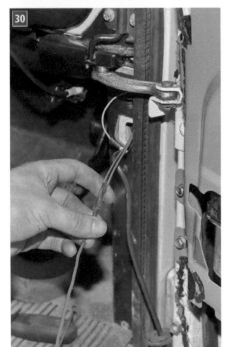

26 To reach the centre console from the A-post, the best route was through the engine bay, so a stiff fish wire was passed down the side of the bulkhead and the electrical wire was attached to it to feed the electrical wire through the maze. Here's how:

27 Inside the door pillar, the courtesy light switch was removed to improve access…

28 …and the end of the fish wire was pulled through the purpose-made hole already in the A-post.

29 Up in the engine bay, the electrical wires were taped to the other end of the fish wire…

30 …and pulled through until they appeared through the wiring access hole.

31 The wires were then passed through Defender wiring grommets.

32 At the other end the grommet is designed to clip into the door subframe. Factory-built electric windows are fitted with purpose-made Defender door cards – which we weren't using. We'll look later at what needs to be done.

33 Once in position the cables could be cut to length and the correct terminals fitted to them for attachment to the electric window winder motor.

34 And this is how it looks with the wiring and grommet in place. The electrical wires are properly protected and have even been cable tied to the door subframe to retain them neatly in position.

35 As well as taking the wiring through to the switches (normally on the dashboard, but in my case on the centre console) there needs to be a power feed. On most Defenders the fuse box is below the dash, but on my vehicle MCL have fitted a separate accessory fuse box in the battery compartment, and it's from this that we took the power feed.

36 The standard door card differs from the electric window door card in just two ways. One is the hole in the standard card where the manual window winder shaft protrudes through; I managed to find some grommets that were a perfect fit for blanking off the holes. The other is clearance for the wiring as it passes through the door card. It's a simple matter to file a suitable rounded slot that's impossible to spot as a modification.

AFTERMARKET KITS AND REAR WINDOWS

Having shown how to fit 'proper' Land Rover electric window gear to the front doors, it's worth mentioning that at the time of writing aftermarket kits are available made by SPAL. These appear to be good quality, though for sheer longevity Land Rover parts are recommended.

37 If you want to add rear electric windows you have no choice but to use a SPAL kit, like the one shown here. It consists of motors and cable-operated winding mechanisms...

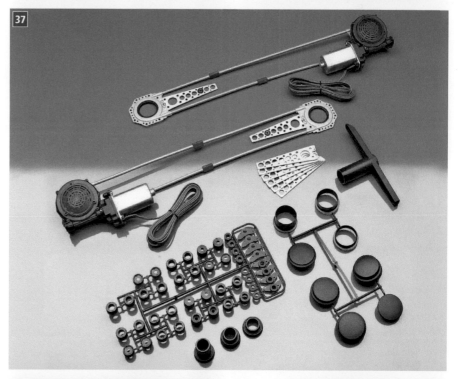

38 ...that work on the existing window winders, using the relevant plastic adapters selected from those supplied with the kit.

39 Fortunately there's room inside the Defender's rear door cards to mount the system, though a little careful planning will be required.

In addition rear door wiring sleeves are available from Land Rover to carry the wiring from the doors to the B-posts. They were originally intended for central locking wiring and they match perfectly the ones for the front doors.

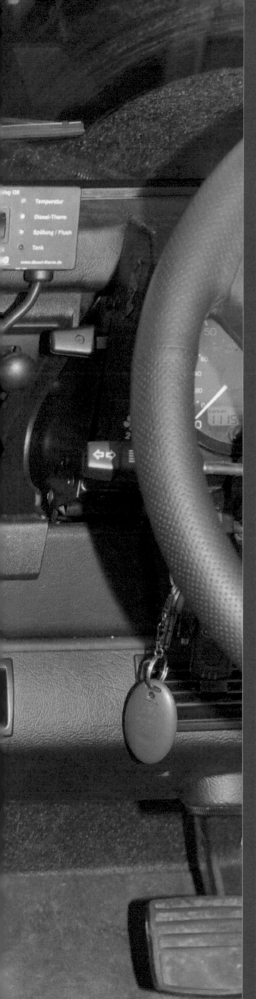

CHAPTER 5

Interior

When you start adding stuff to your Defender you quickly realise the inadequacies of its standard dashboard layout. Here's how my much modified Land Rover got the dashboard it deserves.

It all started when I realised there wasn't enough space on DiXie's dashboard for the switches to operate all the accessories I've fitted and will be fitting in the future. At the time no one was making a replacement dash panel for the Td5-style Defender dash, but then at the *LRM* Show I came across the Raptor range of dashboard modifications. This put in train a surprisingly large amount of further development work carried out by Ian Baughan of IRB Developments and Tim Consolante of MobileCentre, based on the Raptor dash components and a range of Carling switches.

Including various delays and late starts, the work was spread over three days.

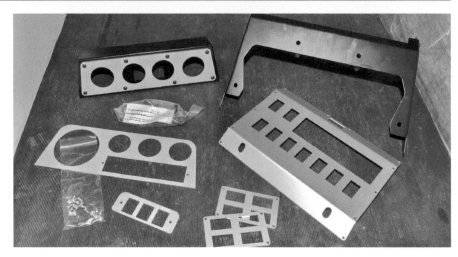

These are the dash parts supplied by Raptor. Top right is the Raptor binnacle mount, a powder-coated steel replacement for the plastic, oft-broken original. This component supports the binnacle that holds the speedometer, gauges and heater controls. Front left are stainless steel screws, also available from Raptor. Other components will become self-explanatory later.

DAY ONE

1 The work on my dash took a lot longer than it would normally because much of the work was exploratory. It started with removing the screws holding the binnacle in place.

2 On the other side of the binnacle you have to remove more screws, after which the instrument panel can be lifted up and the wiring connectors disconnected.

3 Next the right-hand end plate was disconnected, but without disconnecting the heater control knobs – they were left intact.

4 Then the vents were removed...

5 ...and the dash top panel unbolted...

6 ...and lifted away.

7 All of this was so that the centre console panel could be unscrewed and detached. Annoyingly the top three screws are concealed by the dash top panel, hence its removal.

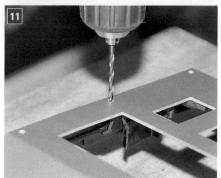

8 Then we removed the radio and disconnected the switches. Fortunately it's almost impossible to confuse Land Rover switch connections because each one is different from its neighbours.

9 With the centre console panel removed, the Raptor panel was placed on top of it and we marked out where the console panel needed to be cut away.

10 We could have used a handsaw but instead chose to use an air-operated cut-off tool. This doesn't run quite as fast as most electrically operated angle grinders so cuts through the plastic without melting it too much, which was what I wanted to avoid.

11 The next step was to place the Raptor panel in position and drill one pilot hole…

12 …followed by a single screw. Then, a second screw was applied on the opposite side before all the remaining pilot holes were drilled in the certainty that all the holes would line up.

13 Rather than use the kit's stainless steel screws we decided to use some black-head self-tapping screws. It's all down to personal preference.

WIRING TRICKS

14 Carling switches are among the best available and Tim sourced the correct legends for the fronts and connector blocks for going on to the backs of them.

15 You have to identify which wire is which using the Land Rover wiring diagram and the switch wiring diagrams available on the Carling website. Wire strippers make the work faster out and do a much more accurate job, with far less risk of cutting through cable strands along with the insulation.

16 Each spade terminal was then crimped on to its wire…

17 …and each connector fed in turn into the relevant socket in the connector block. Each spade terminal clicks positively into position.

18 Now all you have to do is push the connector block on to the relevant switch (at the back of the panel). You'll also need to label each one, because unlike factory switch connectors they all look the same.

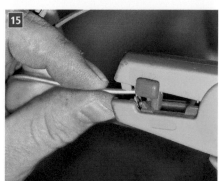

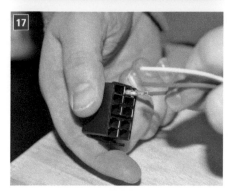

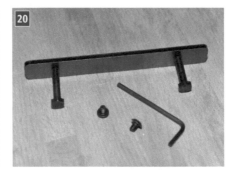

19 After fitting the radio and switches to the panel for the first time it was offered up to the dashboard, at which point it became obvious that a little more cutting away was required.

20 Some time earlier I'd fitted a plastic instrument pod but I wanted to add an instrument, and in any case the plastic pod was nowhere near as robust as the steel and aluminium offering from Raptor. This is the plate and screws that hold the Raptor pod in position on the dash top.

21 After fitting the instruments to the aluminium panel, the panel itself is screwed to the threads in the pod housing. Here we were test-fitting it; you don't actually install the instrument panel until after the pod has been fitted to the dash top.

22 The threaded bar shown two pictures back is inserted beneath the ashtray aperture. Looking inside the pod housing with the front panel removed, you can see the two bolts used for screwing down into the threaded bar.

23 With the pod housing in position these two bolts were tightened.

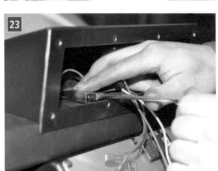

24 With the instruments fitted and the Raptor panel test-fitted, we checked that the radio cleared the Carling hazard switch mounted on top of the panel. This was a layout that I designed and Phil at Raptor was concerned that the two would touch. In the event all was absolutely fine, but it does underline how you need to consider whether components will clash or not when you design your own layout.

DAY TWO

25 There wasn't time to fit the Raptor Binnacle Mount during our first session, so back at the Porter Ranch we dismantled the relevant parts of the dash and removed the plastic binnacle support panel.

26 The Raptor panel is much more robust than the plastic original, though there were a couple of sharp corners to file off.

27 When refitting one of the spire nuts on to this steel projection you can see just how flimsy the original fixing is when all it offers is a tab of plastic.

28 The steel Raptor panel is much more reassuring when you come to screw the dash panels back together.

29 You can also get this fascia plate for the instrument binnacle behind the steering wheel. This was the wrong one for my vehicle, having holes for the two fixing screws on earlier models, but in any case, I chose not to fit one.

30 The next job was to temporarily fit the Carling fan switch to replace the clunky slider switch on the Defender, which can be difficult to operate for those whose hands or arms aren't in perfect working order and tricky to position in any case. Later we'd be using more of those Carling connector blocks, but for now we used regular spade terminals.

31 We also took out the Carling hazard warning switch, simply because I didn't like the way it had to sit horizontally on my dash panel. We went back to the standard Land Rover switch, which meant opening out the hole a little and also that the switch had to be bonded in place, because the fixing clips aren't suitable for the thinner aluminium.

32 Furthermore, another chunk had to be taken out of the backing panel…

33 …so that the Raptor panel could be pushed into position with the hazard wiring plug in place.

DAY THREE

34 Our final session involved another full day's work, though there were few photographs to show for it. Tim and Ian were meticulous in doing everything properly, and took time to make sure whatever they did could be repeated later on customers' cars. Tim used a rather splendid piece of test equipment called the ECT 2000, which has a huge range of test abilities and proved invaluable in confirming what does what in the dashboard wiring.

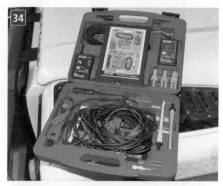

35 Before connecting up my new voltmeter, Tim checked his power supply to ensure that the voltage drop on the cable he chose was minimal before using it to power the voltmeter. Just one of the many ways in which the ECT2000 earned its corn. The ECT2000 is actually a Master Technicians kit, made by Power Probe in the USA.

36 During our second session we'd cut holes in the automatic transmission centre console for Raptor panels designed to take switches for the seat heater, lumbar support and electric windows, all of which are still to be fitted. Vertically, the switches are a touch too close together, so we might have a pair of new panels made later.

37 After our third session the dash was looking splendid! The alarm telltale light had been fitted into one of the Carling switch blanks, while the other switch blank patiently awaits the fitting of yet another component!

If you add extra gizmos to your Defender, you need extra information about how they're all getting on. Here's how we added three extra dash-top gauges.

It took me quite a long time to source all of the bits and pieces you'll see being fitted here. I wanted a pod with a level top, but many of those available are like lesser versions of the Sydney Opera House, which would make them dashboard-top dust-traps. The gauges themselves (all of them said to have been made by the well-known German manufacturer VDO, although only the rev counter was so marked) came from an unusual source – someone on eBay selling stuff taken from ex-military panels – while the adapter for the auto transmission fluid temperature gauge turned out to be relatively sophisticated and, as it happened, a lovely bit of kit.

1 As with most dash-top pods, the front panel is blank and needs to be carefully marked out. I was ending up with odd millimetres all over the place until I realised that it was probably made for the American market. So I switched to inches and it all made sense.

2 We put a large piece of wood in the vice and drilled a pilot hole for each of the three gauge centres. The pilot holes were deliberately slightly narrower...

3 ...than the diameter of the guide drill in the centre of the hole cutter.

4 This looks dangerous but it wasn't really. The guide drill in the centre of the cutter prevented it from moving sideways, and in any case you have to use a very low speed when using a hole cutter because the speed at the periphery would otherwise be very high for what is, in effect, simply a round saw blade.

5 This is how most gauges are fitted to dashboards and gauge panels.

6 You push the gauge into the panel from one side and place the retaining clip over the gauge from the other.

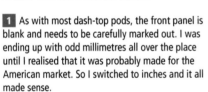

7 On some gauges the retaining clip will only go one way round without fouling on the electrical connections. It's held in place with a couple of nuts. When fixing to a soft plastic housing, make sure the feet on the clip are pressing on the housing directly behind the bezel on the front of the gauge. If you don't, there's every likelihood that the clip will be forced into the soft plastic, damaging it.

8 The VDO rev counter, with its plastic body, was a tighter fit than the other gauges. Also pushed in from the front of the pod...

9 ...it was held in place with this large plastic ring. It's often tricky to get plastic threads to start off properly without crossing themselves. The trick is to stop as soon as any tightness is felt, back off and start again. A spot (no more) of releasing fluid or a squirt of silicone lube will make the task far easier.

10 This is a problem that was exacerbated by the extra thickness of the wall on the plastic-bodied rev counter. Our gauges were quite close together and the legs on the retaining clips needed to be bent inward so that they didn't foul on each other.

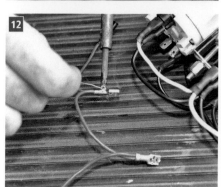

11 Once everything was correctly assembled the nuts holding the steel-body gauges in place were nipped up (though not over-tightened) using my French 'pipe spanners'.

12 We set about making a neat little wiring loom for all the shared lighting and power connections at the back of the gauges. This could be problematical if we decide to change things later but we'll cross that bridge when we come to it.

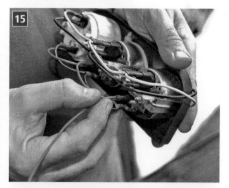

13 Each female spade terminal would have been insulated with a purpose-made sheath, if I'd had any. Instead, we cut lengths of shrink-fit insulation...

14 ...and after sliding each piece over a terminal used a flame to shrink the insulation, especially over the wires rather than over the terminal itself...

15 ...before plugging in at relevant points at the back of the gauges panel.

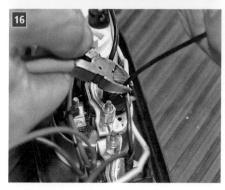

16 Finally, the wires were tidied up by strapping them together with thin cable ties.

17 Meanwhile, I got on with making a non-intrusive mounting for the top of the dashboard. I was quite prepared to sacrifice the ashtray and started by drilling a 22mm hole in its base.

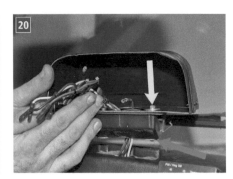

18 I also cut and folded a piece of aluminium plate with a slightly larger hole in the centre, these two large holes having been put there to allow the wiring to pass through. The pod shell was planned to sit on top of the plate and screw to the two flanges that had been folded, one on each end of the piece of aluminium.

19 Here, the aluminium base plate has been painted black and attached to the pod with two screws (arrowed) at each end. No attachments for holding the body of the pod to the front panel were included, so perhaps the expectation is that you'd screw through one piece of plastic and into the other. This

didn't appeal to me, so I fitted the front to the pod, held it in place with masking tape, drilled pilot holes and then used spire nuts raided from my Würth box. I had to grind a bit off each so it wouldn't show and also had to relieve a bit of the plastic at each location so that the holes in the spire nuts lined up with the pilot holes I'd already drilled. (Ideally I should have used the spire nuts to make sure the pilot holes had been drilled in exactly the right position to start with.)

20 I originally planned to screw the aluminium pod base to the ashtray via the flanges on the latter but

then realised that fixings such as nuts or bolt heads would prevent the ashtray from clipping right down into its aperture. So instead I used longer screws inserted from above (green arrow) and passing right through the body of the ashtray, with washers and nuts from beneath (orange arrow). Excess screw lengths were cut back to prevent any risk of shorting on electrical equipment inside the dashboard.

21 I'd curved the aluminium plate so the ends of the pod would be flat on the dashboard top, so now when the ashtray's clicked into place the pod is semi-fixed in position.

22 We now reintroduced the gauges to the wiring we'd run through the dashboard...

23 ...and after pushing the instrument panel into place...

24 ...we screwed it home through the spire nuts on the lip of the pod case.

AUTO TRANSMISSION FLUID TEMPERATURE GAUGE

25 The auto transmission conversion had been carried out by Ashcroft Transmissions. I wanted to be sure that the transmission oil cooler I'd had fitted was going to be up to the job when the vehicle was working hard, towing its maximum permissible weight, without having to fiddle my way through the sub-menus on the Compushift control box inside the vehicle. So Dave Ashcroft recommended that I approach Think Automotive, the UK manufacturers of Mocal oil coolers, and this is what they came up with.

26 I had to send details of the sender unit to Think Automotive – I just bunged it on top of the scanner, which is why it came out a bit fuzzy – and they supplied me with a sender unit adapter (Oil Temperature Gauge Adapter, part number TGA2A). This has a ½in tail for the 12mm transmission fluid hose and a ⅝in UNF female thread for the sender unit.

I wanted the sender unit adapter to be as close to the transmission unit on the outlet side as was reasonably possible. The Think Automotive adapter is quite sophisticated in that while the sender unit is always in the flow of the oil, the adapter has a wide body so that the flow of oil isn't in any way impeded. It also has special fittings on the tails designed to take the amount of pressure involved.

27 We used VDO's instructions, downloaded from their website, on how to connect up the alternator. We soldered a cable for the rev counter on to the existing cable identified (so we thought) by the VDO instructions...

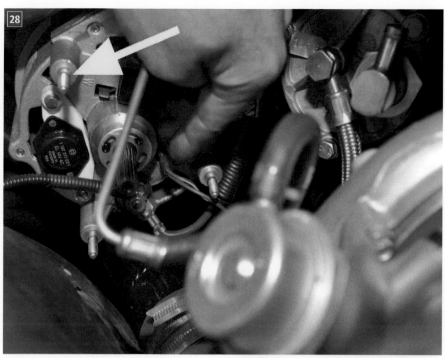

28 ...plugged it in – and nothing happened. It turned out we should have been connecting to the W terminal (arrowed).

29 Incidentally, not all alternators have a W terminal. Some owners have had to swap alternators to get a W terminal. Typically it's a big spade terminal, marked 'W' on the case.

30 VDO also recommend that their tachometers (rev counters) are calibrated using a reference tachometer.

31 This screw is used for tweaking the reading so that it exactly matches that of the reference tachometer.

32 I'm really pleased with the completed job. There's a gauge for the vegetable oil, one to make sure the ATF is running cool enough, and a rev counter just to keep me happy.

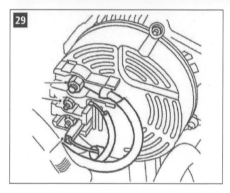

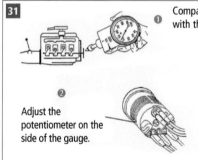

① Compare the VDO Tachometer reading with that of a reference tachometer.

② Adjust the potentiometer on the side of the gauge.

③ The pointer will move clockwise or anticlockwise as you adjust. When the VDO Tachometer reading matches that of the reference tachometer, the adjustment is complete.

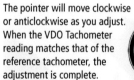

33 Many owners also want to fit extra instruments. As well as the usual 52mm size instruments you can opt for a larger 85mm tachometer, such as this one from the Durite range.

34 Not all dash pods can accept this larger size of tachometer but there was just room to fit one to the standard Raptor Pod after I'd cut it away and sliced a bit off the top of the dashboard to match. (It's hidden by the dash pod.) But you shouldn't go down this route unless you're feeling confident about your skills.

'Wrap your ass in fiberglass,' said the Yanks about the early Corvette. Well, now Land Rover owners can wrap their heads in it too.

I reckon the Spanish company Santana had the right idea when their version of the Land Rover was fitted with a GRP hardtop. Among other things it provided better insulation – *much* better insulation, in fact – as well as a headliner that was extremely difficult to damage. Here we show how we fitted a La Salle Fibreglass headliner to DiXie.

1 There are so many variations, even within Defenders, that LaSalle Trim is to be commended for the range available. Here and in the main picture you can see that this is a 110 headliner but with the speaker pod options and Alpine light inserts.

2 You don't need a huge range of tools but I'd go against LaSalle's recommendations and suggest using a power jigsaw for making cut-outs in the fibreglass where necessary. LaSalle don't recommend jigsaws for a very important reason: fibreglass (GRP) dust can be extremely harmful if breathed in. So whenever drilling or cutting GRP, especially using a power tool, ALWAYS wear an efficient particle mask. GRP contains strands of glass which, when powdered by machining, turn into microscopic flakes of silica which could cause terminal lung damage. As well as wearing a mask I also use a vacuum cleaner to grab the dangerous dust before it gets into the air.

3 A tool you can't do without is a purpose-made trim removal tool.

4 The B-post trim is also held in place by the upper seat belt mounting.

5 You can't remove this long, horizontal piece of trim without first at least slackening the B-post trim, while to remove the grab handle you first have to flip up the covers…

6 …and remove the two screws from each end.

7 This allows the horizontal trim to be lifted away.

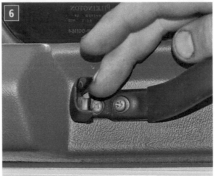

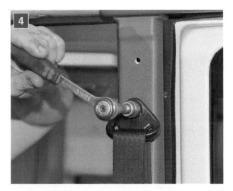

8 Above the rear door, the trim removal tool is again used…

9 …to release the clips holding the trim panel in place. Note that the interior light (arrowed) and the mounting plate behind it also have to be removed.

10 In order to remove the old headlining, lots more trim clips have to be popped out. You have to jiggle the tool carefully behind the clip if you need to preserve the headlining fabric.

11 The centre section needs to be removed first on this model of Defender because it overlaps both the front and rear sections.

12 We lowered it down on to the back seats and then manoeuvred it out through the rear door. It's light but awkward.

13 If you need to in order to clear fixtures and fittings, standard headlining can be bent quite a long way without causing any damage. This section was partially folded so that it could be…

14 …lowered and passed through the door. Note that the interior light has been left connected to the wiring. If you intend refitting the interior light in its original position you'll need to cut a suitable hole in the LaSalle GRP headlining – but that comes later.

15 The interior light at the front end was also removed, as was its metal backing plate. Be sure to disconnect the battery before getting this far, or to insulate electrical terminals as you disconnect them so that you can't cause an electrical short.

16 The Defender rear-view mirror is removed by twisting anticlockwise. The mounting plate from behind it also has to be unscrewed…

17 …as do the sun visors, each fixed to the top of the windscreen surround with two screws.

18 After popping out a few clips down each side of the headlining…

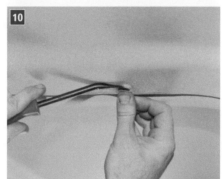

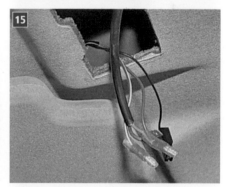

19 …the front section was lowered and removed.

20 At this stage you may need to look at the positioning of the fixed wiring that goes behind the headliner, because whereas the original one is largely made of fabric and has greater flexibility, the LaSalle headliner is rigid and, in places, fits tight against the ribs of the roof. You need to make sure that wiring can pass unimpeded. There's plenty of space between the curved corners of the headliner and those of the roof, so we made sure that any original and extra wiring was run in that area.

TOP TIP
If you think you might be adding lots of accessories in future, why not run a length of seven-core trailer cable from one end of the roof to the other, routing it behind the new headlining, just above the top, horizontal right at one of the outer edges? It'll save a huge amount of time in future should you need to add front-to-back wiring runs.

21 Preparation time is seldom wasted but we spent longer than anticipated getting everything ready before fitting the new headliner. Which leads to the only criticism I have of the LaSalle product: there are too few instructions, and getting the Alpine light trim in the correct position is too hit-and-miss for comfort.

22 I decided that the only way of establishing where the Alpine light cut-out should be made was to remove the glass from the vehicle and use the aperture to mark out the headliner.

23 However, that came later, but it did mean that while the glass was out we could get on with the next stage, which was to fit the optional insulation pads. These have to be measured and marked out, the superimposed grid on the surface of the reflective material making it easier to cut from one side in a straight line…

24 …after which the insulation was folded back on itself and another cut made from the other side, through the white backing paper.

25 Fortunately the insulation is fairly flexible and can be encouraged to follow the shape of the roof. But first, here are some important points:
Be sure to thoroughly clean off the surface of the roof with a suitable degreaser such as methylated spirit or panel wipe. White spirit and even cellulose thinners can leave an oily residue on the latter and could damage paintwork or trim inside your vehicle.
When sticking down the curved section, start by only pulling off the backing paper from the section to go on the curved part of the roof and stick that bit down first, tucking the insulation right down into the bottom corner and pushing it into the curve as you go. Then, when all of the curve has been stuck down, reach behind, peel off the rest of the backing paper and stick down the rest of the insulation.
LaSalle provide plenty of insulation material and it's simple to use offcuts to fill-in where necessary.

26 The insulation is made from non-closed cell foam that's capable of absorbing moisture. That's because a small amount of condensation will always occur and LaSalle consider it's better to have it temporarily absorbed into the insulation, ready to be evaporated off later, than have it run down the inside of the headliner.

27 Test-fitting revealed that there was a small gap between the top of the headliner and the insulation, the headliner itself sounded slightly rattly when tapped, and that wiring draped across the top of the headliner most certainly would rattle when the vehicle was driven. For all of these reasons I decided to use some of the leftover insulation to soundproof and further insulate the tops of the GRP panels – and this seems to have worked perfectly.

28 Another aspect of preparation is the alteration I made to the sun visor fixings. Supplied with the kit is a screw and nut which has the huge disadvantage that you won't be able to remove and refit the sun visor in future with the headliner in place. I drilled out the fixing holes and fitted rivet nuts, so that sun visor screws can now be removed and refitted whenever required.

29 The radio aerial on my Defender has always been poor, so I had a 'Eureka!' moment. Why not fit a roof-mounted aerial – and why not make it a shark's fin aerial at the same time? With no headlining in place, the job was a piece of cake.

30 After carefully measuring and drilling a pilot hole, a tank cutter was used to drill a larger hole in the rib beneath so that the fixing nut could be fitted – and the shark's fin aerial swam into view.

31 This is the rear headliner section. LaSalle recommend that on 110 models you should install the rear section first, but I don't think it makes any difference at all whether you start with front or back.

32 In any event, we started with the rear. You really need a second pair of hands for this job! The headliner has to be held in position so that you can make a mark and then drill a pilot hole for a self-tapping screw. At this stage the rear section can be held in place with just four self-tapping screws evenly spaced around the perimeter.

33 LaSalle recommend fitting the centre section next, but having been there I don't agree. Like the rear section, the front is more or less fixed in position, so I'd recommend fitting that next.

34 It's best to use all three screws holding the rear-view mirror bracket in position but not to tighten any of them at this stage. In practice we had to start things off with a much longer 5mm screw, using that to pull the headliner in so that the standard screws could then be fitted.

35 The rear sides of the front section can be fitted with a couple of self-tapping screws, as used on the rear section. Note that we tried using the depth stop on the Makita drill in an attempt to prevent the drill from penetrating too deeply. There are too many uneven surfaces, however, and it didn't work very well here. These rear screws were left loose so that the centre section could be fitted next.

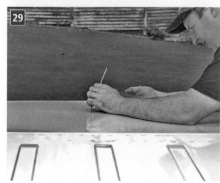

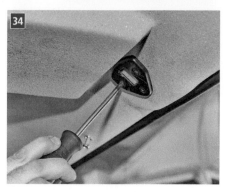

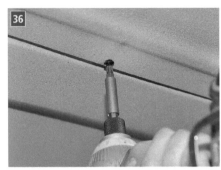

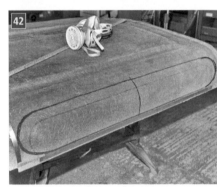

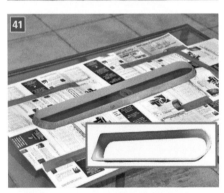

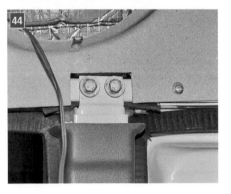

36 The idea of fitting the centre section last is because it's the only one that doesn't have a fixed position, and therefore – bearing in mind that Land Rovers do vary somewhat in their dimensions – you can slide the centre section behind its overlap on the front section, hold it up against the back section and alter its position to give matching gaps at all the joints. Once again, it was a question of drilling tapping-sized holes and inserting self-tapping screws.

37 Once everything was found to fit correctly it was possible to make marks for the various cut-outs that we needed, such as at the tops of the B-posts and the Alpine light apertures from which the glasses had previously been removed.

38 Remembering to don an efficient particle mask before you start, use a jigsaw to cut out the radio aperture from the front headliner section. After marking out the exact size, a hole was drilled in each corner. It was only possible to saw one long cut from one side of the panel, while the other long cut had to be sawn from the other side. The short cuts had to be done by hand. It's best to protect the surface of the inside of the panel with masking tape so that the foot of the jigsaw can't damage it.

39 It's always best to cut a little under size and then open out the hole with a file until the radio fitting cage slides in snugly.

40 The hole size you'll need to cut for the speakers depends entirely on the speaker dimensions, of course. If you've got access to a suitably sized hole saw, so much the better.

41 Unfortunately, simply marking the position of the Alpine lights on the centre headlining section didn't actually tell me where I needed to cut for the trims. So I used a piece of cardboard and experimented until I found the right shape and size to fit over the LaSalle Alpine trim (inset).

42 Here, you can see the original pencil line surrounded by a red line made with a felt pen using the card template shown in the previous shot. You can also see a strip of aluminium glued to the surface of the GRP, following the curve on the left-hand side of what will be the cut-out, and another long strip running down the bottom edge. These strips were glued into place with epoxy resin adhesive to provide extra support. I was concerned about the possibility of the GRP breaking during or after the cutting-out process.

43 You could, I suppose, fix the Alpine light trim in place with screws but I chose to use epoxy resin. As well as taking care not to allow the clamps to mark the finished surface of the headliner, you also have to watch for excess glue oozing out on the visible side of the joint.

44 Meanwhile, the front section was cut out to fit around the top of the B-post. I made a pig's ear of the cut-out…

45 …so turned a problem to advantage by making an aluminium plate to go beneath the bolt heads and washers. As well as covering up my mistake, this has the advantage of clamping the headliner at the top of the B-post. You really shouldn't try to clamp through the fibreglass because this is a major structural body connection and you need to be able to tighten the bolts back to their original torque – and you can't do that against GRP, which crushes. You can tighten them satisfactorily against an aluminium plate, however.

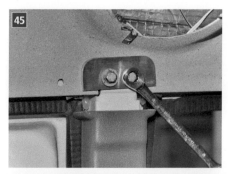

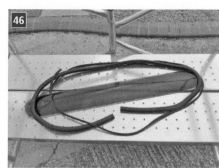

46 With the headliner in its final location it was time to put things back together. These are the new rubbers and inserts I purchased. I reasoned that since the vehicle was six years old, it wouldn't hurt to have new rubbers in place, giving an extra lease of life to an area that's known to crack and leak over time. Unfortunately, however, none of us could get the Alpine glass back in place.

47 So we called in Autoglass, who rapidly found that the aftermarket rubbers (right) were not exactly the correct profile and were larger than the original rubbers (left), so we had to use the latter after all. The moral? Only purchase Land Rover OE.

48 Autoglass started by fitting the main rubber section, with the joint at the bottom.

49 Then the glass was inserted, using a plastic spreader tool to ease the lip of the rubber over the glass. The trickiest job is to insert the glass into its recess in the rubber, which is all but impossible without the right tool. The rubber was lubricated with WD-40 (you could use soapy water) to help matters along.

50 Watching Autoglass finish a job in minutes that we'd struggled with for ages made me realise that spending a few quid on the experts was money well spent.

FITTING CLIPS, FITTING TIPS

51 I'd decided that all the fixings that would be hidden by the trim would be self-tapping screws with washers beneath their heads to spread the load, whereas all the visible fixings would be trim clips. LaSalle supply trim clips with their headliners, but while they're OK much better ones are available. Meanwhile, experience has taught me that the best way of preventing a drill going through a box section and damaging an outer panel is to make a wooden block to fit around the twist drill itself.

52 This is the clip. You can find them for sale by searching for 'VW T5 trim clip' on Google or eBay.

53 You have to make sure the headliner is tight up against the rib to which it will be clipped, then push in the outer part of the clip until you hear a click.

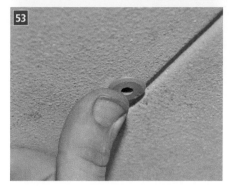

54 Next, push in the insert with your thumb and finish off by hammering home. The insert can be removed by unscrewing it with an Allen key rather than levering it out with the trim tool.

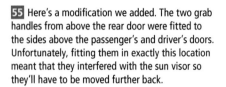

55 Here's a modification we added. The two grab handles from above the rear door were fitted to the sides above the passenger's and driver's doors. Unfortunately, fitting them in exactly this location meant that they interfered with the sun visor so they'll have to be moved further back.

56 Another minor problem was that these raised areas on the side trims (arrowed) push the trim out further than it needed to be, so they were power-sanded off to allow the trim to sit correctly after the grab handles had been refitted.

57 Since the original interior lights were no longer to be used (they were replaced by LED lights from MCL) we decided to fit remote switches, one to the radio housing on the front panel and one to the rear window surround. We'd already run the wiring in place while the headlining was out and drilled a suitable sized hole for the switch. After connecting and fitting the switch…

58 …we checked that the lights worked correctly before refitting the trim.

59 The side trim is now partly held in place by the rear window trim and partly by the seat belt mountings. However, the steel clips that were originally fitted on the rear of the trim, and which hooked over the roof rail, could no longer be used because the headliner covers the rail. If you feel the trim needs more support you may be able to use extra-long self-tapping screws through the trim and into the headliner behind it.

60 Properly finished, with the original trim back in place, the LaSalle Trims headliner really looks as if it belongs…

61 …and at the front you have those additional options of radio and speaker mounting positions.

Overall these LaSalle Trim headliners are well made, well finished and could well last the lifetime of the vehicle, and I'm very pleased with them. They took much longer to fit than I expected, but then I'm a bit obsessive about getting things right! The lack of adequate instructions is really the only criticism I have. The fit is extremely good for what is, after all, an aftermarket product, and the quality of the finish is excellent.

Seat heaters and electric lumbar support

Here's how to fit Rostra seat heaters and electrically adjustable lumbar supports to Defender seats.

1 The Rostra lumbar heater kit for each seat consists of (left to right) pump/pouch, bladder, switch, harness, instructions and hardware package.

2 Rostra's seat heater kit contains (clockwise, from bottom) heater elements, controller, harness, switch and hardware package.

3 The work on the seats was carried out by Britpart's cab trim shop manager, Matt Morgan. He started by removing the backrest from the seat base and unclipping the plastic zip-type connector at the bottom.

4 You don't need to take the backrest cover right off. Just remove it far enough to install the components shown here.

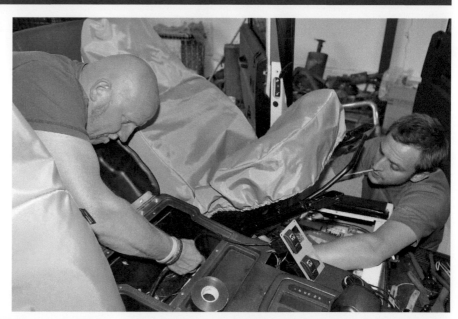

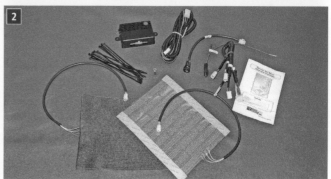

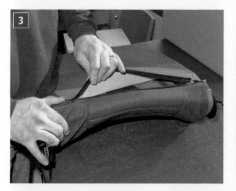

LUMBAR SUPPORT

5 The lumbar support consists of a plastic bladder. Obviously, if you cut into it you'll puncture it, but we found some of the outer edge needed to be trimmed away to make it fit the backrest properly.

6 Seats that have a spring support use a rear-mounted bladder. Defender seats have the front bladder mounted here: inflatable bag toward the cushion, and tube down. Route the tube to the right and guide it next to the seat hinge so that it exits under the seat. Make sure the tube route is inside the seat hinges, not around the outside.

7 Peel off the double-sided tape's backing paper then simply stick the bladder down to the relevant part of the seat back. It's obviously up to you to decide the height at which you want the bladder to inflate.

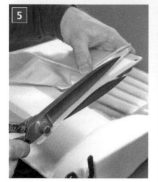

Front Bladder

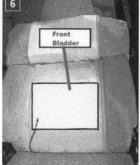

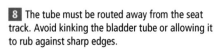 The tube must be routed away from the seat track. Avoid kinking the bladder tube or allowing it to rub against sharp edges.

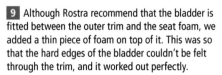 Although Rostra recommend that the bladder is fitted between the outer trim and the seat foam, we added a thin piece of foam on top of it. This was so that the hard edges of the bladder couldn't be felt through the trim, and it worked out perfectly.

10 The bladder is operated by a small pump and electric motor sealed in a bag. Theoretically this could go anywhere within reach of the tubing, but the most sensible place is beneath the seat base.

11 Mount the pouch under the seat and secure it using cable ties in appropriate locations.

12 Just a thought, but you might want to locate the pouch nearest to the front of the seat base because that's where the seat foam is less likely to be compressed.

13 You can now connect the bladder tube to the rubber hose that comes out of the pouch.

14 Secure the bladder tube and the pouch rubber hose with cable ties to prevent them from moving. Rostra say 'Do not add holes to pouch, use existing holes only. Damage can occur to enclosed components and void warranty'; but we were brave and opened up the pouch, and there doesn't seem to be any logical reason why you shouldn't be able to adapt the pouch should you need to – though bear in mind Rostra's point about invalidating the warranty. Also note that the bladder's performance depends greatly on positioning and how well it's secured in place.

15 Before leaving the underside of the seat, plug in the dedicated wiring harness to the socket on the bladder.

16 The wiring will need positioning and can be cable-tied securely in place, making sure that it doesn't foul on the seat runners or mechanism and keeping in mind the planned location of the switch.

17 When you've established where the switch will be located, the wiring can be positioned so that it appears from the trim in the appropriate place.

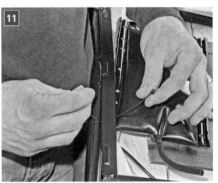

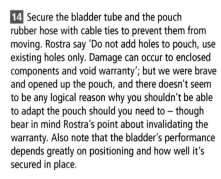

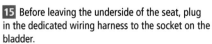

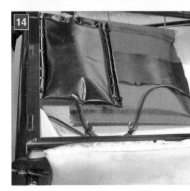

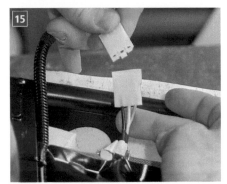

SEAT HEATERS

18 The seat heater pads aren't designed to fit at the back of the foam, otherwise their heat would be dissipated before it reached its target. As with the lumbar support, they're fitted with self-adhesive strips.

19 Before fitting the heater elements, trial-fit the cabling so that you can see which way round the element needs to go. The element for the seat back needs to have its cable facing downwards while that fitted to the seat base needs to have its cable facing backwards.

20 After establishing their correct locations, each pad is placed on the seat foam – note the cover pulled well back – and stuck down. It's important to give special attention to the installation of the seat heater element, since if the element is folded or creased over on itself it may not work. It's also important that you don't pierce or short the element with hog-rings or other metal clips or fittings.

21 After ensuring that the element on the seat base was well stuck down upholsterer's contact adhesive was applied to both surfaces before sticking the seat base trim back into position. In many cases this may not have been fully removed, but it will still be necessary to use adhesive to prevent it from moving around.

22 It's then a matter of stretching the sides of the seat base trim back into place…

23 …ensuring that the heater cable emerges from the correct position.

24 Here the trim is back in place, with the Rostra cable complete with its dedicated plug awaiting later connection.

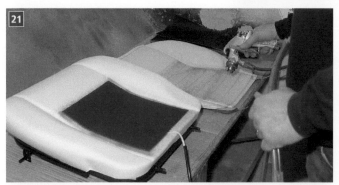

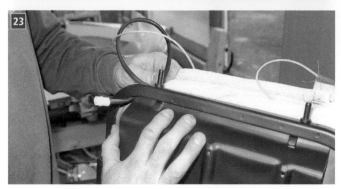

25 The backrest trim had only been lifted up, so it only needed to be pulled back down and stretched evenly into position until…

26 …it was completely in place, with the electrical cables and bladder hose emerging from the required side.

27 The seat heater switch supplied with the kit has high and low positions. The default setting is 'backrest only' mode and 'seat base and backrest together' mode.

28 If you prefer to have both heaters on at the same time, but with high and low mode settings, as I did, cut through the external wire loop on the control box (arrowed).

SWITCHES

29 Lumbar support: cut a ½in x 1³/₈in hole in the console or the seat side panel in order to fit the lumbar support switch.

30 Seat heater: drill a 21mm (¹³/₁₆in) hole for the round switch.

31 Both types of switch clipped into place when pressed in from the front.

32 In this installation we made a custom-built panel and fitted Carling switches from MCL. They don't come with purpose-made connector blocks but they can be purchased separately, allowing the fitting of cables to the backs of the switches in a way that can be connected or disconnected when required.

33 The power supply cable was stripped and a ring terminal crimped on to the end of it…

34 …before screwing it to the extra accessory fuse box (again from MCL) located, in this instance, beneath the passenger's seat.

If you've never had them before, once you've installed seat heaters and lumbar supports you'll soon realise why so many new cars are fitted with them, especially on a cold winter's morning when your Defender's heater is taking its usual long time to warm up. You'll never want to be without them again!

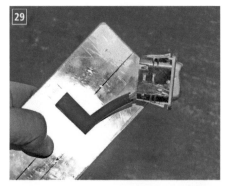

In this section we fit a full set of Britpart's folding individual rear seats and matching lap seat belts.

1 Each seat comes as a self-contained box of parts. Work began with laying out the parts and comparing them with the single drawing on the instruction sheets. We didn't follow the same sequence described in the instructions but it all worked out perfectly in the end.

2 Before starting to fit the seats we offered up the seat bases to work out where the seat belts would be fitted.

3 It's important to drill the mounting holes for the seat belts – or at least the ones in the rearmost corners of the floor – before fitting the seats, because otherwise there's a real risk of damaging the seats with the drill. In practice you're strongly recommended to follow the approach carried out here: mark out drill holes for the seat belts with the seats temporarily fitted into place, then take the seat out, drill for the seat belt mountings and fit the seat belts or the seats in the order you prefer.

4 Each seat back and base has captive nuts built in. Locations are clearly indicated by red dots stuck on the surface of the trim. You need to use a sharp knife to cut the trim so that mounting bolts can be entered cleanly, but you must also take great care not to cut too much material away. You really don't want to see jagged edges of trim protruding from underneath the surfaces of the brackets.

5 The backrest brackets have to be fitted the correct way round as shown in the instructions. It's vitally important that each bolt has its thread started in its captive nut carefully, by hand, before starting to tighten it up. If you accidentally cross a thread you'll almost certainly break the captive nut free inside the trim, making it impossible to bolt the frame in place.

6 In this installation the brackets on the seat backs lined up with existing holes in the bodywork. In addition there are slotted holes strategically placed in the body side rails to enable you to insert the relevant washers and fixings.

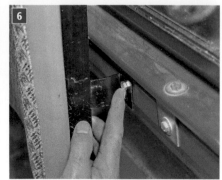

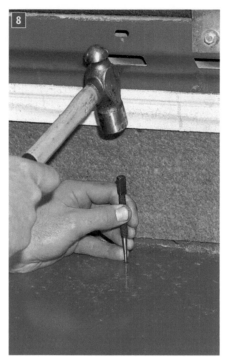

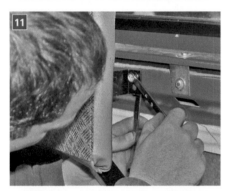

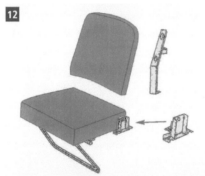

7 With the top brackets in place, the bottom ends of the brackets can be pushed back or forth until they're parallel with the body sides. The positions of the mounting holes can then be transferred to the top surface of the wheel arch box.

8 To centre-punch aluminium, you use a sharp centre punch and give it a single crisp tap with the hammer. If you hammer too hard or give too many blows you'll dent the surrounding aluminium. Remember that it's significantly softer than steel!

9 Then drill clearance-sized holes...

10 ...before fitting the bolts into the wheel arch box, using substantial flat washers to spread the load on the box's underside.

11 Use the slotted holes in the bodywork rail to tighten the upper seat backrest mounting bolts.

12 This Britpart drawing illustrates the swivel bracket that needs to be fitted to the seat base in the position arrowed. It's also the drawing referred to earlier, showing you which way round the seat back brackets have to be fitted.

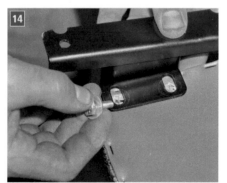

13 Next cut the trim fabric...

14 ...so that the brackets can be bolted into position, remembering as before to start each bolt by hand, ensuring its clean entry into the captive nut secreted behind the trim.

15 A thin black strip has to be screwed to the outer edge of the underside of each seat base...

16 ...but bear in mind that the front two bolt holes are also there to enable the swivel bracket to be bolted down.

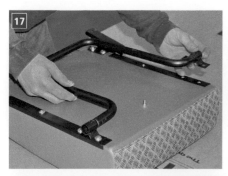

17 Remember to fit the seat support into the first swivel bracket before offering up the second one, otherwise you won't be able to get the support into place.

18 Only then can the second swivel bracket be bolted into position.

19 The next job was to offer up the seat base and mark out the hole positions for the swivel brackets. It's important that the seat backrest is already in place at this stage so that you can check the correct position of the base both when folded away and when laid flat.

20 Off with the seat base. In with the electric drill. Create clearance-sized holes for bolting down the base.

21 What holds the seat base up when it's not in use? This strap does. It clips on to the underside of the seat base, having previously been screwed permanently on to the back of the backrest. And did we forget to fit the first one?

22 We did! So we removed the backrest again. After that we remembered to fit the straps to the rears of all the others before fitting their brackets.

23 Then we fitted the first of the seat belts.

24 You'll need an assistant when tightening both the seat bases and the seatbelts.

25 With all the seats and belts in place you can see the extra versatility that a set of individual folding rear seats brings to the back of both long-wheelbase and short-wheelbase Defenders.

No switches, no electrical connections, no lights, no noises – it just sits there doing its job, and yet it's one of my favourite Defender modifications. Here's how to fit Wright Off-road's Acoustic Mats.

What's an Acoustic Mat?

Acoustic mats are made from dense, cast polyurethane, and are used to drastically reduce noise levels inside operators' cabins in equipment such as diggers, excavators and agricultural tractors. They also provide a hard-wearing, durable surface that withstands the rigours of constant daily use. Their main features are:

■ They reduce the need for engine and gearbox blankets.
■ They're harder-wearing than rubber and will probably outlast your Land Rover.
■ They're easy to clean can be hosed out.
■ They provide insulation to keep heat out (or in).
■ They won't rot or hold water and are fuel, oil, water and sunlight resistant.
■ They're fire retardant and recyclable.

1 The acoustic mat system is designed to replace all the existing trim in the areas it covers. On later models the standard trim in the bulkhead and foot well areas is quite extensive. However, Wright Off-road's Drew Wright says that it's not as effective as the polyurethane (PU) system and may also absorb moisture. Also, you might find that leaving the original mats in place pushes the new ones much too high and won't allow let them to seat down correctly. When stripping out, you need to remove the following the seats, seat base catches, seat belt mountings from the floor, handbrake lever, cable and wiring plug, the screws holding the footwell-side kick plates, and the trim from around the seat box.

BULKHEAD MAT

The smaller, bulkhead mat is fitted behind the fuse box. Remove the cover and detach the fuse box and plate from the bulkhead, then remove the existing trim. It may be possible to fit the bulkhead mat over the existing trim in later models, dependent on how your floor panels are fitted.

On the reverse of the mat are recessed locations for air con pipes, when air conditioning is fitted as standard.

Never crease acoustic mats. They can be deformed or folded and will return to their moulded shape, but creasing them may cause them to crack or permanently distort.

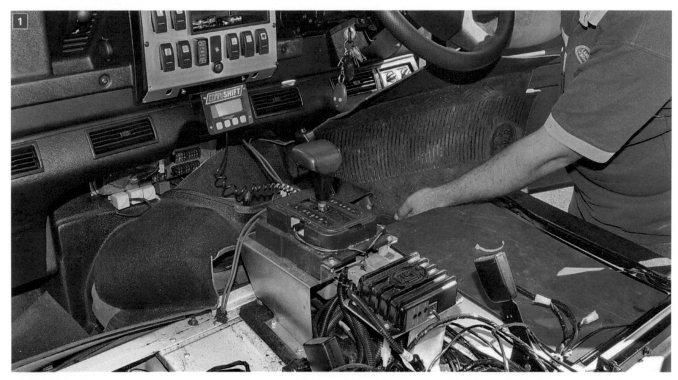

SEAT BOX MAT

This should be fitted next. Position the mat on the seat box and mark through from underneath the seat and handbrake fixing holes, to double-check positions. These positions can then be transferred to the front of the mat.

2 You also have to cut a pair of slots to correspond with the inner seat belt mounts. We started by drilling the ends of the slots. Use soapy water to lubricate the knife blade – it will prevent the blade from sticking as you make the cut.

3 Cutting should be carried out with a heavy-duty craft knife. Make sure you use a new blade and that you have a supply of new blades ready – the mat blunts blades quickly! On the underside of the mat you'll find a number of witness marks that correspond to the features of the seat box. These are the ones for the seat runner mountings. Do remember, though, that you're working with a Land Rover and the positions can vary – so it pays to double-check by measuring first!

4 I decided that the flaps to enable access to the seat box lids would be about 25mm wider on each side than the lids, so measurements were made for the seat box lid cut-outs. There's nothing lost in making the cut in the mat wider than the width of the lid.

5 We tried fitting the lid catches through the material but the thickness of the mat pushed the catches too far forward. So we made slotted cuts where the catches were fitted. Incidentally, we fitted rivet nuts to the holes in the seat boxes where pop rivets had originally been fitted, which enabled us to use 5mm screws instead. Not essential, but nice.

FLOOR MAT

This should be fitted last. If you haven't already done so, remove the gear lever gaiter. You should retain the piece of foam that goes under the gaiter because it provides the sound deadening for the top of the gearbox.

90/110 LT77 (EARLIER) GEARBOX MODELS ONLY

The transmission tunnel opening and middle seat channel will require cutting to the shape of the recess on the vehicle.

Seat fixing holes are also marked. Select the required ones and drill, but make sure you *are* using the correct ones – Land Rover modified the seat box around the introduction of the 200 Tdi and moved the seat fixings by about 25mm (1in) inboard.

Position the mat on the seat box and mark the seat fixing holes from beneath.

6 As the new mat is lowered into position, make sure its leading edge is pointing upwards. Lower the mat over the gear lever, angling it downwards at the front. Aim the leading edge under the pedals and feed the gear lever through the hole. You can then refit the gear lever gaiter using the new cable tie

supplied. Ensure the pedals have full range of travel and don't foul the mat.

Once the mat is in place on the seat box with all the cutting complete, you can refit the handbrake lever and gaiter and the fuse box cover.

7 Acoustic mats for the rear come in 8ft x 4ft chequer-plate finished sheets. You need two full sheets for a 110 Station Wagon. Because they were to be glued down I used soapy water and a pressure washer to wash off all the slippery release agent before starting.

8 It's a painstaking business measuring, marking and cutting each individual piece. I found a pencil worked best. Felt pen can be difficult to remove from the surface.

9 Use panel wipe (or methylated spirits) to clean the mat and painted metal surfaces, having keyed the paint surface with light abrasive first. After spreading a thin, even smear of contact adhesive on both surfaces...

10 ...this vertical sheet was carefully positioned while it was being stuck down. Be sure to follow the important safety instructions on the contact adhesive tin, especially regarding fume hazards and flammability.

11 I purchased aluminium trim, intended for household tiling, to finish off the corners. (Regular aluminium angle has sharp edges, so beware!) It's available with a self-adhesive option, but PU sheet is very choosy about what it'll stick to. I used Würth PU Bond & Seal. Not too much, though, or it'll spread everywhere!

12 The finished mats not only look great but have fantastic qualities that make you wonder why Land Rover don't fit them from new.

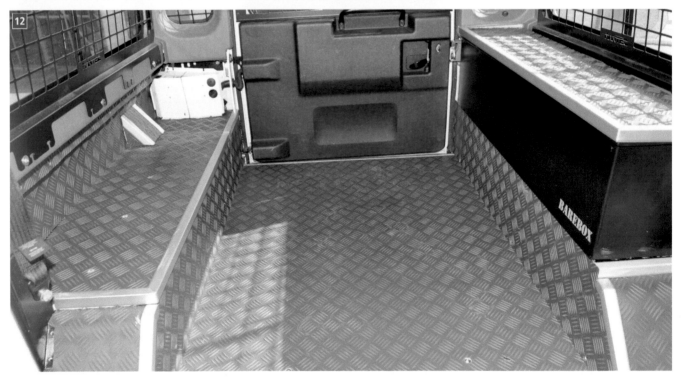

They're called BareBoxes, but ours aren't bare! This is how we fitted BareBoxes to my project Defender.

Mr BareBox himself, Steve Motts, came over to Ian Baughan's place near Tamworth, where we carried out most of the work involved in fitting a complete set of BareBox storage boxes to the back of my Defender. The majority of their boxes are supplied fully constructed but in an unfinished or 'bare' state – whence 'BareBox'. This gives customers the freedom to select their own finish. I chose to have mine powder-coated black and to have locks fitted, though I'm not convinced about the latter, as you'll see…

1 This is a BareCub steel cubby box, which is supplied powder-coated inside and out in satin black. The BareCub also features a removable cup holder, an internal coin/key tray and a radial security lock, complete with two keys. The box is first positioned and then drilled to pilot holes through the bottom of the box and into the steel plate beneath. You also drill through the front of the box and into the hollow box section that runs right across the front of the seat supports.

2 Each hole was then opened out to the correct size for a rivet nut – a threaded insert into which…

3 …fixing screws for both the inside of the BareCub…

4 …and the outer part, the front oddments tray…

5 …were inserted. The front screw is concealed by the cup-holder tray.

6 This is the oddments tray that sits inside the lid of the BareCub. As you can imagine, it's all inclined to rattle around a bit unless you add anti-rattle pads.

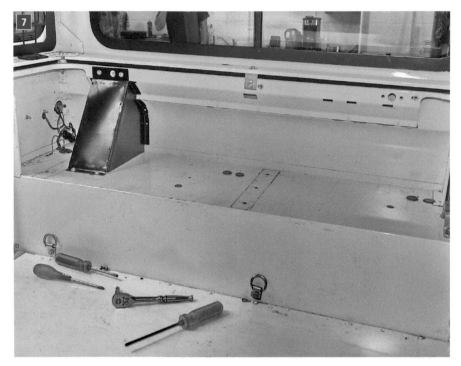

7 The main BareBox is shaped to fit the space above the wheel box on both 90s and 110s. In my case, there's a unique fuel filler for a tank slung beneath the wheel box. Earlier I'd fabricated and fitted the black cover for the filler hose, seen here.

8 On standard Defenders the fuel filler on the right side of the vehicle is much less obtrusive, but the principle of how to cut out for the fuel filler cover remains the same – except that on the standard version you'll need to cut less away than shown here.

9 Another probably unique modification was carried out to the aluminium rear lights cover. We reshaped it so that it protruded no further than the flange around the door frame, allowing the BareBox to go as far back as possible.

10 Steve demonstrated one of the smaller BareBoxes, and if you're not interested in completely filling the back of your vehicle you won't have to carry out the cutting and shutting shown here.

11 Here the longest BareBox is lifted into position…

12 …and the position of my filler hose cover marked out. A fairly generous amount of material was to be cut away to ensure the box would fit into position.

13 The measurements were transferred on to the back of the BareBox…

14 …and a hole was drilled in each corner.

15 The angle grinder was then used to 'join the dots'…

16 …and the redundant steel taken away before carefully smoothing all the ragged edges. The edges were painted later.

17 The BareBox slipped into place first time.

18 Here's how a rivet nut is compressed, gripping it into place.

19 This enables you to bolt down the box. In this instance the bolts doubled as fixings for the tank beneath, hence the reinforcing strap beneath the bolt heads.

20 Here's one of the smaller boxes in position on the other side of the vehicle. You can see how neatly it fits the available space, but you can also see how the key on top of the lock tends to bang against the side wall or sliding glass. You can't open the box without the key being in place, so that's a disadvantage.

21 And here's the finished rear end – the rest is a work in progress – showing the tremendously useful amount of space available using various lengths of BareBox.

The only other quibble I've got is that each lock requires its own key, which really could be a nuisance. However, these are minor criticisms and these extremely useful boxes are an invaluable addition to the rear of any Defender.

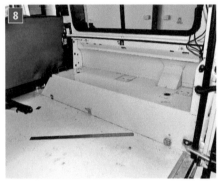

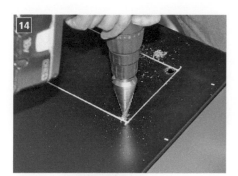

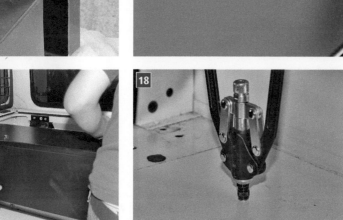

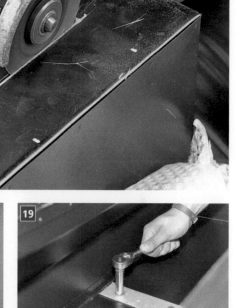

CHAPTER 6

Security

This is how one of the ultimate anti-theft devices can be fitted to your Land Rover.

My Defender DiXie is precious to me in more ways than one. Not only has it had a small fortune spent on it, but I'm also aware that it would be practically irreplaceable if it was ever stolen. So in addition to an alarm, I wanted a tracking system fitted. With more than 300,000 vehicles stolen every year, the UK is the worst-affected country in Europe.

I've had experience of CobraTrak before, because it's fitted to our caravan, and I know from first-hand experience just how friendly and efficient Cobra's customer liaison people are. You see, if your vehicle shows up on Cobra's system as possibly being stolen (for example, if you disconnect the battery and forget to tell them...) they get straight on the blower and tell you about it.

The main advantages of CobraTrak systems are:

- All are Thatcham accredited and recognised by the majority of leading insurers.
- They're all Sold Secure Approved (an important feature for caravans, as far as caravan insurers are concerned).
- You can normally expect to qualify for a discount on your insurance premium.
- They come with a three-year warranty.
- Your system can usually be transferred if and when you change your vehicle.

The CobraTrak First system detects unauthorised movement of a vehicle when the ignition is switched off (eg if the vehicle is towed away), and uses the latest GPS/GPRS/GSM technology to provide pinpoint accuracy to track a stolen vehicle.

Reassuringly, police liaison is conducted in local language through Cobra's network of secure operating centres across 36 European countries, Russia and South Africa. Every one of Cobra's operating centres is secured to Home Office standards against attack, which involves, among other things, being situated in a windowless, well-protected building.

1 CobraTrak's engineer discussed with me the type of wiring connections used. He's not the first engineer to have told me recently that some manufacturers don't allow the use of soldered connectors, claiming that their own approved crimped connectors are best. My personal view is that while crimped connectors might conceivably be best on Day One, what about several years down the line, after corrosion may have set in? And what about crimps that haven't been carried out perfectly in the first place? The engineer and I agreed that we prefer soldered connections. So work started with stripping and twisting cables...

2 ...then soldering them together.

3 Interestingly, Gary likes to wrap the soldered connection in plastic insulation tape...

4 ...followed by a layer of fabric tape, to match, he said, the installation's original wiring as far as possible.

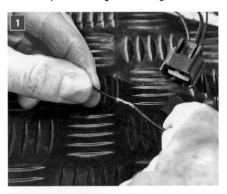

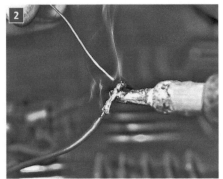

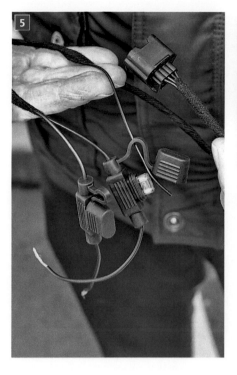

5 As with all electrical installations, the unit is safely fused before the installation is finally connected.

6 We can't, for obvious reasons, show you what the CobraTrak unit looks like, but I can assure you that it's even smaller than the shape shown here. It's installed covertly so that thieves have no way of even knowing that a tracking system is present. Since our first CobraTrak unit was installed the company has replaced both hardware and software with new versions. The latest version has integrated GSM/GPRS and

GPS antennae; a built-in LED for auto-diagnostic during installation; a waterproof housing (to IP67 standards), so there's no need to worry if you go wading; and an internal, rechargeable backup battery. In addition there's a high-sensitivity GPS receiver, a quad-band modem (including GPRS) and even a three-axis accelerometer sensor for movement/shock and crash detection. Impressive stuff!

7 An alternative system is CobraTrak First Mobile, which offers all the benefits of CobraTrak First but with the addition of having your vehicle position delivered directly to a map on your mobile phone or PDA, and the ability to self-set and un-set transport mode (if you want to move the vehicle on a trailer, for instance) or garage mode (when it goes into a workshop) via your mobile phone or PDA. The only downside is that there's a fixed annual subscription, without the option of being able to purchase a lifetime subscription.

ONE THIRD
of all vehicle thefts in Europe occur in the UK – the vehicle crime capital of Europe

£39K
The average value of a stolen vehicle fitted with **CobraTrak**

TEN
The level of accuracy in metres of the Cobra tracking software

NW
The UK regions reporting the highest levels of stolen vehicles
SE

92%
of vehicles fitted with CobraTrak were stolen **WITH THE KEYS**

23:00
the most common time of day for an vehicle to be stolen
06:00

50 50
the odds of a vehicle being recovered without CobraTrak

4.1
the average number of minutes taken for Cobra and the police to recover a vehicle

£150,000
the value of the most expensive vehicle recovered by Cobra UK in 2009 – a Lamborghini Gallardo

96%
Of all vehicles were recovered undamaged

36
The number of European countries with full Cobra service coverage

£1950
The LEAST valuable vehicle recovered by Cobra in 2009 – a Volkswagen Polo

£2.5bn
the value of vehicles stolen in the UK and not recovered in the last 3 years***

72hrs
the average time before a high value vehicle is shipped overseas

900
the number of vehicles stolen every day in the **UK**

24/7
Cobra Secure Operating Centres across Europe are manned round the clock 365 days a year

3yrs
the warranty on the CobraTrak hardware

180+
countries where the Cobra roaming SIM card operates

FURTHER UP THE RANGE
The next system up, in terms of features, is CobraTrak ADR, an automatic driver recognition system. The idea is that you carry a pocket-sized ADR card that communicates with the vehicle and 'allows' you to drive it. When you leave the vehicle the system automatically arms itself. If the vehicle is moved without the ADR card present, Cobra's secure operating centre is alerted instantly to a potential theft. This means that even if your vehicle is taken using your own keys, the theft is detected immediately.

CobraTrak 5 is the top-of-the-range system. It incorporates all the benefits of CobraTrak ADR, plus the added protection of Remote Ignition Lock. Remote Ignition Lock technology enables the police to authorise Cobra to send an alert to the vehicle and prevent the engine being restarted once it comes to a standstill. This significantly increases the chance of your vehicle being recovered undamaged, and can also help Police avoid high-speed pursuit of suspect vehicles.

These are the parts supplied, together with optional accessories, for the Visionaire Tracker:

A Main control box.
B Optional remote-control switch box.
C In-line fuses.
D Optional remote immobilisation relay.
E Wiring harness.
F Warning light (optional).
G Remote control (optional).
H Defender-specific bonnet catch (optional).
I Key-operated switch (optional).
J Waterproof key cover (optional).

The Land Rover Defender is now one of the most nicked (and most easily nickable) vehicles in the UK. They're usually stolen for parts, so the chances of ever seeing your Defender again should it be stolen are pretty remote. If you go in viciously – and thieves invariably do – a Defender can be stripped in no time at all, and once stolen it's a race against time to find it. So what can you do?

There's been a huge increase in the popularity of trackers in recent years and, as with so many other electronic goods, costs have fallen, so that trackers are becoming increasingly easy to afford. Unfortunately they all have a downside, depending on what you need from your tracker.

Some claim to do all the tracking for you and will alert you in the event of an apparent theft. These are expensive to buy and expensive to subscribe to. In addition, most can only be activated once you have a crime reference number. And by the time

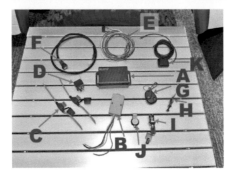

you have that your Defender is likely to be in a thousand pieces.

1 At the time of writing, the Visionaire tracker is the only one of its type known to this author. Its main features are:

■ It can alert you if the vehicle is moved, hotwired or started (even with its own keys), towed or lifted.
■ 24/7 access from any Internet PC or mobile phone.
■ It records mileage, journey times and speeds.
■ It can alert you if the vehicle is being tampered with, has the bonnet up, the power disconnected or a low internal battery, and has an optional panic alert.
■ The unit is 'live' at all times – you can log on and see it move live across the screen on Google Maps. Updates come through in two-second intervals when it's moving – all the time, not just when you tell it to.
■ Alerts can be sent to up to three people by SMS and/or email (email contains a map showing vehicle location).

■ It gives further information to the user – 12 months' history with snail trail.
■ You can 'share' the information displayed with others and remove that access when you wish.
■ You can fit the unit yourself, although we recommend it's fitted by a professional installer.
■ It comes with its data plan already in place so that all you need to do, once it's installed, is start using it. You don't have to wait while you set up a GPRS plan.
■ There's an internal back-up battery.
■ There are no subscription charges.

2 Ian Baughan of IRB Developments carried out the fitting. Obviously, you need an ignition feed as well as a permanent live. Not all of the mass of wiring shown here is relevant to this particular job – we were carrying out other work at the same time!

3 It's recommended that you install the wiring loom first in order to prevent shorting the system or incorrectly activating it. Once it's in place you simply connect the wiring to the unit and wait around five minutes for the device to configure itself.

4 This is the optional, extension GPS antenna, used if you want to bury the unit deep within the vehicle.

5 This is the 'panic button' which you can use to instantly get in touch with your selected contacts, in the event of a breakdown or accident for example. An optional warning LED can also be fitted, to remind you when the unit is armed.

Overall, fitting the device is quite straightforward, provided you have a certain degree of technical ability, and any competent vehicle electrician would find installation a doddle. Also, the people at Visionaire are on hand to guide you through the process if necessary.

The unit is of reasonably compact size, and interestingly Visionaire have developed several specific Land Rover locations that allow it to work perfectly while ensuring that it's very well concealed. The objective is that in the event of a theft, the Visionaire

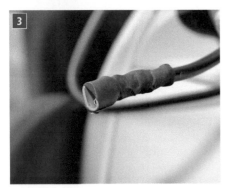

will remain undetected long enough to allow you to contact the Police and tell them where to start looking.

Incidentally, we don't think there's any problem with showing here what the unit looks like. Almost all tracker units have images that can be found online, and even if not, if a thief comes across the unit with a well-known tracker manufacturer's name on it they don't need to know what the unit looks like! And if they tampered with it you'd be alerted immediately.

SETTING UP

6 After entering your login username and password, you open the control panel.

7 This enables you to choose the parameters within which the tracker system sends its notifications. These include ignition on, tow alert, bonnet open, power loss, low internal battery, panic, speeding or aggressive driving, which can let you know if someone else has been driving your vehicle in an inappropriate manner.

8 This is the page for setting your preferred unit for distances, but there are a large number of tweaks that you can carry out to suit your own preferences.

9 A specially useful feature is that you can share the transmitted information with anyone else you choose who has a computer-based or mobile phone-based email address.

10 Having multiple user access could have a variety of uses. Visionaire told me about a young Defender owner who was exploring in Tunisia. His mother was watching his progress online and, having been given an itinerary in advance, knew he'd taken a wrong turning. She contacted him on his mobile phone and sent him off in the right direction before he got into trouble!

11 Previous events are recorded on a calendar, which enables you to go back to any day or trip during the previous 12 months. The calendar also shows each day's mileage and engine operating hours, with running totals.

12 Don't forget that you can also receive alerts and view the map and location information on a mobile phone. This can be great when you're away from your computer. And the device can alert you if your vehicle is started with stolen keys. Since the Government reports that 85% of cars in the UK are stolen using the original keys this is a useful feature, giving you a head start in locating the vehicle and engaging with the authorities to secure its speedy recovery.

13 If you want to you can set the system to send an email or message every time your Land Rover starts up. It means you receive a huge number of emails on occasion, but it's an option I've selected by default.

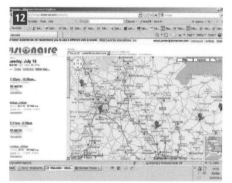

14 Being able to log every step of a trip has many other uses, including keeping a record of where you've been on a green-laning adventure. If you're at all familiar with computer maps you'll see that Google Maps are used for relaying location data. This has the huge advantage that you can take advantage of all the options available on Google Maps.

One remarkable feature I've discovered is that the tracker works even in an area that's too weak to receive or send a mobile phone call, such as where I live. Most reassuring!

CHAPTER 7

Comfort

Here's how you can make your Defender's screen vents work like those on a modern design of vehicle by fitting a DefenderVENT kit, produced by Danish specialists Wiberg & Wiberg. MM 4x4 show us how it's done.

Clearing a Defender windscreen when it's icy or misted-up has always been a combination of wiping and waiting. And as for those side windows, forget it! All of which can be a bit heart-stopping when you can't see where you're going. Or where you've been, or who's coming up from behind. Because, those misted-up side windows perfectly obscure the view through the door mirrors.

So I was delighted to hear about the DefenderVENT kit. Fitting it takes a few hours, but the work is straightforward enough, as you'll see here.

The kit consists of two side nozzles, two DefenderVENTS, a length of flexible hose (to be cut to length), two plastic hose clips, and installation instructions.

The manufacturers optimistically claim assembly time of one to two hours, but that depends on the model of Defender and the amount of 'stuff' that has to be

disconnected or dismantled for access.

Here's what's involved on the Td5-type Defender dash, as explained by the impressive skills of top Land Rover mechanic Andy at MM 4x4.

Be sure to disconnect the battery before starting work to avoid the risk of dashboard shorts. Make a note of any radio code and turn off your alarm to prevent it from sounding, if appropriate.

1 First the instrument panel surround has to be removed. You'll need a small screwdriver for the cross-head screws in the heater lever knobs. Be careful – they're easy to drop and lose!

TOP TIP
After removing the screws and knobs from the heater levers, we fitted the tiny screws back into the levers for safe keeping.

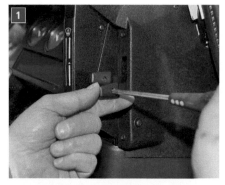

2 It's easy to get carried away and remove all the screws you can see in the area, even though only some of them need to be.

3 It's not exactly the end of the world if you take out more screws than necessary because no harm will be done...

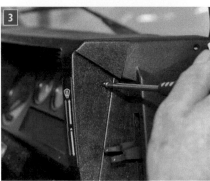

4 ...provided you make a note of which screws went where. And no, you almost certainly won't remember unless you keep some sort of record.

5 At the other end of the instrument panel, you don't need to remove the knob from the fan adjustment lever because it doesn't have to pass through a slotted hole, like the levers at the other end.

6 Note that other screws hold the fan adjustment block in position and don't need to be removed – it can stay where it is.

7 The instrument panel has to be freed before the end panel can be removed, because the former clips over the latter. You have to wiggle the cranked heater levers through the slot in the end panel.

8 At the passenger-end of the dash, you have to carefully lever out the push-in 'Land Rover' logo plate, which exposes an Allen-head screw holding the top of the end panel in position.

9 A bog standard cross-head screw has to be removed from the candy-floss material beneath it. This material is so soft that the thread often strips. I'm not even sure what useful purpose this screw serves...

10 ...because there are two pegs that push into sockets in the lower dash, thus retaining the dash end panel at its lower end. You have to lift upwards, sometimes quite sharply.

11 Now you can attack the screen vent trim. Take out the two screws. You'll need a stubby screwdriver because the windscreen is in the way of a longer one.

12 Then, remove the screws on the underside of the dashboard top...

13 ...ease the top rail up to see if you've missed anything, and when all fixings are clear lift the top rail away and remove it.

14 There are two more or less horizontal screws in the underside of the centre console. Note that we decided to leave the radio attached.

15 Now the top rail has disappeared you can see three more screws holding the centre console in place...

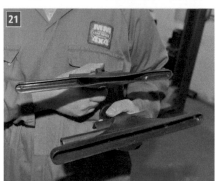

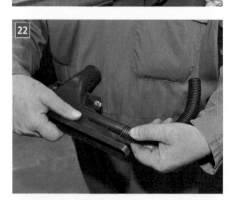

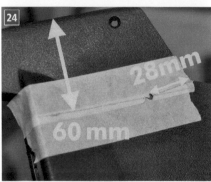

16 ...and when they're out, the whole centre console can be pulled forward. We left it there because all we needed to do was gain access, and this can be done with the centre console and radio just eased away.

17 Before you can remove the centre dash panel on this model you must unscrew the vent knobs and remove the fixing screws.

18 These screws are very obvious across the front of the panel, including the screw for the much shorter section on the driver's side.

19 With the longer centre dash panel eased forward we were able to get a screwdriver on the two screws (arrowed)...

20 ...that pass through the steel dash frame and into the two spire nuts (arrowed) on the body of the old vent. Here it's been slipped out of its air hose before removal.

21 Just look at the difference here! The original vent is at the top. Typically, the slot has partly closed up, as if the quality of the plastic is poor and/or the moulding process is faulty. The DefenderVENT (bottom) has a much larger opening and is made of much more rigid plastic. We switched the spire nuts from the lugs on the old vent to the new one. They just push off with a flat-blade screwdriver and push on to the new one.

22 We cut the hose to what we thought would be the right length, but note: don't do this! Instead, cut the supplied hose in half and cut it to length later. You'll see why in a mo. Anyway, you push one end of the hose over the outlet tube on the side of the new vent. You have to push really hard, working it over the raised area at the end of the tube.

23 No pipe clips are supplied but why risk the darned thing coming off again for the cost of a hose clip?

24 A side nozzle has to be fitted in each end panel. Positioning is tricky. Here's how we did it. Place masking tape on the driver's side end panel so that you can draw a line parallel with the top edge, 60mm down. You need to drill a pilot hole, positioned on this line, 28mm from the corner shown here.

25 If you don't have access to a square, you can use a piece of machine-cut card from the box in which the kit is supplied to establish a line 90° from the edge of the panel.

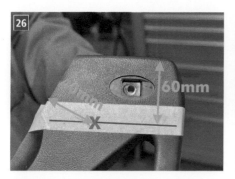

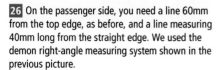

26 On the passenger side, you need a line 60mm from the top edge, as before, and a line measuring 40mm long from the straight edge. We used the demon right-angle measuring system shown in the previous picture.

27 As with the other end, you'll need to drill a small pilot hole, right through the steel strengthener inlaid into this panel.

28 Then we deviated from the supplied instructions again. Using a hole cutter, a slow cutting speed and plenty of Morris' cutting fluid, we drilled a 20mm hole in the position of the pilot hole.

29 The side vents each have a bulge on their ends (arrowed), but we felt this hindered rather than helped. The tube at the bulge measures 22mm but the main section of tube measures 20mm. So if you drilled a 22mm hole to allow the bulge to pass through, the tube would be loose. Instead we filed off the arrowed bulges to make the tubes parallel, which is why we made 20mm holes.

30 Muggins here then dropped a minor clanger. After cutting away part of the foam at the back of the end panel I decided to use Würth Bond & Seal PU sealant to bond the tube in position. Trouble was, Andy would need to push the hose on and couldn't avoid getting sealant all over his hands.

31 The new vent has been fitted on to the hose and screwed in place. This allows you to route the hose and cut it to length, leaving enough slack so that you can push it on to the vent.

32 So, the hose went on to the vent tube (it's a tight fit even without the bulge)...

33 ...and the supplied hose clips were used to clamp it in place.

34 We made sure the vent deflectors were both in the vertical position – it seems to be best – before offering up each end panel...

35 ...and reassembling the dashboard.

Once finished there's very little to show for your work except the certain knowledge that you've fitted OE-quality parts to improve one of your Defender's functions in a way that Land Rover certainly should have done – but didn't. And at the end of the day, correct function is what the Land Rover Defender is all about.

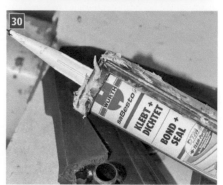

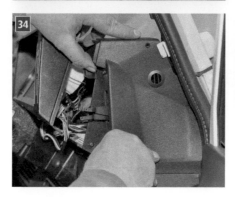

Cruise control once seemed like Space Age magic but it's a regular option on most new cars these days. In some ways, the slower Land Rovers are even better suited to cruise than nippier motor cars. And here's how you add it.

When you're doing a long haul on a motorway it can be difficult to maintain a steady speed without both your brain and your right foot going to sleep. I've been using cruise control on almost every modern vehicle I've owned for the last 30 years and I simply wouldn't be without it. Conrad Anderson have been fitting cruise controls for just about as long as I've been using them and really know their stuff. They're more than happy to fit cruise control for you or to sell you the parts to fit it yourself.

HOW IT WORKS
The vacuum actuator or electrically operated servo pulls (with the help of two solenoid valves and a cable) on the throttle cable, thus maintaining the desired set speed. The computer receives and interprets signals sent by the speed sensor, which it uses to regulate the servo. The command module is used to tell the computer at what speed to hold the vehicle and whether to increase or decrease the setting.

1 The cruise control system fitted to my project Land Rover Defender has an electrically operated solenoid, which is the only realistic option for diesel-engined vehicles. (You could tap into the vacuum pump, when fitted, but it's not ideal.) An alternative for petrol-engined vehicles is this vacuum-operated version.

2 Conrad Anderson also have different types of operating switch available. The two stalks shown here fit to the housing around the steering column while the optional memory switch can make your vehicle go to any one of three speeds that you've programmed into it. This is useful on a motorway run with a lot of roadworks where you need to keep to 50mph for a stretch before speeding up again later.

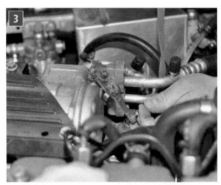

3 This is the throttle quadrant from the fuel pump on 300 Tdi-type engines. Td5 models have 'fly-by-wire' throttle operating systems with no cable between throttle pedal and injection pump. On these and similar later engines the cruise control simply plugs into the electronics.

4 The first attempt to attach a cable to the quadrant on my 2.8 TGV engine's injector pump involved grinding a flat on a redundant ball on the quadrant, centre-punching it…

5 …and attempting to drill a hole. But drat, the material was too hard!

6 Plan B was to weld a bracket to the quadrant into which a suitable cable nipple could be located.

7 As well as finding a location for the end of the cable inner, the cable outer also has to be located. When you get a suitable fixed bracket in just the right location…

8 …you thank your lucky stars and start drilling.

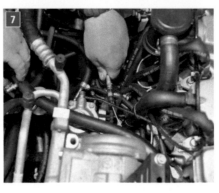

VACUUM OR ELECTRIC SERVO?

Conrad Anderson say that the reason they fit electric servos to the Defender range is because there's very little room above the pedal, and the vacuum actuator with it's fixed stroke of 38mm wouldn't fit. The electric servo GC55 has four different stroke lengths to choose from, done by means of two pulleys with two different internal diameters. They can therefore reduce the stroke length and the bracket length to attach to the pedal. They normally fit vacuum servos to diesels because they almost always have a vacuum pump, but electric servos to petrol-driven models.

9 You can then make a cable mounting…

10 …to be bolted to this conveniently situated engine bracket.

11 The standard clamp nuts on the end of the outer cable were then used to fix the outer in position.

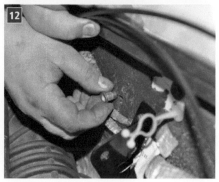

12 After a bit of head scratching, the best place for locating the electrical actuator servo was found to be the middle of the bulkhead. This is a hollow section so it's necessary to use rivnuts.

SERVO MOUNTING NOTES

The servo is best mounted inside the engine compartment, on to the vehicle body or a handy bracket. If mounting directly on to the bulkhead, use rubber mounting washers to lessen any transmitted noise. Never attach to the engine unit.

- The actuator should be mounted at least 30cm away from high-tension leads, such as distributor, coil, ignition leads or alternator. Keep it away from hot parts such as exhaust and radiator systems and also any moving parts.
- Keep the servo a minimum 30cm from high-tension wiring and major electrical power sources.
- Be sure the actuating cable will reach the throttle linkage without bending tighter than a 15cm (6in) radius.
- The mounting bracket may be attached to the actuator in one of four different positions.
- If aftermarket solid core spark plug wires are installed, make sure the flexible cable is mounted away from them.

In most instances where a vacuum system is used it's connected from the brake servo feed pipe. If a non-return valve is in the line, attach the T-piece between the NR valve and the pump.

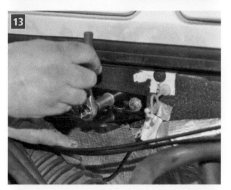

13 The correct size holes were drilled, and after fitting the rivnuts the actuator's mounting bracket was bolted into place.

14 Here you can see the two optional sizes of cable pull cam for the actuator. Note the difference in distance between the outside of the cam and the cable nipple fittings.

15 After calculating the amount of cable pull required, an appropriate sized cam was selected and fitted to the actuator shaft…

VACUUM-OPERATED SYSTEMS

When a system with a vacuum-operated actuator is fitted, the vacuum connection can be made with one of the three T-pieces supplied. If in doubt about the seal, always use a hose clip.

Vacuum connection on petrol engines

Locate a good non-restricted vacuum source from the intake manifold. Don't use a ported source such as the distributor advance or EGR vacuum regulator. On smaller engines the brake booster may be the only suitable source. To verify a good vacuum source unplug the hose while the engine is running. If the engine stalls or 'runs rough' then this is a good source to use.

Diesel engines with a vacuum pump

You're recommended to make the connection between the pump and the non-return valve on the brake servo feed pipe.

ACCELERATOR CABLE ARRANGEMENTS

The stroke of the servo cable has to be between 38mm and 50mm with petrol engines, and 38mm to 42mm with diesel engines. The setting of the servo cable should be done with a warm engine, to prevent any interference with cold-starting settings and idling speeds.

BEWARE! Always ensure the smooth operation of the accelerator mechanism by testing using the pedal, and by hand at the actuating arm. Check that neither accelerator cable nor servo cable can become obstructed. If there's a stationary contact or kick-down switch behind the accelerator pedal, the servo cable must be directly connected to the accelerator pedal.

16 …before slotting the cable in place…

17 …and fitting the actuator to its bracket.

18 Having shown how to fit the cable to work off the injector pump quadrant, Conrad Anderson went on to show how, with an automatic gearbox, it's necessary to connect the cable to the throttle pedal. A bracket had to be welded to the throttle pedal assembly (arrowed)…

19 …to secure the outer cable, while the inner was attached to another bracket welded to the throttle pedal lever.

20 With pedal finally connected and pull lengths correct, the actuator cover was finally fitted.

21 To connect the operating lever, the Defender's steering column shroud was removed…

22 …and a suitable power source was established.

23 Fortunately the standard grommets in the Defender's bulkhead are ideal for passing additional electrical cables through.

24 Electrical integrity is all-important, and for that reason all the joints were soldered rather than crimped.

WARNINGS FROM CONRAD ANDERSON

- Do not use a test lamp or bulb. Always use an LED tester, or multimeter.
- If you disconnect the vehicle battery, be aware of the possible loss of radio codes, computer settings, alarm systems and other transient electronic data.
- To ensure that the engine doesn't over-rev when changing gear, it's *essential* that the clutch switch is installed, to cut the cruise control when the clutch pedal is depressed.

25 On vehicles without electronic speedometers, a rather crude magnet and pickup device has to be fitted to a drive shaft or prop shaft. However, with the Td5-type of speedometer a speed pickup can be soldered to the relevant cable on the back of the unit.

SPEED SENSOR CONNECTIONS

Manual transmission vehicles without a coil (generally speaking, diesels) must use the automatic transmission method for speed sensing and will require a mechanical clutch switch or over-rev protector.

Automatic transmission vehicles, early models: vehicles that don't have an electronic control module (ECM) will need to use magnet sensing on the drive shaft, or order a speed pulse generator. Later vehicle models may use magnet sensing, or you'll need to order a speed pulse generator, or connect directly to the electronic control module (ECM) speed signal wire, if the vehicle has one.

More information is provided in the comprehensive instructions supplied by Conrad Anderson.

26 After the position of the operating shift has been established, a hole can be drilled in the steering column shroud...

27 ...and the operating shift can be offered up...

28 ...and fixed in position.

29 There's quite a lot of adjustment available and you may have to fit and remove several times until you achieve the angle and position you want.

30 Mounting the command module: after routing the wires, press home the six wires into the eight-way plug, paying attention to the colours and the pin direction, then plug into the corresponding socket on the cruise wiring loom.

31 Surplus cabling should be carefully wrapped and cable tied before being hidden from view. It's worth making a note in your handbook of the location of the in-line fuse.

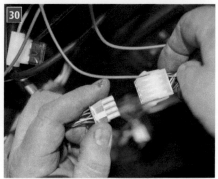

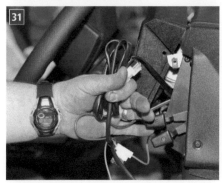

32 There's a choice of two different covers for the memory control. You'll want to sleeve the wires that come out of the top of the unit to improve their appearance.

33 The cruise control's paddle switch looks neat and fits in well with the Land Rover's switchgear. In this location it's easy to operate and difficult to confuse with the horn and indicator stalk.

It's fitted, it's finished, and I use it regularly. Great result!

Since my 300 Tdi Defender DiXie started out as a Third World export spec vehicle, it lacked any sort of soundproofing. Here Noisekiller's Steve Bithell demonstrates how you can have a quieter Defender without ear defenders.

1 Depending on the model of vehicle you own and amount of soundproofing you're looking for, the Noisekiller kit consists of mostly pre-cut sheets, some of them self-adhesive, with the option of adding extra sheets that you can cut yourself. Full sheets measure 2m x 1.2m.

2 Self-adhesive acoustic mats are of class 'O' fire-rated acoustic foam sandwiched inside two self-adhesive rigid damping sheets for maximum noise reduction. The damping sheets help to block road noise, exhaust noise and vibrations, while the acoustic foam absorbs frequencies that pass through the damping sheet. Flat sheets are ideal for the seat box, though you might need to trim according to positions of clips.

3 Inside, pre-cut sections quieten the bulkhead. That's factory sound deadening at the top, fitted by Nene Overland. Thanks for trying, Land Rover, but it's a bit minimal!

4 There are more sections for the footwells...

5 ...pre-cut to fit driver's and passenger's sides.

6 The gearbox tunnel was removed from my vehicle at this stage but it's all the same. You mark and cut out where the fixings bolts go...

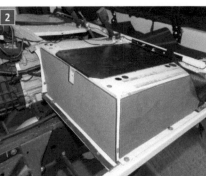

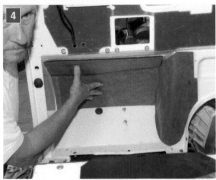

7 ...peel off the protective covering to expose the self-adhesive backing...

8 ...and glue down, starting from the top and doing your best to make a flat sheet bend around three-dimensional curves.

MAKING IT STICK

There's a lot of misunderstanding about what's needed to make self-adhesive panels stick. This applies to all self-adhesive panels, not just those under the bonnet.

9 The undersides of bonnets become especially mucky after a while and just wiping off the muck WON'T be enough. You also need to remove all traces of invisible grease and, where polish or releasing fluid might have found a home, silicones too. Clean off heavily encrusted areas with degreaser followed by a high concentration of detergent in warm water.

Follow up with a degreasing agent such as bodywork panel-wipe, methylated spirit or surgical spirit. Petrol is not only dangerous, it's also greasy, as is white spirit, though to a lesser extent.

Use spirits outdoors, in a well-ventilated area and away from all flames and other sources of ignition.

When peeling off the backing paper you have to hold the panel, obviously – so make sure your fingers are clean too.

10 With the bonnet off the vehicle, the first of the foil-covered under-bonnet panels is accurately positioned and pressed on from the top downwards, to exclude air pockets.

11 Then a paint roller is used to help the adhesive make even contact.

12 You then work across the bonnet until all areas are covered.

13 We cut pieces of Noisekiller's non-adhesive acoustic floor mat and used contact adhesive (such as Bostik) to glue to this bulkhead section normally covered by the front wing. If you can't get at it because the wings are in place, don't worry; it's not critical.

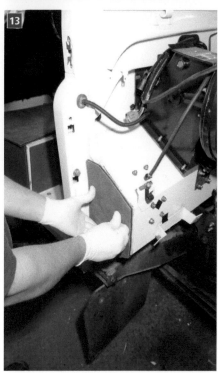

14 Noisekiller's barrier mat is a heavy-duty polymer damping sheet with a self-adhesive backing and foil facing. It's particularly useful around bulkheads, wheel arches, doors, under spare wheels and on the rear wings, and is used extensively to enhance the bass sound quality of rear sound systems and to block out noise and vibrations from exhausts. Unfortunately there's no ready-made panel for the engine side of the bulkhead so I made a template out of a sheet of cardboard. In practice there's a lot to be said for this approach because of the huge variety of fixtures and fittings to be found on different Defenders' bulkheads.

15 Barrier mat is easy to shape, making it perfect for the bulkhead. Its foil finish and cellular structure also help to keep excess heat from the engine out of the passenger compartment.

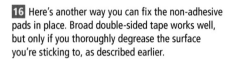

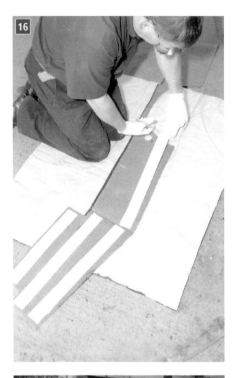

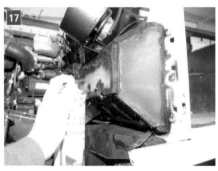

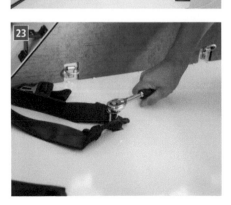

16 Here's another way you can fix the non-adhesive pads in place. Broad double-sided tape works well, but only if you thoroughly degrease the surface you're sticking to, as described earlier.

17 Aerosol spray contact adhesive can also work well provided there's no risk of overspray on to important surrounding panels or components.

18 We really went to town on the bulkhead and...

19 ...in conjunction with the bonnet soundproofing, engine noise is massively reduced, which is especially noticeable when the bulkhead vent flaps are open. Replacement foil can be stuck down with contact adhesive.

20 For that extra touch of luxury, you'll want to do the rear of the vehicle. These are the ready cut-out parts prior to fitting, again made of A-class 'O' fire-rated acoustic foam sandwiched inside two rigid damping sheets. They're usually used on the floor surface and along the sides of transmission tunnels, such as under the existing carpets.

21 Slots were cut out where the tie-down eyes were fitted.

22 Then the backing paper was peeled off and the foam sheet stuck to the vertical face of the wheel box before the paint roller was used again to achieve maximum adhesion.

23 When rear seat belts are fitted, you have to disconnect them first.

24 We laid down the floor mat and felt through it for the seat belt mounting positions. These were marked out with tailor's chalk before cutting through with a sharp craft knife.

25 The best way of attaching the panels that go behind the seats is to cut and remove...

26 ...half of the backing paper, to reduce the risk of the pad sticking where you don't want it to before inserting the pad, peeling off the remaining backing paper then sticking it down thoroughly as before.

27 First mark the locations of the rear seat bases and the seatbelt mounts...

28 ...and measure their positions side-to-side...

29 ...before marking all the cut lines.

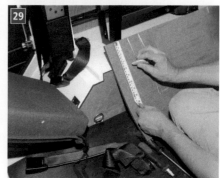

30 Remove the pad from the vehicle and cut it carefully on a cutting board. Those of us who are less experienced should use a straight edge to cut against.

31 Then remove the backing paper and stick down the pad.

32 Steve was concerned (needlessly, as it happened) about fouling the rear seats, so used thinner soundproofing material in this location. Obviously, this only applies to Station Wagon vehicles.

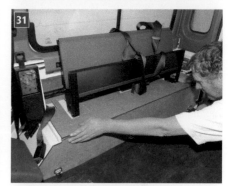

33 However, the rear seats did require the soundproofing to be cut away where the seat frames rest against the floor, otherwise the safety catches won't locate correctly.

34 An acoustic pad was plopped on the rear floor with thinner sections on the outer edges. Both the rear floor...

35 ...and the rear load area are covered by the original rubber mat.

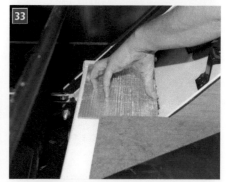

There's one more product that hasn't been fitted here but which I've tried in the past and can thoroughly recommend: Noisekiller Lead Sandwich. This is a sheet of lead sandwiched inside two layers of class 'O' fire-rated acoustic foam with a self-adhesive backing. The lead layer acts as a barrier to sound and the two layers of foam absorb the airborne sounds that have been blocked. It's blooming heavy, but you place it over the top of the engine and/or the transmission and you'll be surprised how much noise it cuts out.

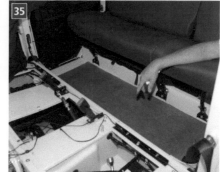

I can thoroughly recommend the use of a Noisekiller soundproofing kit. It would be foolish to think it's going to turn the sound levels inside a Defender into those of a modern Range Rover, but the difference is enough to make journeys far less tiring, normal conversations possible and – most importantly – to allow me to listen to Test Match Special on the radio.

Elite Automotive Systems were suppliers of air conditioning to Land Rover for many years and also specialise in smaller run installations, such as for military vehicles and Morgan cars. Indeed, Elite used to take delivery of new Land Rovers from the factory, fit the a/c and ship them back again. But when the new owners came along, it was, in the words of Elite themselves, ta-ta to the contract. So managing director Paul Miller came up with the idea of supplying units direct to enthusiasts as well as to specialist Land Rover parts suppliers such as Bearmach. My Defender DiXie went to Elite to receive one of their user-friendly kits.

First, a word about 'gassing' the installation, because it's something that you emphatically can't do yourself – there's the difficulty of getting the correct gas, the need for specialist equipment to create a partial vacuum in the system before inserting the gas, and the all-important health and safety plus environmental issues to consider. But *nil desperandum*; there are loads of places around that will do this work for you.

It's important that you follow the instructions supplied by Elite when fitting one of these kits. They contain vital safety information, as well as the correct torque settings.

1 Elite's engineer removed my KBX grille to start fitting the extremely comprehensive set of parts. Two really great things about this kit are the 'factory' dashboard assembly and the compact Elite condenser components, which mean you get to retain the standard grille instead of having to fit an extended one and don't have to worry about a winch if you've had one fitted. Incidentally, it's also worth pointing out that contrary to appearances this a/c panel doesn't affect legroom. It looks as if it's going to get in the way of your knees or your feet, but in practice it's no bother at all.

2 After removing the grille, the surround's bottom bolts were removed...

3 ...followed by the top ones. The grille surround was then temporarily removed.

4 With the surround out of the way, the bonnet slam panel and supports were unbolted...

5 ...and laid carefully on top of the engine with release cable still attached.

6 In order to remove the surround, the radiator top brackets had been detached. Bear with us; there's a story here!

7 Next attention was turned to the condenser radiator and fan assembly.

8 We lifted first one side of the radiator and slipped the condenser mounting bracket over the mounting pin, and then did the same on the other side. The radiator hoses remained attached and no draining-down was required.

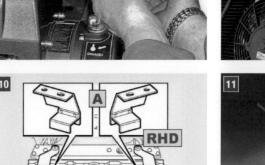

9 The condenser top brackets simply slide on to the top of the frame and lined up with the holes for the radiator top bracket bolts.

10 The 300 Tdi's LHD version is similar to the RHD shown here but the pipes (B) will come in from the other side. The slam panel supports need the supplied spacers to be fitted (C) so that the support tubes clear the condenser radiator.

11 In our case, one spacer was added on the left and two were needed on the right. There are three spacers in the kit.

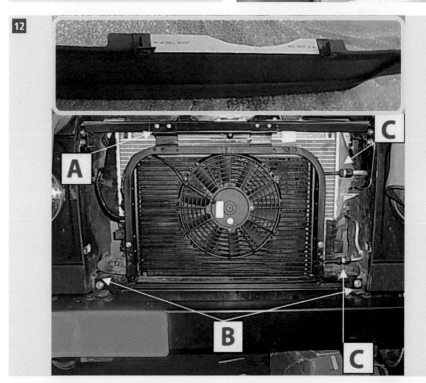

12 The Td5's condenser has a free-standing frame. Here's how it's fitted:
- Remove the bonnet latch anti-tamper bracket from the slam panel by carefully drilling out the four rivets.
- Adapt the top panel (inset) using the template supplied with the kit.
- Bolt to the slam panel at the top (A), via in-built brackets.
- Bolt the lower to the chassis rails mounts at the bottom (B).
- Refit the bonnet latch anti-tamper bracket to the slam panel along with the condenser upper mounting brackets, ensuring the upper brackets are slid over the condenser frame using the four rivets supplied in the kit.
- The pipework (C) comes past the coolant radiator in a similar way to the 300 Tdi.

13 This is the rear view of the factory-fit dashboard assembly. It contains the fans, ducting and electrical control gear.

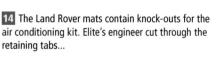

14 The Land Rover mats contain knock-outs for the air conditioning kit. Elite's engineer cut through the retaining tabs...

15 ...and removed the circles of mat and the body grommets from beneath. They *nearly* line up! Two new grommets come with the Elite kit. Lubricate them with washing up liquid (*not* grease – it damages some types of rubber) to help the grommets go in and the dash panel tubes to be inserted into them later.

16 You have to temporarily remove the speakers and permanently remove the heater outlet elbows.

17 The two outer speaker screw holes are used for mounting the outer ends of the a/c panel and have to be drilled out to 6.5mm ready to take the 6mm bolts supplied.

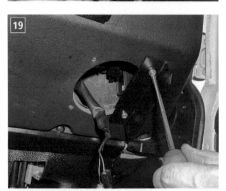

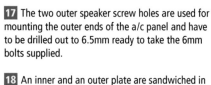

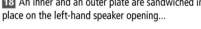

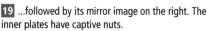

18 An inner and an outer plate are sandwiched in place on the left-hand speaker opening...

19 ...followed by its mirror image on the right. The inner plates have captive nuts.

20 At this stage we test-fitted the a/c panel. You need a helper to align the panel with the dash while holding one end in position. You also need to be sure that the panel is located in such a way that the gear stick and handbrake lever both clear it. Holding the panel end tightly against the bracket, we used the holes in it to drill pilot holes before lightly inserting each pair of fixing screws.

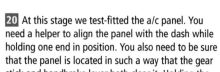

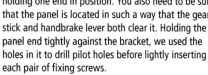

21 An extra-long 5.5mm drill and fixing screw are provided with the kit.

22 After we'd used the drill...

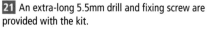

23 ...we added the fixing screw but didn't tighten it right up at this stage. Being happy about the fit of the a/c panel, we removed it again.

24 Though it wasn't strictly necessary to do it at this stage, we bolted the two relays to the supplied bracket...

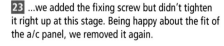

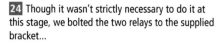

25 ...before screwing the bracket to a suitable location on the bulkhead (top arrow). Also, note the correct location of the large grommet where it protrudes through the footwell.

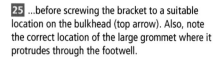

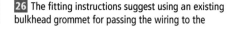

26 The fitting instructions suggest using an existing bulkhead grommet for passing the wiring to the

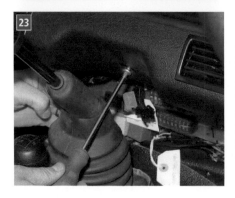

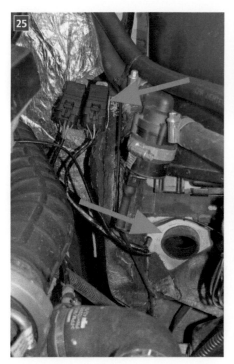

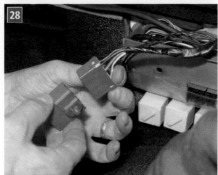

interior of the vehicle. But as all Land Rover owners will know, no two seem the same, and ours didn't have a grommet where we needed one. A fresh hole was drilled.

27 After removing the fuse box cover, pliers were used to pinch the clip...

28 ... holding the factory-fitted spare socket for connecting the a/c wiring loom found in later vehicles.

29 The wires from the relays in the engine bay have been passed through the hole we'd drilled (we'd stripped the plug so that each individual wire could be passed through, then reassembled the plug inside the vehicle), and you can see the white plug from the relays in the footwell. The new kit comes with a Y-piece section of loom. There's the white connector that plugs into the relays and a brown one for the a/c connector on the vehicle, which then leaves a 'spare' brown connector for plugging in the new a/c panel.

30 Then the dash panel was refitted and permanently screwed it into place. Before doing so it's worth checking that the heater outlets on the a/c panel are properly aligned. Ours had slipped out of position slightly and this would have reduced the hot air flow in winter.

31 The final job on the dash panel was to reconnect the speakers and screw them into position on the new panel.

32 With the supplementary dash panel fitted, the next job was to fit the compressor to the 300 Tdi engine. This involves fitting this additional tensioner assembly for the air conditioning belt. The slotted plate replaces the timing chest cover and the pulley is the smooth one of the two supplied. The black disc is a dust cover.

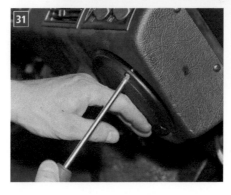

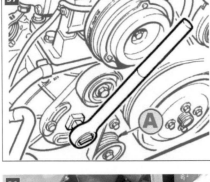

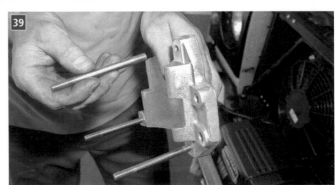

33 A quick way of relieving the tension on the existing belt is to use a long lever on the tensioner pulley (a quick-fix method that is/was once used in the factory, it seems).

34 The old belt is removed.

35 Off came the cover plate (bottom), and the pulley was bolted to the new adjuster plate to the recommended torque.

36 Getting at the pulley with the adjuster in place is a pig so you must be sure to tap its tight-fitting dust cap into place *before* hand tightening the adjuster bolts to the engine.

37 The other pulley supplied with the kit (A) is ribbed and is fitted to the engine timing chest with the M10 x 30mm bolt supplied. So how do you install its tight-fitting dust cap, eh?

38 The long lever was used again, and by tapping and pushing it the cover was made to click fully home.

39 The compressor will fit into an aluminium cradle. The three studs supplied have to be screwed in, shortest-thread first.

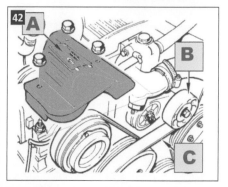

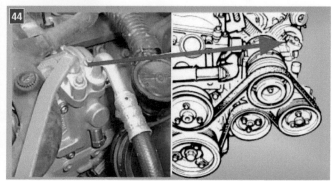

40 The cradle is bolted to the engine using the four supplied bolts with the two studs nearest the engine. The throttle cable bracket can be refitted, if it's had to be removed. The compressor is slid on to the three studs.

41 Next the new belt was slipped into position, making sure the grooves in the belt and the ribbed bottom pulley were aligned.

42 But before tightening the tensioner (B) on the belt (C), the three flange nuts on the compressor must be torqued down. The compressor cover (A) fits on to the three mounting studs. See the illustration in Step 37 for the way a half-inch drive torque wrench is used in the square hole in the tensioner to tension the belt to between 33Nm and 36Nm before tightening the three M8 bolts holding the tensioner tight.

43 All the plugs and sockets on the wiring loom have unique connections so they can't be confused.

44 This shows the different location of the Td5 engine's compressor – on the other side of the engine to the 300 Tdi.

45 The latest Puma-engined Defenders also have an Elite kit available, and this shows the compressor fitted to that particular power unit.

46 Back to the 300 Tdi. The next component to be fitted was the dryer (or 'receiver/dryer') to the left-side (passenger-side on RHD models) chassis rail, just ahead of the suspension bump stop. It's marked with 'IN' and 'OUT' pipe positions.

47 On Td5 models the dryer fits inside the engine bay, next to the intercooler hoses (R = RHD models) or to the front right-hand chassis (L = LHD).

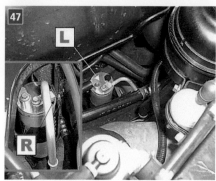

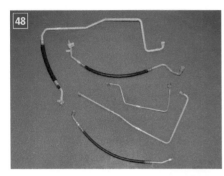

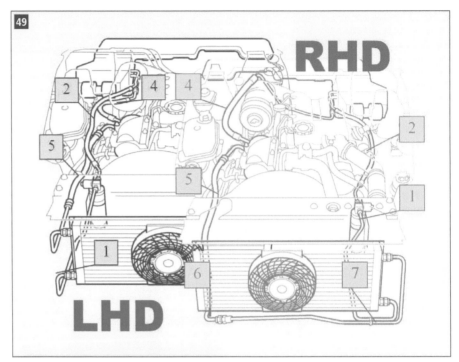

RHD

LHD

48 Now all the components were in place, all the aluminium pipes to be fitted were laid out.

49 Each set of instructions sets out clearly where each pipe run should go. However, these runs were designed with factory-build in mind, and – especially bearing in mind the way in which extras and accessories have often been fitted – you'll probably need to bend the rules (or at least the pipes) to some extent.

50 This flexible pipe runs from the compressor to the condenser radiator. Feeding it through was something of a challenge!

51 The evaporator is built into the under-dash assembly and the pipe fitting points appear through a hole in the passenger-side footwell on the engine side. You first peel off the self-adhesive protective cover...

52 ...then offer up and fit the two pipe ends. The connectors locate with push-in stubs and O-rings, and it's important that they line up *precisely* before you tighten the fixing bolts. You usually have to bend the pipes in order to achieve perfect alignment.

53 Note that all O-rings must be lubricated with PAG oil, as used on air conditioning systems, before inserting connectors into place. It doesn't seem that any is included with the kit so you'll need to get hold of some from an a/c specialist.

54 At the compressor pump, there are two plastic blanking plugs that have to be unbolted and removed before the pipes can be aligned and fitted.

55 This particular condenser fitting had a roll pin in it but there was no corresponding hole in the condenser, so we simply extracted it with pliers.

56 With the front pipes in position, we prepared to fit them to the condenser radiator.

57 When tightening pipe unions – and especially when screwing on to a component with fixed threaded stub – always use two spanners, one to grip the fixed hexagon. If you don't there's a real risk of twisting the soft aluminium union right out and ruining the component or pipe.

58 Some pipe clips are provided, such as this double clip that holds the pipes together. If you want to avoid rattling noises, spend some time clipping pipes securely into place so that they don't rub on fixed bodywork.

59 The condenser on the Td5 has its own self-contained frame that fits direct to the bodywork (A). These are the RHD version's pipe connectors (B).

60 And this is the system used on Puma-engined Defenders.

61 You'll have noticed how vehicles with a/c appear incontinent. It's because they extract moisture from the interior and deposit it on the ground. This is the drain hose that fits to the evaporator and passes through the floor, under the dash. I asked for a pipe clip to be added because I've encountered these pipes being accidentally kicked off, which then leaves water inside the vehicle.

62 The fan wiring was connected and the cable carefully clipped in position.

63 The kit includes an anti-theft device for fitting to the lock assembly. My 2006-built vehicle had one as standard, but if yours doesn't this is a useful mod. It stops someone levering open your bonnet catch with a screwdriver through the grille.

64 Naturally, Elite have their own in-house gas charging system. First, the system is checked for gas tightness using dry air, then a partial vacuum is created in the system, drawing out air and moisture, and a/c gas is introduced.

65 The engine was run once charging was complete and, though the temperature on the outside was in the high 20s, this electronic thermometer showed that the air coming from the a/c grille was a lowly 7°C.

66 Incidentally, in my case, the handbrake knob caught on the new a/c fascia. Even though there was a cut-away, the handbrake didn't line up with it. The solution was a typical Land Rover one – I pushed the handbrake lever sideways until it did line up, and now everything's fine. I've even got more sideways legroom than before!

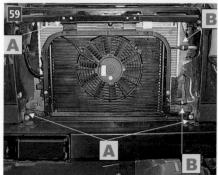

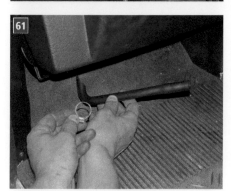

Here we see how an Eberspächer II Hydronic D5W S engine pre-heater was installed in DiXie.

Eberspächer's system has the advantage of pre-heating the passenger compartment as well as the engine, using the vehicle's own fuel as well as its own engine coolant system. This makes starting easier, protects the engine against the rapid wear that takes place when an engine is running cold, saves fuel and, according to Eberspächer, is kinder to the environment Other optional benefits include:

■ Warm air distribution using the vehicle's own air vents.
■ Heating started by timer, radio remote control or telephone.
■ Pre-cooling possible in summer.

The main picture shows most of the components used in this particular installation. Reading roughly from left to right, and ignoring the peripheral pipes, hoses, brackets and wiring looms supplied with the kit, the main components are EasyStart Mini Timer control unit, fuel pump, water pump, hydronic heater unit and EasyStart remote control kit.

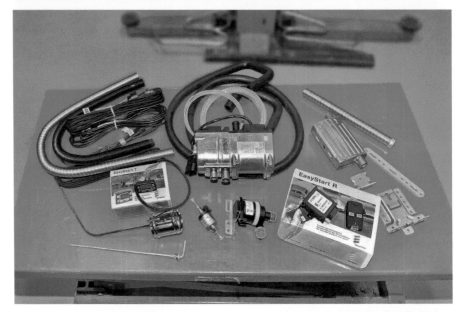

1 The Easystart Mini Timer control unit has to go somewhere on the dash. My vehicle was fitted with a Raptor dash panel. The self-adhesive template supplied was located there and drilled as instructed.

2 With its own self-adhesive backing paper peeled off the timer was stuck down, screwed into position, and the cover cap clipped into place.

3 The Eberspächer Defender kit is produced primarily for Td5 models and these are the brackets...

4 ...the lower one of which fits on these two M6 studs under the fan matrix. You have to cut off the holder bracket foot. (Picture courtesy of Eberspächer.)

5 On my (originally) 300 Tdi version, we decided to use the bracket that secures the inner wing. Jon Jennings, Eberspächer UK's sales engineering manager, who was overseeing the project, fabricated this plate and bolted it into place...

6 ...ready to take the dedicated mounting bracket on to which the heater unit has to be mounted.

7 This shot shows how the Hydronic unit fits neatly in position in the left-hand side of the engine bay.

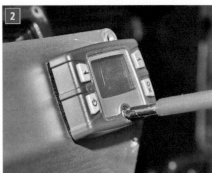

8 The next problem was deciding where to mount the water pump. Eberspächer provide an option for mounting the pump bracket on the side of the heater body, and in our case this proved to be the perfect location.

9 However, water hose stubs sticking straight up out of the top cover were going to cause a problem, so it was unscrewed and clipped off…

10 …the hose stub retaining clips were carefully broken off (the only way of removing them)…

11 …and the optional right-angle stubs supplied with the kit were fitted along with their new O-rings and replacement retaining clips.

12 You have to set the angle of each water stub before screwing the top down because they clip into place and can't be swivelled later.

13 On most Defenders installation of the cooling system pipe work is quite simple, as shown here. The coolant hoses supplied are correct for the Td5 engine but these can easily be cut and adapted for use on the earlier engines.

14 Td5 one-way valve from radiator to header tank: there's a black nylon 8mm OD expansion pipe from the top of the radiator to the header tank. When the engine cools down air is introduced into the top of the engine, and when the pre-heater switches on, air goes straight to the heater water pump.
    To prevent this from happening, Eberspächer install a one-way valve to the black nylon pipe on the flow from the engine to the header tank. This prevents air entering the top of the engine when the engine cools down but allows water expansion from the engine. The valve is included in the Defender Td5 dedicated heater kit. (Picture courtesy Eberspächer.)

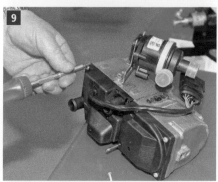

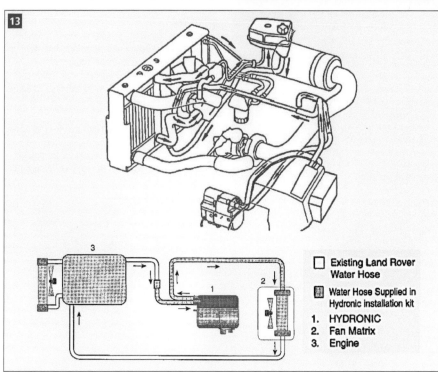

Existing Land Rover Water Hose

Water Hose Supplied in Hydronic installation kit

1. HYDRONIC
2. Fan Matrix
3. Engine

15 My hoses already had T-pieces fitted to them because of the engine's veg oil conversion. We clamped off the heater and adjacent pipes, removed and cut pipes as required…

16 …and plumbed the Hydronic unit into the heater hose circuit.

17 On Td5-engined Defenders the water feed hose running from the engine to the fan matrix should be taken off at the fan matrix and routed to the Hydronic. (Picture courtesy Eberspächer.)

18 Having found a route for the flexible stainless steel exhaust pipe…

19 …we fitted these heatproof silicone rings, sliding them into position over the exhaust pipe so they protected potentially vulnerable components that had been identified along the exhaust pipe's route.

20 For now the silencer has been fitted just behind the mudflap but it's going to have to be moved in future so that it doesn't hang vulnerably lower than the bottom of the chassis rail.

21 This is where Eberspächer recommend mounting the silencer on Td5 models.

22 There's also a combustion air inlet hose. It pulls in cold air, of course, so it's easier to locate than the exhaust. You just need to make sure that nothing can easily drop or be pulled into the open end of the hose, that the hose points away from the vehicle's airstream and that the inlet is as high as reasonably possible to prevent water ingress.

23 There's a fuel pickup pipe supplied with the kit that can be fitted at the filler neck on Td5 models. You can't break into the fuel line as with 200 and 300 Tdi models, because unlike them the fuel line is pressurised.

24 Eberspächer instructions showing where to cut the fuel filler pipe to enable fitment of the dedicated Td5 fuel pickup pipe say 'Cut rubber pipe at line. Secure with 2 off 50 to 70 mm clips'. (Picture courtesy Eberspächer.)

25 Jon made the important point that the fuel hoses supplied with the kit, if cut with side-cutters, will flatten (inset, arrow), so you should use purpose-made cutters to ensure that the full bore of the pipe is retained.

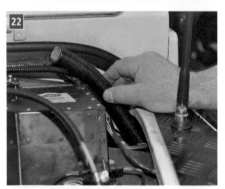

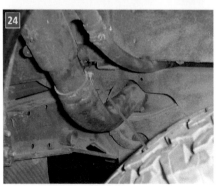

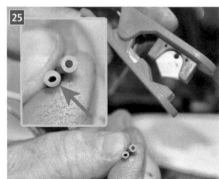

26 There's a choice of straight or angled fuel hose connectors for the fuel metering pump, depending on its location. In this instance diesel was picked up from the fuel line adjacent to the pedal box, so the fuel pump was located on a bracket fitted there, mounted at a 15° to 35° angle.

27 The other end of the fuel line was fitted to the stub on the top of the heater unit.

28 Before finally routing the fuel pipe and holding it in position with cable ties, it was sheathed with the convoluted split hose supplied with the kit.

29 You have to fit the Hydronic relay base next to the fuses holder within the battery box under the passenger seat. An alternative position for the relay base and fuses is next to the fan matrix, on the front bulkhead under the bonnet. Fit the relay into the base.

30 The instructions tell you to find the route of the black and black/violet wires to the fan matrix under the bonnet. Cut the violet/green wire going to the Land Rover two-way plug, close to the fan motor. Fit terminals and housings to the violet/green wire and connect the black and black/violet wires from the Hydronic loom as shown. (Picture courtesy Eberspächer.)

31 With the loom connected into the Land Rover wiring circuit, it only remains to connect the heater unit to the newly installed loom using the plug and socket provided.

32 Similarly, another branch from the loom is routed over to the fuel metering pump and plugged into the pump connector.

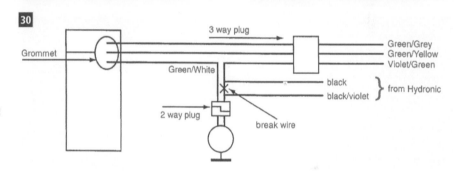

33 Apparently, not many people go for this option but I think it's of tremendous benefit. It's a remote control unit that you carry on your key fob with a receiver unit built into the vehicle. The remote has a stunning 1km range (in open line of sight, though much less in a built-up area) and I've already found it invaluable for firing up the Hydronic before I get to a car park or without even having to step outside the house.

34 After a couple of dummy start-ups to pump fuel through to the unit, the Eberspächer Hydronic fired up for the first time and almost instantly began heating the coolant. When a unit of this type first fires up there's inevitably a small amount of smoke and steam given off as the new furnace clears its throat.

There's no doubting the superb quality of this Eberspächer equipment. In warmer weather it means that my engine is up to operating temperature almost immediately and therefore operating at full efficiency, and in colder weather the heater is immediately capable of producing warm air to defrost my toes and demist the windscreen.

It's worth pointing out that because these heaters are integrated in the engine's cooling water system the Hydronic's programmer is capable of turning on the heater fan to blow warm air into the interior through the air vents, should you want to.

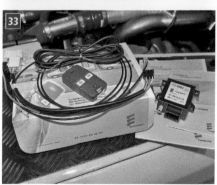
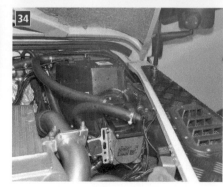

It freezes hard in winter in the Atlas Mountains, as Moroccan trekkers will tell you. It freezes hard in Headingley, Hereford and Hemel Hempstead too, as Land Rover drivers with numb fingers will agree. One solution is to use a diesel-powered cockpit heater, such as the well-known Webasto Air Top 2000, more the sort of thing frequently fitted to motorhomes. Here's how we fitted a Webasto to my Defender DiXie.

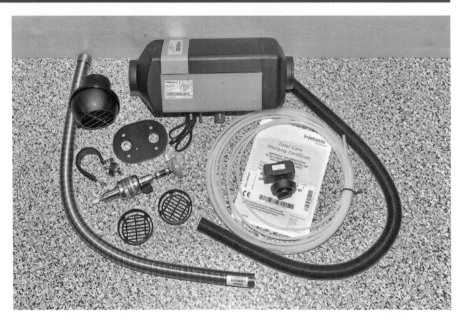

1 The Webasto Air Top 2000 comes as a kit. Do watch out if you see them being advertised cheaply on eBay because essential components such as the fuel pump, operating controls and hoses frequently aren't included, and they're very expensive to buy separately. Thoughtfully, Webasto include several different shapes of brackets and clips to allow for almost all installation requirements.

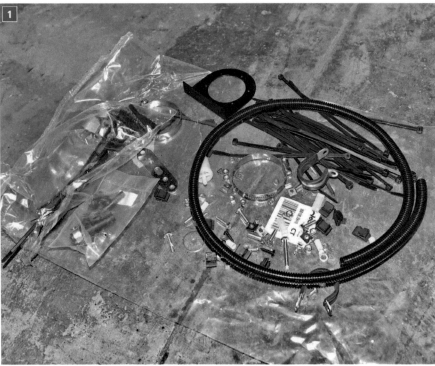

2 The Air Top 2000 fits very well beneath DiXie's driver's seat. In most cases there'll be components such as a fuse box and associated brackes that'll need to be removed and resited first.

3 It's worth taking time to check that the location you choose is right, bearing in mind the need for holes in the floor and also the requirements of an air inlet and outlet for the heating system.

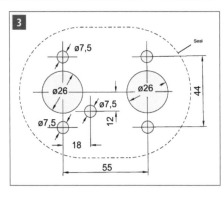

4 Once we'd established the mounting position, we measured up the exact location for the inlet, exhaust and fixing holes, using the sealing gasket as a guide.

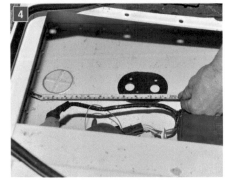

5 A stepped hole cutter was used to drill the holes to the required size…

6 …and a magnet was used to pick up the steel chippings. Of course, aluminium is non-magnetic, so when the aluminium side panels were drilled later a workshop vacuum cleaner was used. Bare steel should, of course, be protected with primer then finish paint.

7 As you can see from the earlier pictures, the vent outlet supplied with the kit is a domed affair, but AC-Automotive also stock a flatter version that protrudes less. Although it may not direct the flow of air quite so well, we felt this version to be better suited to a vehicle's foot well.

8 Location of cold air inlet and hot air outlet are a matter of choice but I decided that it would be better to have warm air directed towards the rear of the vehicle in view of the large unheated space in the back. So having established the location of the air inlet…

9 …a pilot hole was drilled, followed by a larger hole to take the inlet connector.

10 The same procedure was followed at the back of the seat box. You need to avoid any mounting bolts already found in that area.

11 The bottom of the Air Top 2000 was prepared by fitting the sealing gasket and tucking the cable neatly into its access hole.

12 After locating the unit from above, the four mounting nuts were fitted and carefully tightened from beneath the vehicle.

13 It was now time to start making all the right connections so the kit's wiring loom was prepared for installation.

14 There are several cables in the loom that weren't required in this installation, although they would be if you had, say, a remote control or timer unit fitted. So we snipped off the unwanted cables and started connecting the others into, in this case, the fuse holder connector block.

15 The loom needs to be positioned neatly and carefully, both inside the vehicle and where it runs beneath. It must be strapped and clipped in position, emulating the way the original manufacturer's loom is fitted. Above all it mustn't foul on any mechanical components or hot parts such as the exhaust system.

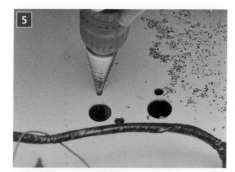

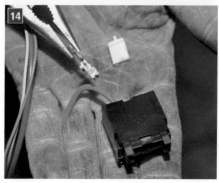

16 Webasto supply a large P-clip and an anti-vibration connector…

17 …for fitting the fuel pump in a suitable location, preferably beneath the vehicle. Its exact location will depend to some extent on the location of the fuel tank – see later.

18 A good length of fuel pipe is included with the kit, as well as an angled union for fitting it to the underside of the Air Top unit.

19 We connected the loom cables into the plug for the fuel pump, ensuring that the waterproof sealing grommets were carefully pushed home before plugging the loom into the pump connector.

20 After establishing where it was going to go and how much would be needed, the exhaust pipe was cut to length.

21 Using the brackets and connectors supplied with the kit, the exhaust pipe was fitted beneath the vehicle. You can also see the black inlet hose for burner-air that's also been connected to the base of the Air Top unit. The exhaust outlet needs to be angled down and slightly away from the direction of travel and the inlet hose opening needs to be pointing directly away from the direction of travel.

22 Back on the electrical theme, we decided that the control switch would be fitted on my vehicle's centre console. The switch base and a tape measure were used to establish the correct location…

23 …before drilling out the necessary hole in the console.

24 The wiring loom, having been run into position already, was simply plugged into the connector on the switch…

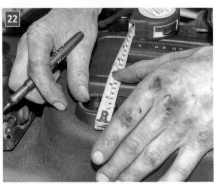

25 …which was fixed to the centre console panel with the large brass nut provided, before being tightened with a socket, remembering that the nut is being tightened on to a plastic thread.

26 Because Webasto have no way of knowing the location of the battery in the vehicle to which the heater's being fitted, a length of cable and various connectors are supplied. We crimped a ring terminal to one end of the power feed cable…

27 ...and a terminal for the fuse holder to the other end before connecting everything together – except for the fuse at this stage, of course.

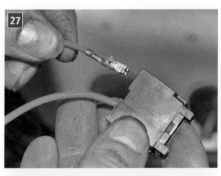

28 Next we dismantled the vent components before gunning some silicone sealant into place and fitting the inlet and outlet vents to the seat box.

29 There's lots of air hose supplied with the kit, but it's easily capable of being concertina'd to slot comfortably into position, after first putting the hose clips on, to be tightened when in place.

30 Webasto supply components for fitting a fuel supply pipe to a drain tap (top) or to a standard plastic tank (bottom). Dale, owner of Webasto dealers AC-Automotive, says he's not a fan of the drain tap connector because of the risk of picking up muck from the bottom of the tank, although the drawing here shows a pipe stub sticking up into the tank, presumably above the level of any debris that might be in there. Even so, Dale prefers to pull fuel from a cleaner supply, higher up in the tank.

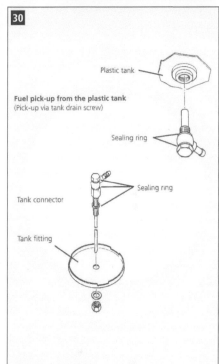

Plastic tank

Fuel pick-up from the plastic tank
(Pick-up via tank drain screw)

Sealing ring

Sealing ring

Tank connector

Tank fitting

31 My Land Rover has a steel auxiliary tank. We removed it from the vehicle and drilled a hole large enough to take the slot-in connector, which after it's been inserted...

32 ...has a large washer and connector nut fitted to the top. We'd already cut the pickup pipe on the lower end of this connector to the required length.

33 The fuel line, just like the wiring, has to be carefully and securely strapped and clipped to the underside of the vehicle, well away from any hot components.

Once everything was connected and the fuse in place, we turned on the switch, the pump ran – and nothing happened, as we'd already been forewarned. This is because when first installed the system has to pump fuel all the way from the tank to the burner, and several restarts are needed before the smooth whoosh of the burner firing up takes place.

Now, even on the very coldest days, the cockpit starts to warm up within a minute or so (as opposed to the 10–15 minutes it takes for the engine to deliver heat to the occupants). And if we need to leave the dogs in the back when it's 10° below, or if I'm sitting around for an hour typing into my laptop (not an uncommon occurrence!), I know the interior can be maintained at a civilised temperature. In other words, not like a standard Land Rover at all!

CHAPTER 8

Battery set-up, lights and towing

MCL's Tim Consolante and Ian Baughan from IRB show how you can not only fit twin batteries to your Defender but also make them charge and work properly together.

It's obvious that doubling up on your battery power can only be a good thing, but what most people don't realise is that the majority of twin battery installations have fundamental design faults.

The primary purpose of a standard vehicle battery is to serve as a store or reserve of electrical power to start the engine. All the electrical loads in the vehicle are supplied by the alternator whilst the engine is running. A standard starter battery is designed to be kept in a charged state and not deeply discharged.

With the addition of supplementary accessories, and the requirement for power whilst the engine isn't running, the risk of having a flat battery is greatly increased. This is inconvenient at best, but in the case of an overland expedition vehicle it could almost be a life or death situation.

In order to preserve the main starter battery it's good practice to move ancillary loads to a second battery that's isolated from the main starter battery when the engine is stopped. Once the engine is running both batteries need to be charged.

Winching is an emotive subject with many opinions. The fact is that a large winch can demand over 400A, and in order to provide this sort of power for any period of time you'll need an uprated electrical system. As to which battery to attach the winch to, we've gone traditional with DiXie and treated it as an auxiliary load. Therefore we've used the auxiliary battery. When winching, with the engine running, both batteries will be combined in parallel to deliver maximum current and capacity.

TYPES OF BATTERY

- Standard starter battery – a battery producing a large current for a short period of time to start an engine, designed to be kept fully charged.
- Leisure/deep cycle battery – designed to deliver a low current over a long period of time and cope with deep discharge cycles.

As we're using a battery separation charging method (see below), we'll be using two identical brand new Yellow Top batteries supplied by Optima. Because we're joining them in parallel the make-up of the batteries and their internal resistance need to be as similar as possible, so that there's no risk of a charge imbalance caused by the batteries having different charging requirements.

The Optima 4.2 Yellow Top is a dual-

purpose starter and deep cycle battery, so it's ideally suited to our twin battery set-up. Capable of delivering 765CCA (cold cranking amps), when most standard Defender batteries 'only' deliver 630CCA, this means more cranking power than the original unit on the starting side. At the same time, the battery is capable of deep cycle discharge with rapid recharge rate for the auxiliary battery function.

The Optima Yellow Top is an AGM (absorbed glass mat) battery, meaning the electrolyte is suspended in a mat so that it's spill-proof and much more resistant to vibration and impact. Optima batteries also utilise a spiral-wound cell as opposed to conventional flat plate, providing more surface area. Optimas will even work underwater! Perhaps these are the reasons

why the MOD picked the Yellow Top for its latest Land Rover Defender FFR (fitted for radio) vehicles.

TYPES OF CHARGING

- Twin alternator – a dedicated alternator for each battery. Requires extensive fabrication and engineering but very effective.
- Alternator charge controller – takes a single alternator output and directs charging current to batteries proportionally depending on state of charge.
- Battery separation – connects batteries in parallel via a switch/relay/solenoid.

Battery separation is our preferred choice here because it's cost effective and can deliver the performance required. It also has a higher current-carrying capability than the other methods. And in the top-of-the-range Blue Sea system it incorporates the ability to manually combine the batteries to self jump-start if required.

Battery separation in its simplest form involves the connection of the two batteries

CABLE SIZE AND WINCH POWER

Cable is sold in different sizes of CSA (cross sectional area). This is different to diameter. A 60mm² CSA cable will have a diameter of approximately 15mm. Always try to use the largest cable you can afford; this IS one of those times where big is best!

Winch HP	Amps @ 12V	Minimum CSA
1	70	16 mm²
2	140	25mm²
3	210	30mm²
4	280	40mm²
5	350	50mm²
6	420	60mm²
7	490	70mm²
8	560	90mm²

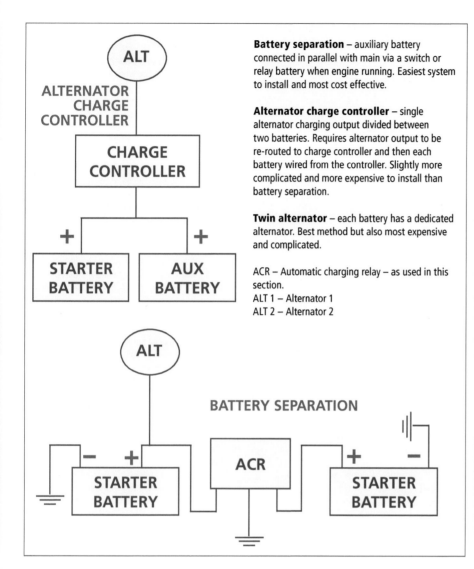

ALT

ALTERNATOR
CHARGE
CONTROLLER

CHARGE
CONTROLLER

+   +

STARTER
BATTERY

AUX
BATTERY

ALT

BATTERY SEPARATION

– +   + –

STARTER
BATTERY

ACR

STARTER
BATTERY

Battery separation – auxiliary battery connected in parallel with main via a switch or relay battery when engine running. Easiest system to install and most cost effective.

Alternator charge controller – single alternator charging output divided between two batteries. Requires alternator output to be re-routed to charge controller and then each battery wired from the controller. Slightly more complicated and more expensive to install than battery separation.

Twin alternator – each battery has a dedicated alternator. Best method but also most expensive and complicated.

ACR – Automatic charging relay – as used in this section.
ALT 1 – Alternator 1
ALT 2 – Alternator 2

manually, via a switch. The process can be semi-automated, using a relay and a suitable trigger such as an ignition live. The option we're using is a fully-automated ACR (automatic charging relay). The ACR senses when the voltage of either of the batteries rises to a level indicating that a charge source is active, this level being 13.0V for two minutes. When this occurs the ACR's contacts connect and the ACR allows the charge to both batteries. If the voltage on both of the batteries subsequently drops to 12.75V for 30 seconds, the ACR will disconnect, isolating the batteries. So using this system, if you were to connect, say, a solar panel to your auxiliary battery and the voltage rises above 13.0V for more than two minutes the relay will combine the two batteries together, also topping up your starter battery without even having the engine running!

A side effect of combining two batteries together is that, if one is deeply discharged and the other fully charged, there will be an inrush of current when they're first combined whilst they equalise. High currents through the relay can also be experienced when

extreme loads are placed on the system, such as winching, where currents of up to 500A aren't uncommon. The majority of relays on the market today are rated at less than half of this, some as low as 30 amps!

The Blue Sea unit is rated at 500A continuous and 2,500A in rush, making it the highest spec unit currently available – but at the same price-point of lower spec systems. A lower priced Blue Sea unit is also available rated at 120A continuous and 250A inrush.

MCL's choice is ANL fuse holders, available in ratings up to 750A. MCL recommend the fitment of a main protection fuse as close to the second battery as possible before any other load is connected.

Blue Sea, as the name suggests, are manufacturers of high quality marine electrics, and as such their products are designed to the highest standards using some of the best materials available. A by-product of this marine spec is that a number of products are submersible waterproof, including the charging relays – a great feature on adventure-seeking Land Rovers!

INSTALLATION
MCL's Tim Consolante uses a system that not only keeps both batteries in tip-top condition but also ensures that if the main battery runs flat, the second battery can be connected as a kind of internal jump-start battery merely by pressing a switch on the dashboard. As part of the battery box project Tim also installed a new fuse box. This is a huge improvement overall over loose accessory fuses added on an ad hoc basis as new components are fitted to one's Land Rover.

1 Anderson connectors can be fitted to the front and rear of the vehicle, providing power as required without the need for connecting jump leads to the battery. It's a minor pain to have to lift the seat base and the battery cover in order to get at the battery terminals in a Defender, and crocodile clips can't possibly make as good a contact as Anderson connectors, while there's also the risk of creating a short.

2 Some of the heavy-duty cable from the battery box was run to both the front and rear of the vehicle.

3 At each end, an Anderson connector was fitted and bolted to a bracket on the bodywork.

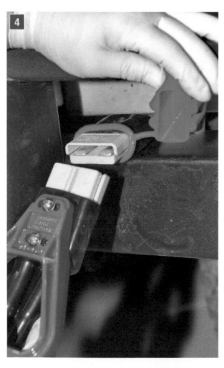

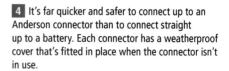

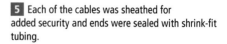

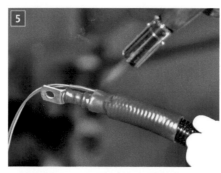

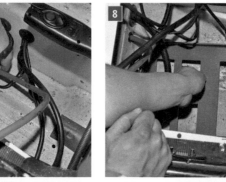

4 It's far quicker and safer to connect up to an Anderson connector than to connect straight up to a battery. Each connector has a weatherproof cover that's fitted in place when the connector isn't in use.

5 Each of the cables was sheathed for added security and ends were sealed with shrink-fit tubing.

6 It was necessary, of course, to drill new holes in the battery box to take the heavy-duty cables. Ian prefers to use a stepped hole cutter rather than a tapered one because it gives a square-sided hole and the size can be judged more accurately.

7 Note that each hole was fitted with a grommet to create a seal and prevent chafing before each length of cable was fed through into the battery compartment, ready for connecting to the batteries later.

8 Into the bottom of the compartment we lowered the base for the special battery carrier that IRB had made, specifically to suit batteries such as the highly regarded Optimas supplied by MCL. So far, so conventional!

9 Of crucial importance is the American-built Blue Sea automatic charging relay supplied in the UK by MCL. This has several vital functions and operates in conjunction with a switch on the dashboard that we'll be looking at later. For now it's enough to point out that we had to find a suitable location in the battery box for the relay unit.

10 We also needed to find a location for the heavy-duty fuse unit, also supplied by MCL.

11 After removing the batteries once more from the battery box a suitable location was found for the fuse unit alongside the battery carrier.

12 Having worked out, when the batteries were still in place, where the automatic charging relay would be situated, we screwed it into position on the side of the battery box.

13 The comprehensive auxiliary fuse box supplied by MCL came mounted on a substantial bracket which was also fixed to the side of the battery box, but high enough for one of the batteries to be installed beneath it.

14 Both batteries have to be lowered into place in the rear half of the battery box because of the location of the fuse box. Tim lowered the first Optima battery into position on the carrier base, then slid it to the front of the battery box…

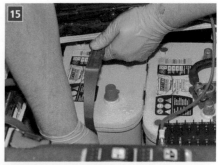

15 …before lowering and locating the second battery on the carrier base.

16 A purpose-made battery strap runs front to rear, and here it's being carefully tightened down over the centres of the two batteries.

17 Once the main cable connections had been made to the fuse, the Blue Sea automatic charging relay and the two batteries, and the subsidiary supply connections had been made to the auxiliary fuse box, fuses of an appropriate size were fitted to provide power to relevant accessories.

18 The fuse box lid has provision for labelling the fuses to indicate which fuse is for which accessory, which is something we need to do.

19 Here's the switch I mentioned earlier, fitted to the dash panel. In normal use the rocker switch remains in its central position and allows both batteries to be properly charged by the vehicle's alternator. When it's in the down position the charging relay in the battery box is turned off and there's no connection to the second battery. In the up position the solenoid in the automatic charging relay engages and power is supplied from the second battery to the first – a fantastic way of charging your Land Rover in the event of a flat battery.

20 Of course, if there's next to no power remaining in the first battery the switch on the dashboard can't operate the solenoid in the charging relay. In this event the knob on the top of the relay can be pushed in and the lever turned to operate the relay manually, bringing the secondary battery into play.

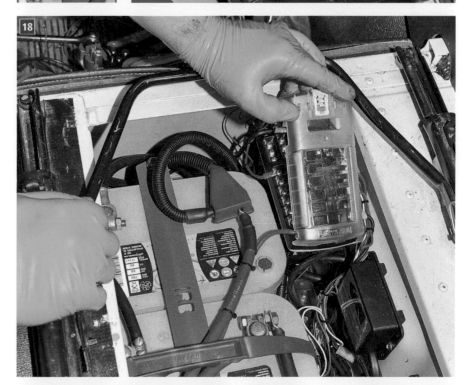

Without doubt, this MCL-developed system is a hugely superior way of running two batteries. With this system in place you have the benefits of:
- Being able to use your secondary battery for all auxiliary activities such as jump-starting, winching, running a cockpit heater or auxiliary lighting.
- Charging both batteries to their fullest capacity – essential to ensure battery longevity.
- Being able to use the secondary battery as a full backup for the main battery next time you leave an interior light on and drain it.
- Having both batteries properly clamped in place – vital for safety and, again, battery life, because a rattling battery is not only an acute safety hazard, but having a battery on the loose will severely diminish its life expectancy.

Interior LED lights

Fitting LED interior lights means you'll consume less electricity and have a brighter Defender interior.

1 These units are completely encased within a polycarbonate extrusion, which protects against moisture ingress. Mounting holes only past halfway through so, after checking that I wouldn't be drilling through anything electrical, I completed the hole front-to-back. Other ways of fixing include using an adhesive strip, or fixing with purpose-made clips or brackets.

2 By a surprising coincidence, the hole mounting centres matched exactly the centres of two of the headlining fixing clips. I needn't have done it this way round but I marked the positions with a 1.5mm drill…

3 …then removed the two clips with a trim removal tool so that a self-tapping screw could be inserted into each one, cutting the thread for later use.

4 The light unit diffuser was unclipped…

5 …and the light unit itself unscrewed to gain access to the wiring behind it.

6 After identifying the correct power supply terminal shown here we soldered a new cable on to it. Note that there's a push-fit terminal at the other end of this white cable, enabling the connection to be made after the original light unit has been screwed back in place.

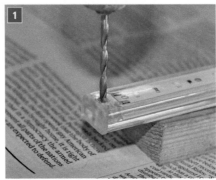

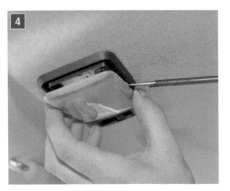

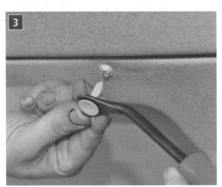

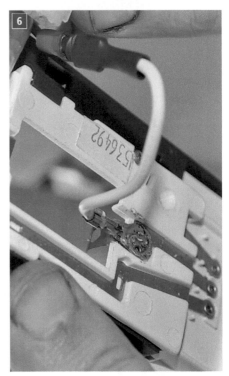

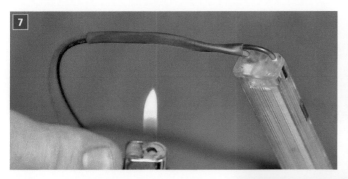

7 Next we prepared the LED light cable ready for feeding it through the roof space. The cables come out of the end of the LED unit so can't be fully concealed. To improve their appearance we decided on a piece of shrink-fit insulation.

8 The cable supplied wasn't long enough so we soldered an extension in place...

9 ...using narrow shrink-fit on each cable to insulate it.

10 Then, a larger piece was used to further insulate both cables. Finally, belts-and-braces, we slid a piece of narrow trunking over the remainder of the cable that didn't have its own sleeving and used yet another piece of shrink-fit insulation to connect it to the already sleeved cable.

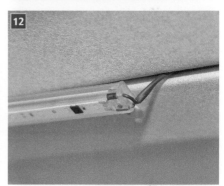

11 If you pull down the headlining where the front and middle sections join you can slide a fish wire underneath, then tape the electrical cable to the end of the fish wire and pull it through.

12 The idea was to leave just enough sticking out for the LED light to be fixed in place.

13 Then all the headlining clips were refitted, making sure that the two pre-drilled, pre-screwed clips went into the correct locations for the light unit fixing screws to be added.

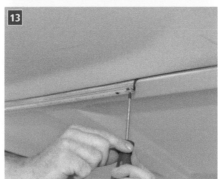

14 Further electrical work was needed on the back of the original light unit where the connector block held here had been cut away and replaced with two separate connectors. The negative cable for the LED light was added into one of them. Note that LED lights are polarity sensitive and will only work if connected the right way round.

15 In addition to the front light two LED strip lights were fitted at the rear of the vehicle, held on with double-sided tape. The rear lights were connected to the original rear lamp unit and the bulbs from both front and rear original lamps were removed, leaving them to operate simply as switching units for the new LED lights.

The difference in brightness is remarkable! That's because the properties of the LEDs used in these lights give greater luminosity and a brighter unit, while using fewer LEDs and less power. There's a choice between a 522mm length strip, with 24 high-intensity LEDs, and a 1,020mm strip with 48 LEDs.

Driving lights

Driving lights come in all shapes, sizes and prices. Beyond saying that you get what you pay for and that you can't expect cheap driving lights to last very long or give the finest light output, you'll also have to pay attention to the light-fixing system on your Land Rover, and if the lights you're purchasing aren't compatible you'll have to make brackets or other modifications, similar to those described here.

1 The Hella Luminator driving lights shown being fitted come with a number of wiring diagrams to accord with different types of installation. One shows the auxiliary lamps connected so that they're switched on with the headlights. This one shows them being connected so that they're switched on in addition to the headlights but only when selected via a separately installed switch. Incidentally, the numbers shown on this drawing correspond with the terminal numbers on a standard relay.

2 Our first installation was carried out by Tim Consolante of MCL Ltd, who supply all the Speaker Corporation LED driving lights shown. Here Tim is measuring out the wiring runs. The relay was mounted on the inside of the left-hand wing in the engine bay.

3 The cable was introduced into the space behind the grille via this aperture adjacent to the back of the radiator.

4 Connectors were crimped to the ends of the cables ready for inserting into the Speaker-compatible cable plugs...

5 ...before applying shrink-fit insulation to seal the cables' entry into the plug.

6 Next a relatively inexpensive lamp back made by NBB of Sweden was fitted to the mounting on the soft A-bar.

7 Then the cable ends were stripped, standard terminals were crimped on...

8 ...and, after being pushed through the lamp backs, were plugged into the terminals on the back of the reflector before halogen bulbs were fitted.

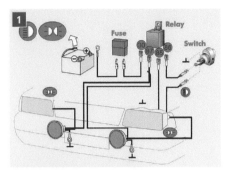

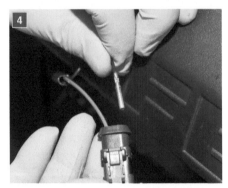

9 You can see that these units give out a perfectly respectable beam of light, but comparing the yellow of the halogen bulb with the clear white of the LED headlamp alongside certainly puts it into perspective.

10 The Speaker Corporation TS3000's LED light beam is intensely bright even when compared with the LED headlights alongside. However, remember to look at the manufacturer's published beam pattern, because brightness isn't everything! A very narrow, pencilled beam with illuminate a small area a long way away, whereas a wider beam disperses the light and thus appears less bright, but illuminates a wider area.

11 While the shallow and lightweight NBB spotlights bolted straight on, the LED driving lights shown here needed to be fitted with specially made 5mm-thick plates with studs in them to allow enough room between the fixing point and the grille.

12 If you're fitting very expensive lights, you may wish to consider using stainless steel shear nuts (arrowed) such as these inexpensive examples from Screwfix Direct. As you tighten the nut the hexagon reaches a point where it shears off, leaving just the threaded cone in place, which is extremely difficult to remove. Therefore you need to be certain you won't want to move anything later on!

13 This drawing shows the Hella Celis Luminator driving lights that I finally fitted. It's important to note that I deliberately disregarded the Hella instructions, but you're not recommended to do so! These driving lights have 'Angel eyes' LED bulbs around the periphery, designed to come on with the side lights.

14 We started by accessing one of the side-light units by removing the wheel arch extension...

15 ...and unplugging the side-light terminal.

16 The Hella instructions suggest the use of Scotchlok connectors, but I really dislike these because damp gets into them and they lose their electrical connection. Have a look online if you're not familiar with them. Instead, we decided to make a soldered joint using a Power Probe gas soldering iron.

17 A Würth wire stripper was used to stretch the insulation open, leaving a piece of bare wire without having to cut into it.

18 Both pieces of wire were 'tinned' with solder before being soldered together.

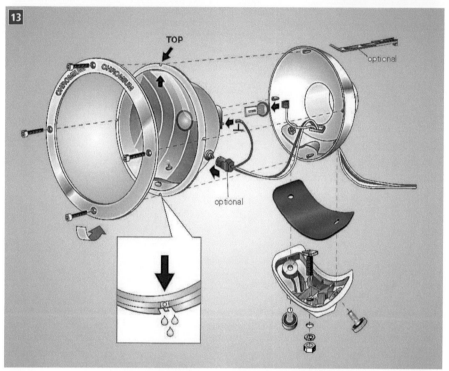

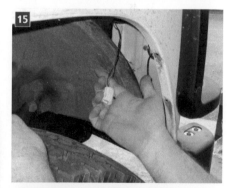

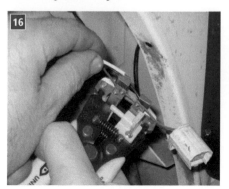

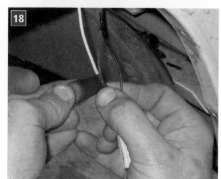

19 Würth self-amalgamating insulation tape wrapped around the joint is close to being waterproof, and, because it bonds itself together, it won't come undone.

20 The connectors used behind the grille were also by Würth. As with the connectors seen earlier, terminals have to be crimped to the ends of the cables...

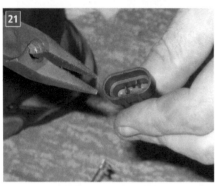

21 ...and inserted into the connector block.

22 These connectors are waterproof and incorporate grommets to seal the cables' entry into the connector body.

23 The Hella Celis Luminator driving lights have their own stainless steel mounting plates. I fitted these modified versions of the steel brackets shown earlier. The grille needed to be cut to accept the full depth of the lamp bodies.

24 Hella recommend that these lights aren't fitted upside-down – so we did! As far as I could see, the only possible reason for not inverting them was because there were no drain holes, so, using my Dremel, I cut a small slot in what was the top of each housing to precisely match the one that was in the 'bottom'.

25 The only other potential problem I could see was the cable entry and fixing holes, but a little extra sealant overcame that objection.

26 I was confident that the main fixing bolts would be almost impossible to access, but the large, knurled thumbscrews you can see at bottom right of the exploded parts drawing were replaced by M8 security bolts, though you need to be sure you have the correct fitting tool. I bought four stainless steel bolts and a set of security-bolt fixing tools from Amazon for just a few quid.

27 The security bolts were used to fix the main lamp bodies in position...

28 ...and the Würth waterproof connectors were pushed together then hidden out of sight behind the grille.

29 Although these are halogen bulbs and most comparable Hella driving lights are much brighter HID bulbs, they look satisfyingly bright to me!

LED rear, work, fog and reversing lights

LED REAR AND WORK LIGHTS

We decided that the space above the Defender's rear door was crying out for one of MCL's Model 9049 12V four-module work light units. This particular lamp gives the output of six halogen work lamps whilst using just over the power of one.

1 Work started with Ian Baughan removing the rear trim panel found on Station Wagons, which simply unclips.

2 The trim panel over the top of the rear door is held on with these push-in clips. You'll need a proper trim removal tool to remove these clips without risk of damaging them.

3 After all the plastic clips have been removed the panel is loose and ready for removal.

4 Just one small example of the superior quality of these MCL units is the gland nut assembly used for passing the electrical cable through the vehicle's bodywork. On the right is the nut that holds the unit to the body, while on the left is the gland nut that tightens on the gland in the body of the fitting after the wire's been passed through it.

5 During the offering-up process seen in the heading picture we'd marked the bodywork to indicate the best place for passing the wiring through. A stepped hole cutter was used to drill the correct-sized hole for the gland nut. Even though you're dealing with aluminium it's best to apply primer to the edges of the drilled hole, because while aluminium doesn't corrode anything like as quickly as steel, it does corrode in time.

6 The connector on the MCL light unit is an industrial push-fit plug and socket, waterproof to IP68.

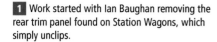

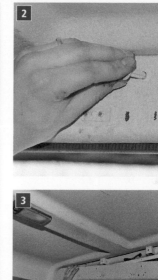

7 Ian pushed the cable through the gland fitting…

8 …leaving an appropriate amount of cable for plugging in to the light unit. First he tightened the attachment nut on the inside of the body, then the gland nut which closes the gland into the electrical cable. Once the gland nut has been tightened the wire can only be moved by slackening off before sliding the cable through.

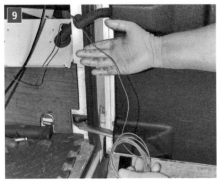

9 Meanwhile, MCL's Tim Consolante was busy running the wiring into position.

10 If you want an option to use the work light as a reversing light you'll have to take a feed from the reversing light circuit. Road vehicle regulations prevent the use of the lights I've got fitted as reversing lights, but there would be nothing to prevent you from using a pair of MCL's single-unit LED lights as reversing lights, as well as work lights, if you wanted to.

11 This is the bracket holding the light unit to the body. The threaded components supplied with the light are stainless steel, so we used some of the stainless mounting bolts and washers I buy in packs from Screwfix Direct.

12 After attaching the two brackets to the ends of the light unit we prepared the fixings to go on to the bodywork. There would be a nylon washer between bracket and body, and on the inside a plain washer, spring washer and nut.

13 Tim held the unit in position…

14 …and when all bolts were in place Ian tightened the fittings and reattached the trim panel that goes above the door.

15 Note that when refitting the window trims all you have to do is line up the spring clips with the edge of the aluminium panel to which they're being fitted, start them off with a push and then bang them in place with the flat of your hand.

16 MCL supplied all the Carling switches fitted to the Raptor dash panel and we found one to match the rear work light, connecting it up to provide power from the auxiliary battery under the passenger seat.

17 As an alternative (or in addition, if you prefer) to switching the work lights on from the dashboard, you could use a remote-control wiring kit such as that from Ring Automotive (inset).

18 However you look at it, MCL's high-powered LED work lights throw a whole new light on the business of getting jobs done after dark in the vicinity of your Land Rover. The final verdict – literally brilliant!

LED FOG AND REVERSING LIGHTS

Here we look at how to fit original-looking but superior performance LED fog and reversing lights that MCL source from Land Rover's own lighting suppliers.

19 One of the great things about MCL's fog and reversing lights is that they come complete with standard Land Rover plugs, enabling them to be simply plugged into the existing wiring.

20 After unscrewing and detaching the existing fog light unit the wiring plugs and sockets were unlatched and separated.

21 New sealing rings come with the MCL lights and the first job is to remove the surplus material from the inside of the ring. Use something like surgical spirit or panel wipe to clean the edge of the mount on to which the light is fitted…

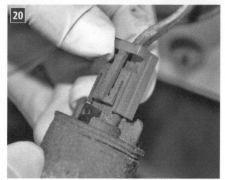

22 …then remove the backing paper, pass the wiring through the sealing ring and use the self-adhesive surface to stick it in place.

23 Provided that no repairs are required to the existing wiring or socket (which can deteriorate over time) you simply plug in the new light…

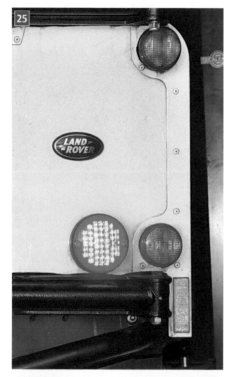

24 …and screw it into place, using the original fixing screws.

25 The light is slightly more directional than that emitted by an incandescent bulb fitting but that's OK, because a fog light is for warning traffic that's following behind. You can see from this shot taken in daylight that the brightness of these LED lights is far better than that from conventional lights. And when you bear in mind that you're never going to get a blown bulb and that the lights are completely sealed against the elements and thus against internal corrosion, LED lights are a real no-brainer.

26 The process for fitting the reversing light is exactly the same.

27 This time the benefits are, if anything, even greater…

28 …because you'll have a perfectly legal but much brighter reversing light with far greater longevity than a standard unit, which justifies the greater cost of these lights compared with the old-fashioned incandescent sort.

Fitting a winch

Thanks to torrential rain it was so muddy at a show I attended that people were glad of a winch when they got stuck. And Britpart's Stuart Harrison fitted one to our project Defender, Wilfred, at this very show.

We'd opted for a Britpart DB 12000i winch and winch bumper. Britpart's own-brand DB8000, DB9500i and DB12000i electric winches all feature an automatic load-holding brake; a hardened drum; a galvanised cable (minimum brake force 14,400lb) – though most people switch to nylon straps before long; weatherproof and dustproof contactor controls; a thermal overload protection (DB9500i and DB12000i models); a planetary gear system for fast line speed, and free spooling.

1 The job began with removing the screws holding the grille in place.

2 After lifting off the grille, we unbolted and removed the front bumper.

3 The Britpart winch bumper usually bolts straight on in place of the standard one, but we'd had replacement bumper irons welded on as part of Wilfred's refurbishment, which had access holes that weren't as large as those on the originals.

4 This made it impossible to insert and hold in position the nut plate to which the bumper bolts are screwed, as demonstrated. But we came up with a cunning plan! A hacksaw blade was taped to the nut plate...

5 ...which could then be inserted through the narrow slot in the bumper iron. With a little jiggling, the new bolts were inserted and lined up with the threads on the nut plate, starting them all off before tightening any of them.

6 In fact the A-frame is also held on with the bumper bolts, so a little more jiggling than normal was necessary in order to line everything up.

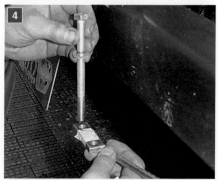

7 We decided not to fit the front-most of the three bolts per side, but when you do, you need to use the fitted A-frame as a guide for drilling the extra holes needed in the bumper plate.

8 The winch is a bit of a lump and it's safer (and therefore strongly recommended) for two people to lift it.

9 We positioned the winch on the bumper then suddenly realised that, with the winch bolted down, it would be impossible to fit the roller cage, or 'fairlead' as it's called.

10 With the winch pushed right back there was room to introduce the two bolts supplied as part of the kit...

11 ...and to fit and tighten the lock nuts.

12 Now, the bolts – four of them – can be introduced into their holes in the base of the winch body. The bolt heads sit in slots which prevent them from turning as their fixing nuts are tightened.

13 The winch body has to be placed on the bumper so that the bolts protrude through its base, seen here from beneath; the captive nuts are screwed on...

14 ...then fully tightened once all four bolts and nuts are in place.

15 There's a full range of winching accessories in the Britpart range. Here we're using a bow shackle

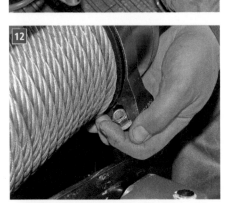

between the winch hook and the eyelet on the winch bumper.

16 Next we prepared to fit the isolator switch and the heavy-duty cables, available from Britpart as extras.

17 You can fit the isolator switch wherever you want it. A favourite spot is beneath the bonnet but Stuart favours a bulkhead mounting, accessed from the driver's seat. This hole in the 200 Tdi bulkhead is almost ready to go.

18 We had to drill two fresh holes for switch mounting screws.

19 They're close to the edges of the hole so you have to be careful you don't break through. It's best to start off with a centre punch before drilling a pilot hole.

20 Although this is a separate installation (on a Series 3, as it happens), the wiring principles are exactly the same. Once the position of the switch has been established the wiring has to be neatly run. You should use cable clips to fix the wiring safely in position after the runs have been made.

21 The cables come ready-fitted with terminals, but you'll probably have to fit new ones after the cable's been cut to length.

22 Finally, the cables are connected to the battery. There's no fuse so you must make sure that there's absolutely no possibility of cables shorting out. They'd almost certainly cause a fire and/or a battery explosion. Better still, fit a heavy-duty fuse to the positive cable, adjacent to the battery. Make sure the isolator switch is turned off whenever you're not using the winch. Consider fitting the switch as close to the battery as possible.

23 Most installations require that the grille is cut away to avoid fouling. The plastic material is easy to cut with tin snips.

24 Be prepared for several trial-fits before you get it right. It's better than cutting away too much and leaving an ugly gap.

25 Last job was to screw the grille back in place.

Our Britpart winch has been a great success and is made even better if you pay extra for fairlead rollers made from stainless steel, available as optional extras.

Tow ball and winch receiver plate

How about a detachable tow connection for your Defender? And why not have the option of a tow ball on the front – and with detachable winch connections too? Then why not build the whole thing into a front steering guard and an NAS-style rear step – is that Extreme enough for you?

The Extreme 4x4 rear receiver we fit here comes built into an NAS-style rear step (shown being fitted in Chapter 4), while the front receiver is incorporated into an extremely useful heavy-duty steering guard. Extreme 4x4 also offer a simpler, conventional-looking tow bracket but with the same type of receiver shown here.

And in case you're wondering, a front-mounted tow ball is fantastic for manoeuvring large trailers and caravans in confined spaces, and with great accuracy too.

1 In the main picture you can see how the tow ball plate is used at the front of the vehicle while, at the rear, the same assembly can be fitted to the rear receiver, as required.

2 This is the Extreme 4x4 steering guard with tow hitch receiver built in. It comes with longer, replacement mounting bolts and the required fixing pin for when the tow ball mount is in place.

3 The steering damper passes through the steering guard, so we began by removing the pivot pin on the driver's side…

4 …followed by the retaining nut and washers on the passenger side.

5 The two through-bolts, passing through the chassis and holding the towing eyes in place, were unscrewed next…

6 …and the towing eyes were dispensed with – the steering guard comes with towing eyes built in. We also removed the two bolts further back along the chassis, forming part of the connection to the steering link on the driver's side and its unused bracket on the passenger's side (see below).

TYPE-APPROVED TOW BRACKETS

In the UK, only type-approved tow brackets should be used for towing on the road on vehicles registered after 1 August 1998. All tow bars must carry a 'type approved' label indicating:

- Maximum nose-weight.
- Type-approval number.
- Country code showing where tow bar was tested. (*eg* UK = e11).

However, this law only appears to apply to cars, not commercial vehicles.

The tow bars shown here have not been type-approved for vehicles first registered after 31 July 1998.

7 Würth copper grease was applied – we really do get through it – and the new bolt was inserted into the mounting point on the passenger side.

8 On the driver's side the new bolt was pushed all the way through, but on the other it was left flush with the end of the mounting, as shown.

9 The inner surfaces of the chassis rails, where the steering guard would be fitted, were coated with cavity wax, then we lifted up the steering guard and hooked one end of it on to the bolt which had been left sticking through the chassis. You'll need to lift up the other end of the steering guard with your knees, then reach round…

10 …and push the other bolt through the chassis and the mounting hole on the rear of the steering guard, which was now suspended on the two rear mounting positions.

11 The front bolts, now stripped of their towing eyes, each required a large washer to be added where the bolt head fitted against the chassis rail.

12 It was much easier lifting the front of the steering guard than it had been lifting the back. Getting the nuts back on to the bolts was a little tricky, however, because of the narrow space remaining.

13 The front bolts were tightened by locking the nuts with a spanner inserted into the space between bumper and steering guard…

14 …while the rears were much easier to access. This is the steering link side…

15 …while this is t'other.

16 You can see here how the steering damper passes through this hole in the steering guard. After fitting the compression nut, you need to hold it with one spanner while tightening the lock nut on to it with another.

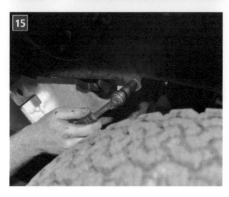

17 The open end of the receiver really needs a cap to blank it off when it's not in use. I bought this rather flimsy one cheaply on eBay but have since found that Extreme 4x4 sell better ones.

18 The front receiver protrudes a little way but when my front protection bars have been refitted it'll be just right.

19 At the back, we started by checking the NAS rear step for fit. It comes with spacers for the two end plates in case they're needed, but in this instance they weren't.

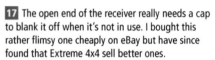

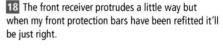

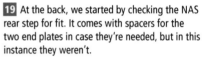

20 Both the pegs that fit into the existing jacking points, as well as the insides of the jacking points themselves, were given another dose of cavity wax.

21 Two large Allen bolts hold the step to the rear cross member. A couple of the rubber pips on the step plate had to be cut off with a sharp knife to give the bolts sufficient clearance.

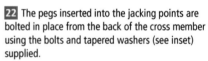

22 The pegs inserted into the jacking points are bolted in place from the back of the cross member using the bolts and tapered washers (see inset) supplied.

23 The two ends of the step bolt to the cross member using existing chassis bolts…

24 …while strong reinforcing bars are fitted underneath, from the chassis to the bottom of the step.

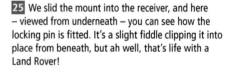

25 We slid the mount into the receiver, and here – viewed from underneath – you can see how the locking pin is fitted. It's a slight fiddle clipping it into place from beneath, but ah well, that's life with a Land Rover!

26 This is an AL-KO tow ball. So what? Well, AL-KO hitches, increasingly being fitted to caravans and some trailers, have a built-in anti-snake mechanism and are greatly superior to the non-damped sort. Trouble is they're physically larger on the outside and you need a hitch whose ball is a little further away from the vehicle. AL-KO tow balls are perfectly compatible with regular hitches, so if you're fitting a new tow ball you might as well go for the AL-KO type.

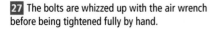

27 The bolts are whizzed up with the air wrench before being tightened fully by hand.

28 So now we had a tow ball mount that could be transferred to the front of the Defender when required, only needing the fixing pin and retaining clip to be fitted before swinging into action. The difference it makes both connecting up to the trailer and manoeuvring it around is really significant. It makes you realise why every campsite has a tractor with a front-mounted tow ball for moving caravans around on-site.

29 This is the Extreme 4x4 winch tray. It fits to the receiver, front or rear, in exactly the same way as the tow ball mount.

30 The business-end of a plasma rope, complete with fairlead, were fed through the opening in the front of the winch tray.

31 Popping the winch in position…

32 …and bolting it down using the pre-drilled holes in the tray were the easiest part of the job.

33 When fitted to the rear of my Defender the winch has to be used with the door open because of my door-mounted spare wheel carrier, but that's no big deal. Perhaps a winch with a lower profile would clear the door? But I'm happy enough with things the way they are.

ANDERSON ELECTRICAL CONNECTORS

34 In order to make it possible to use the winch easily in either location, Tim Consolante from MCL had already fitted Anderson sockets to the front and rear of the vehicle. So now we just had to fit the matching plug to the winch and away we could go! The winch cover was lifted…

35 …so that we could fit the connector cables, once new ends had been crimped and soldered on to them.

36 To the other end we fitted a male Anderson connector, making it dead easy to attach and disconnect the winch as required.

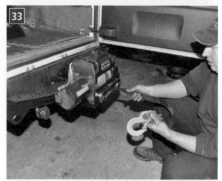

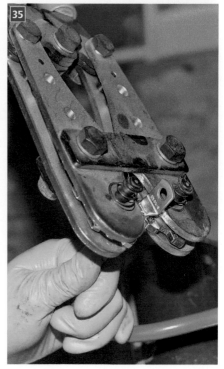

Specialists & Suppliers

4x4 Reborn
Unit 3, Quarry Farm, Old Milverton,
Warwickshire, CV32 6RW Tel:
01926 258894 Mob:07979 806906
www.4x4reborn.co.uk

AB Parts
65 Parkside, Spennymoor,
Co Durham, DL16 6SA. Tel: 01388 812 777
www.abpartsstore.co.uk

AC Automotive Limited
Unit 4, Llanthony Business Park,
Llanthony Road, Gloucester. GL2 5QT
Tel: 01452 309983
www.ac-automotive.co.uk

AL-KO Kober Ltd
South Warwickshire Business Park,
Kineton Road, Southam, Warks, CV47 0AL
Tel: 01926 818 500
www.al-ko.co.uk

Allard Motor Sport
Cae Pen House, Lone Lane, Penault,
Monmouthshire NP25 4AJ
Tel: +44 020 8133 9108
www.allardaluminiumproducts.co.uk

Allisport Ltd
23–25 Foxes Bridge Road, Forest Vale Ind. Est.,
Cinderford, Forest of Dean GL14 2PQ
Tel: 01594 826045
For the full range of intercoolers, covering
most Land Rover vehicles,
see www.allisport.com

ARB Corporation Ltd
42–44 Garden Street, Kilsyth, VIC 3137,
Australia. Tel: 03 9761 6622 www.arb.com.
au. ARB's products are distributed in the UK
by GKN Driveline.
See www.gkndriveline.com

Ashcroft Transmissions Ltd
Units 5 & 6, Stadium Estate, Cradock Road,
Luton, Beds, LU4 0JF. Tel: 01582 496040
www.ashcroft-transmissions.co.uk

Autoglass Ltd
Autoglass operate the well-known, nationwide call-out service for emergency glass
replacement.
Ring Freephone 0800 36 36 36 for details of
your local branch.
www.autoglass.co.uk

Autoland 4x4 Services
Unit 8, Houghton Regis Trading Centre,
Cemetery Road, Houghton Regis,
Dunstable, LU5 5QH Tel: 01582 866680
www.4x4service.co.uk

Barebox
PAR Technical Services Ltd,
Tel: 01252 860488
www.barebox.co.uk

Bearmach Ltd
Bearmach House, Unit 8, Pantglas Industrial
Estate, Bedwas, Caerphilly, CF83 8GE
Tel: 0292 085 6550
www.bearmach.com

BFGoodrich Tyres
Campbell Road, Stoke-on-Trent,
Staffordshire. ST4 4EY
www.bfgoodrich.co.uk
See the website for a complete list of tyres
and their qualities as well as a list of dealers
from where you can purchase these superb
on- and off-road tyres.

Blue Sea Systems
www.bluesea.com

Bolt On Bits
12, Tofts Rd, Cleckheaton, BD19 3BE
Tel: 01274-869955

Britpart
The Grove, Craven Arms, Shropshire, SY7
8DB. Tel: 01588 672711
www.britpart.com

Carrotech Ltd
Norfolk, IP20 9NH, Tel: 0845 5575594
www.carrotech.com

Clarke International Ltd
Hemnall Street, Epping, Essex, CM16 4LG.
Tel:.01992 565 300
www.clarkeinternational.com

Climair UK Ltd
197 Days Lane, Sidcup, Kent, DA15 8JX
Tel: 020 8309 7744
www.climairuk.com

CobraTrak
Cobra Information and Order Line:
Tel: 0844 239 0034
www.cobravehiclesecurity.co.uk

Conrad Anderson L.L.P.
57–59 Sladefield Road, Ward End,
Birmingham B8 3PF.
Tel: 0121 247 0619
www.conrad-anderson.co.uk

Durite
The full range of Durite electrical equipment
is available from **Extreme 4x4 Ltd,**
Tel: 01255 411411
www.extreme4x4.co.uk

Eberspächer (UK) Ltd
Eberspächer have a fully trained and
approved nationwide dealer network,
or you can contact them to locate your
nearest dealer at:,
Headlands Business Park, Salisbury Road,
Ringwood, Hants, BH24 3PB
Tel: 01425 480151
www.eberspacher.com

Edward Howell Galvanizers
Watery Lane, Wednesfield,
West Midlands, WV13 3SU.
Tel: 01902 637 463
www.wedge-galv.co.uk

Elecsol Europe Limited
47 First Avenue, Deeside Industrial Park,
Flintshire, CH5 2LG
Tel: (Free) 0800 163298
www.elecsol.com

Elite Automotive Systems Limited
Elite House, Sandy Way,
Amington Industrial Estate, Tamworth,
Staffs B77 4DS
Tel: 01827 300100
www.eliteautomotive.co.uk

Europa Specialist Spares Limited
Fauld Industrial Park, Tutbury, Staffs, DE13 9HS.
Tel: 01283 815609.
www.eurospares.com

Extreme 4x4 Limited
Durite Works, Valley Road, Dovercourt,
Essex, C012 4RX. Tel: 01255 411411
www.extreme4x4.co.uk

Fertan UK
14 Broadwater Way, Worthing,
West Sussex, BN14 9LP. Tel: 02380 456600
www.fertan.co.uk

Handirack UK Ltd
C/o Kamino International Transport Ltd, Unit
4 Mereside Park, Shield Road,
Ashford, TW15 1BL
Tel: 0870 961 9130
www.handiworld.com

Holden Vintage and Classic Ltd
Linton Trading Estate, Bromyard,
Herefordshire, HR7 4QT
Tel:01885 488488
www.holden.co.uk

Illbruck Sealant Systems UK Ltd
(butyl tape) Trade Division, Coalville,
Leicester, LE67 3JJ
Tel: 01530 835 722
www.illbruck.com

IRB Developments
Ian Baughan, Unit C, Middleton House Fm, Middleton, B78 2BD
Tel: 0121 288 1105 or 07, Mob: 0773 092 0431
www.irbdevelopments.com
Please be aware that, at the time of writing, Ian holds a full-time job and can sometimes be extremely difficult to contact.

KBX Upgrades Ltd
AB Parts Store, 65 Parkside, Spennymoor, Co Durham, DL16 6SA. Tel: 01388 812 777
www.kbxupgrades.co.uk

LaSalle Interior Trim
Roughburn, Dundreggan, Glenmoriston, Inverness, IV63 7YJ. Tel: 01320 340220
www.lasalle-trim.co.uk

Makita UK Ltd
Michigan Drive, Tongwell, Milton Keynes, Bucks. MK15 8JD. Tel:01908 211 678
www.makitauk.com

Mantec Services (UK) Ltd
Unit 4, Smart Drive, Haunchwood Park Ind. Est., Galley Common, Nuneaton, Warks CV10 9SP. Tel: 02476 395 368
www.mantec.co.uk

Maplin
The electrical and electronics specialist. Stores all over the UK or buy online at www.maplin.co.uk.

MM 4x4
Droitwich Road, Martin Hussingtree, Worcs, WR3 8TE. Tel: 01905 451 506
www.mm-4x4.com

Mobile Centre Limited
PO Box 222, Evesham, WR11 4WT
Tel: 0844 578 1000 www.mobilecentre.co.uk

Morris Lubricants
Castle Foregate, Shrewsbury, Shropshire, SY1 2EL. Tel: 01743 232 200
www.morrislubricants.co.uk

Motor & Diesel Engineering (Anglia) Ltd
Rowan Farm, Priory Road, Ruskington, Sleaford, Lincs. NG34 9DJ. Tel: 01526 830 185
www.mdengineering.co.uk

MUD UK
Unit 20, Moderna Business Park, Mytholmroyd, West Yorkshire HX7 5QQ
Tel: 01422 881 951 www.mudstuff.co.uk

Nene Overland
Manor Farm, Ailsworth, Peterborough, PE5 7AF
Tel: 01733 380687 www.neneoverland.co.uk

Noisekiller Acoustics (UK) Ltd
Unit 7, Parkside Ind Est, Edge Lane Street, Royton, Oldham OL2 6DS
Tel: 0161 652 7080
www.noisekiller.co.uk

Optima Batteries
www.optima-batteries.com

Pela Extractor Pumps
www.pelapumps.co.uk Retail: Craythorne & de Tessier, 7 Sawmill Yard, Blair Atholl, Perthshire, PH18 5TL
Tel: 01796 482119 www.cdet.co.uk

Pentagon Auto-Tint (Reading)
Unit 3B, 175/177 Cardiff Road, Reading, RG1 8HD Tel: 0800 107 5518 You can speak to fellow Land Rover nutcase and regular off-road competitor Kevin Thomas at Pentagon Auto-Tint (Reading) by telephoning Freephone 0800 107 5518. He just loves talking land Rovers! Go to www.tintyourglass.co.uk for more information and some superb video footage of how Supaglass can protect your Land Rover.

Prins Maasdijk
Postbus 39, 2676ZG, Maasdijk, Holland
Tel. 0031 174-516011 www.prinsmaasdijk.nl

Raptor Engineering
Phil Proctor, Mob: 07503 12 22 23 (Call Mon-Fri after 5.30pm, Sat/Sun anytime)
www.raptor-engineering.co.uk

RH Nuttall Limited
Great Brook Street, Nechells Green, Birmingham, B7 4EN Tel: 0121 359 2484
www.rhnuttall.co.uk

Richard Cusick
Maintech Solutions, 30 Mountstewart Road, Newtownards, Co. Down BT22 2AL
www.maintechsolutions.com.
Tel: 07980 292182

Ring Automotive Ltd
Gelderd Road, Leeds, LS12 6NA,
Tel: 0113 213 2000
www.ringautomotive.co.uk

R T Quaife Engineering Ltd
Vestry Road, Otford, Sevenoaks, Kent, TN14 5EL
Tel: 01732 741144 www.quaife.co.uk

Sam's 4x4
14 Deykin Park, Witton, Birmingham, B6 7HN
Tel: 0121 328 3322 Mobile: 07946 663 428

Scorpion Electro Systems Ltd
are owners of Soundlinx, Sigma and Toad Security. Drumhead Road, Chorley North Business Park, Chorley PR6 7DE
Tel: 01257 249928 www.scorpionauto.com

Screwfix Direct Ltd
www.screwfix.com

SPAL Automotive UK Limited
Unit 3 Great Western Business Park, McKenzie Way, Tolladine Road, Worcester, WR4 9PT Tel: 01905 613 714
www.spalautomotive.co.uk

Stig's Stainless Fasteners
19 Leith Road, Darlington Co Durham DL3 0GL. Tel: 01325 464243
www.a2stainless.com

Think Automotive
292 Worton Road, Isleworth, Middlesex TW7 6EL. Tel: 020 8568 1172
www.thinkauto.com

Towcraft Ltd
22 Birmingham Road, Rowley Regis, West Midlands, B65 9BL
Tel: 0121 559 0116 www.towcraft.co.uk

Tyresave
Duncan Clubbe, 4 Dock Road, Connah's Quay, Deeside, Flintshire, CH5 4DS
Tel: 01244 813030
www.tyresave.co.uk

Tyron Developments Ltd
Castle Business Park,Pavilion Way, Loughborough, Leicestershire LE12 5HB
Tel: 0845 4000 600 www.tyron.com

U-Pol
automotive refinish products.
1 Totteridge Lane, London N20 0EY
Tel: 0208 492 5900 www.u-pol.com

viaMichelin
www.viaMichelin.com

X-Eng (PSI Design Ltd)
Units 5c & 5d Sumners Ponds, Chapel Road, Horsham West Sussex, RH13 0PR
Tel: 01403 888 388
www.x-eng.co.uk

Webasto
Say, "Our Sales Team will be pleased to provide you with general product information and provide you with details of your nearest Webasto Authorised Main Dealer. Please email your full contact details to: info-uk@webasto.com."
www.webasto.co.uk

Wiberg & Wiberg
Nyrupvej 70, Vielsted, 4180 Sorø, Denmark
Tel: 0045 5760 1002
www.wiberg-wiberg.com

Witter Towbars
Drome Road, Deeside Industrial Park, Deeside, Flintshire, CH5 2NY
Tel: 01244 284 500
www.witter-towbars.co.uk

Wright Off-road
Tel: 01604 882990 or 07950 633712
www.wrightoffroad.com

Würth UK Ltd
1 Centurion Way, Erith, Kent, DA18 4AF.
Tel: 020 8319 6000
www.wurth.co.uk